"If you enter this world knowing you are loved and you leave this world knowing the same, then everything that happens in between can be dealt with."

—Michael Jackson, 1958–2009

It was greed that killed Michael Jackson.

"The vultures who were pulling his strings somehow managed to put this [London] concert extravaganza together behind his back," said one aide. "They told him that this would be the greatest comeback the world had ever known. That's what convinced him."

Meanwhile, everybody around him noticed that Jackson had lost an astonishing amount of weight. His medical team even believed he had become anorexic. One of Jackson's closest friends claimed a month before Jackson died that Michael told his daughter, Paris, he had only weeks to live. "He called her into his room and told her not to get mad at him if he didn't make it to Father's Day. He had a premonition that his days were numbered."

Praise for *New York Times* Bestselling Biographer Ian Halperin and His Books

"A stunning exposé."

—*Maclean's* (Canada)

"Valuably different in tone to everything else you'll read on the subject."

—*The Guardian* (UK)

"A judicious presentation of explosive material."

—*The New Yorker*

This title is also available as an eBook.

UNMASKED

THE FINAL YEARS OF

MICHAEL JACKSON

BY

IAN HALPERIN

POCKET BOOKS

NEW YORK LONDON TORONTO SYDNEY

Pocket Books
A Division of Simon & Schuster, Inc.
1230 Avenue of the Americas
New York, NY 10020

Copyright © 2009 by Ian Halperin and Transit Publishing

First Pocket Books paperback edition November 2009

POCKET and colophon are registered trademarks of Simon & Schuster, Inc.

For information about special discounts for bulk purchases, please contact Simon & Schuster Special Sales at 1-866-506-1949 or business@simonandschuster.com.

The Simon & Schuster Speakers Bureau can bring authors to your live event. For more information or to book an event contact the Simon & Schuster Speakers Bureau at 1-866-248-3049 or visit our website at www.simonspeakers.com.

Cover design by Michael Nagin.
Front cover photo © 2009, Matthew Rolston/Corbis Outline, all rights reserved.
Back cover photo Time & Life Pictures/Getty Images.

Manufactured in the United States of America

10   9   8   7   6   5   4   3   2   1

ISBN 978-1-4391-8348-9
ISBN 978-1-4391-7719-8 (ebook)

To Michael's fans who stood by him no matter what and to his three children for whom he was a most proud and dedicated father.

RIP, Michael.

ACKNOWLEDGMENTS

Thanks to:

Pierre Turgeon: For your inspiration and incredible insight. For being a brilliant strategist and for being one of the most professional editors I have ever worked with. Merci, Pierre!

François Turgeon: For your unwavering support, artistic vision, whimsical genius and for being a great friend. BTW, this book would not have been the same without the support of your incredible husky, Emo.

Anthony Ziccardi: When we first met face-to-face we didn't really know where this was all going. Your determination and dedication will never be forgotten.

Elisa Rivlin: A very special thank-you for your amazing work and going above and beyond the call of duty, especially on a Sunday!

Max Wallace: For polish and sparkle and for keeping it real. You are one of the industry's finest. Here's to many more *New York Times* bestsellers that I'm sure represent your destiny.

Nachammai Raman and Dwayne Lawrence: You are both so cool to work with. Congrats on an excellent editing job.

Isabelle Dubé: Without your input and vision none of this would have been the same. You are the smartest and most talented publicist I have ever worked with.

Gratia Ionescu: Meticulous, polite, and a world-class person. It is always a pleasure to work with you.

Jarred Weisfeld: The most charismatic literary agent in the world. Every day I have worked with you has been a blessing. Here's to many more years together.

Noah Levy (Senior Editor, In Touch): You had the vision and courage to publish my story when I claimed Jackson had six months to live. I was criticized worldwide for disclosing this. You saw the goods I had and had the vision to publish it and stand by it.

George Thwaites (London Daily Mail): You are the best. I have known you many years and you have been the most straight-up person. Thanks.

Dawn Olsen (GlossLip): You are the nicest and most dedicated person I have met.

Page Six: Always a pleasure—thanks for your unwavering support.

Marie Joelle Parent: Un grand merci. Je suis un fan.

All the people who were brave enough to speak on the record. And a big thanks to the people close to Michael who spoke to me off the record. I guaranteed their anonymity because they had signed confidentiality agreements. You all are extremely brave. I can't thank you enough.

Without you there would be no book.

The L.A. hairdresser who trained me: I didn't think I could ever pose undercover as a hair stylist. You made me believe. And you certainly deserve full credit for making me pull it off.

The entire staff at Transit Publishing: Whenever I visit the office, I leave with a smile. You are all a ray of light.

My precious daughter, Clover Sky: When you were fifteen months old, I used to blare Michael Jackson singing "Bad" on the car stereo and you'd dance to it in the driveway. When you were eighteen months old, you used to say: "Daddy, I love Michael Jackson, but he sounds like a girl." Thank you for all the joy you have brought me since the day you came into this world.

I'd like to thank the entire Simon & Schuster team for their hard work and determination. I'd especially like to thank Jennifer Robinson, Lauren McKenna, Jennifer Bergstrom, and the entire production team at Simon & Schuster for somehow, someway getting this book into stores so quickly.

MICHAEL JACKSON'S OWN WORDS

"If you enter this world knowing you are loved and you leave this world knowing the same, then everything that happens in between can be dealt with."

"In a world filled with hate, we must still dare to hope. In a world filled with anger, we must still dare to comfort. In a world filled with despair, we must still dare to dream. And in a world filled with distrust, we must still dare to believe."

"I wake up from dreams and go 'Wow, put this down on paper.' The whole thing is strange. You hear the words, everything is right there in front of your face . . ."

INTRODUCTION

When, before Christmas 2008, I revealed on my celebrity blog, ianundercover.com, that Michael Jackson had a life-threatening condition, it set off an international media frenzy. Publications ranging from *US Weekly* to the *Washington Post, U.S. News & World Report* to *Rolling Stone* reported my exclusive, along with thousands of other newspapers, TV stations and magazines throughout the world, including eleven outlets in China alone.

On December 24, In Touch magazine quoted me as saying Jackson had "six months to live." That day, Jackson's official spokesman, Dr. Tohme Tohme, called my report a "complete fabrication." The singer, he assured the media, was in "fine health." Most of the media took his word for it and the feeding frenzy came to an abrupt halt.

Six months and one day later, Jackson was dead.

My involvement in the Michael Jackson story actually began four years earlier, on June 13, 2005. As a breaking news alert flashed on CNN announcing that the jury had reached a verdict in Jackson's molestation trial, I knew that American legal history was about to be made. Finally, justice was going to be served, I remember thinking. This was not going to be another O. J. Simpson travesty where an uneducated group of twelve unqualified jurors fell sway to a high-priced legal team that helped a celebrity get away with murder by playing the race card. No, this was by all accounts a mostly white, middle-class, educated group of citizens—eight women and four men—that was smart enough to weigh the evidence and come to a credible conclusion about innocence and guilt.

I hadn't been following the trial very closely but I had caught enough snippets on TV and newspapers that made it fairly obvious he was guilty of some very heinous acts.

And so I fully expected the jury to return a guilty verdict on the most serious counts for which Jackson had been indicted, especially the charge that he had sexually molested a thirteen-year-old cancer patient whom he had taken under his wing the year before.

As the banner moving across the screen announced that the verdict would be read in open court at 4:45 p.m., the commentators who had been following the case since the beginning seemed reluctant to hazard a guess about the outcome. I figured that they were just trying to remain objective for the cameras. Like me, they must have seen enough convincing evidence throughout the trial to make Jackson's guilt a foregone conclusion. Hadn't the boy's entire family, after all, been witness to the crimes? Hadn't a stewardess seen Jackson plying the boy with alcohol on board an air-

plane? Hadn't members of the staff at Neverland testified to some highly suspicious shenanigans that pointed
to only one conclusion? And what about reports that
Jackson had been accused before of molesting a boy
and had apparently offered a multimillion-dollar settlement to avoid going to trial years earlier. Where there's
smoke, there's fire, his detractors argued convincingly.
And, most telling of all—the only evidence that I really
needed to convince me—hadn't Jackson actually admitted to letting the boy sleep in his bed?

All very damning evidence and surely enough to
send Jackson away for a very long time to a place where
molesting children would not be likely to elicit him a
warm welcome from his new roommates.

As I waited for the fateful moment of justice, the
scene outside the courthouse resembled a circus as
crowds of Jackson fans and detractors competed for the
attention of the hundreds of television crews who had
assembled from all corners of the globe to report on the
latest trial of the century.

"MJ innocent. MJ innocent!" came the cries from
his large contingent of loyal fans. They were met with
cries of "Fry him. Fry him!" from the equally boister-
ous crowd of child advocates across the street. The cre-
scendo built to a deafening roar as a motorcade pulled
up in front of the courthouse. As the doors of a black
SUV opened, a phalanx of bodyguards surrounded its
occupant, an uncharacteristically normal-looking Michael Jackson, wearing a dark suit and tie. This was a
far cry from the day he arrived 20 minutes late in the
middle of the trial wearing a pair of pajamas.

The legal commentators were reporting that the district attorney, Tom Sneddon, was very confident—cocky, even—as he entered the courthouse, convinced that a conviction was imminent. This was the man who had spent more than a decade determined to bring Jackson to justice for the unspeakable crimes he was sure the singer had gotten away with when he settled with the first boy in 1994. A modern-day Inspector Javert, he had more than ten years to gather evidence, assemble witnesses and wait for the victim he knew would eventually come forward to secure him the long-awaited indictment he had been itching for all these years. Surely he would not have gone forward unless he had an airtight case.

And so I waited along with the rest of the world for the only possible verdict: guilty. The word that would finally erase the stench that had been lingering over the American justice system ever since the O.J. trial, when the jury pronounced a cold-blooded killer not guilty on all counts.

Four forty-five p.m., the time we had been promised an announcement, came and went. "I think we're going to see convictions here," declared one legal analyst as the wait dragged on, noting that the jury had deliberated too long for an acquittal.

The judge had not allowed cameras in the courtroom but he had authorized an audio feed so that we could hear the verdict in real time along with the defendant, who faced as much as twenty years in prison if found guilty. Reporters in the courtroom informed us that the verdict had been handed to the judge and that two of the jurors were staring at him on the bench instead of at Jackson.

"When the jury stares at the judge, it's not an 'innocent,'" announces a seasoned legal observer. "They do not want to look at the defendant that they have just convicted."

Finally the talking heads shut up and the audio feed begins.

"The People of California, plaintiff, vs. Michael Joe Jackson, defendant. Case #1133603. Count one, verdict. We the jury in the above entitled case find the defendant not guilty of conspiracy as charged in count one of the indictment. . . . Count two, verdict. We the jury in the above entitled case find the defendant not guilty of a lewd act upon a minor child."

By the time the second count was read, I was hardly listening anymore, and neither were the cheering fans outside who realized the implications of the foreperson's words. The case had collapsed like a house of cards and the prosecution had completely failed to get even one conviction. Jackson was free. I was stunned.

As the father of a young child, I found the idea that a sexual predator had evaded justice repugnant. Having not followed the trial closely, I assumed that Jackson's all-star legal team had simply outmaneuvered the less accomplished civil servants who were responsible for prosecuting him. Something snapped. I decided on the spot that I was going to bring Michael Jackson to justice in some way and make him pay for his sickening acts. Around that time, I had just begun a new career as a documentary filmmaker and I figured the best method at my disposal would be to make a film and finish the job started by Martin Bashir, the British filmmaker whose special, *Living with Michael Jackson*, had been the catalyst for Jackson's prosecution. With my decades of experience as an investigative journalist, I intended to find and present the evidence that the jury had never got to see and which I assumed existed in abundance. I would in effect prosecute him once again in front of the cameras, but without the archaic rules of evidence that handicapped Tom Sneddon and Marcia Clark before him, and which usually favors the rich and powerful.

Like a prosecuting attorney, I was in no way objective. But that didn't mean I couldn't be fair. A hatchet job accomplishes nothing except to tarnish the reputation of the person doing the hacking. I was determined to let the facts speak for themselves.

By the time I stumbled upon the Michael Jackson case, I was already somewhat of a veteran in the field of celebrity justice. In fact, it was another notorious case involving a music icon a decade earlier that had carved out my journalistic reputation, for better or worse.

In 1994, I was on tour with my band, State of Emergency, in Seattle, Washington, where Kurt Cobain had allegedly killed himself a few months earlier. During this tour, I met a number of people who had known Cobain, including one of his heroin dealers and his best friend, who told me that everything was not as it appeared. They were convinced that the rock star had not in fact killed himself, but that he had been murdered.

I assumed that the whole thing was a typical conspiracy theory until I heard about Tom Grant, the respected Beverly Hills private investigator who had been hired by Cobain's wife, Courtney Love, to find Cobain after he fled from a Los Angeles rehab center shortly before his body was found in a room above the garage. Grant, a former L.A. sheriff's deputy, worked for Courtney for months after the suicide until he quit abruptly and publicly accused her of having her husband murdered.

When I returned to Canada, I wrote a magazine article about the case with my writing partner at the time, leading to the offer of a book, which was eventually published in 1998, entitled *Who Killed Kurt Cobain?*

The book looks in depth at the case for and against the murder and presents some very damning circumstantial evidence. It reveals that there were no fingerprints found on the shotgun that Cobain allegedly used to kill himself. It reveals that he had a triple lethal dose of heroin in his blood at the time of his death and that such a dose would have rendered him unconscious before he could have neatly put away his heroin kit, picked up his shotgun and pulled the trigger. It presents evidence on tape proving that at the time of the death, Kurt and Courtney were in the middle of a very messy divorce. He had recently asked his lawyer to take Courtney out of a new will, which had not yet been signed at the time of his death. Because the two had a prenuptial agreement, Courtney would have received virtually nothing if the divorce had gone through. Instead, she inherited an estate that is worth hundreds of millions of dollars in future royalties. We interviewed Eldon Hoke, a former friend of Courtney's who revealed that she had offered him $100,000 months earlier to blow Kurt's brains out and make it look like a suicide. He declined the offer.

He passed a lie detector test administered by the world's top polygraph examiner. A week after he told his story to the BBC, he was himself mysteriously found dead. We obtained a tape recording of Courtney's own entertainment lawyer and godmother to the couple's daughter, who said she believed that Kurt was murdered and that the so-called suicide note he left was "traced or forged."

Yet, despite the abundance of damning evidence, we also debunk many of the conspiracy theories surrounding the case, present exculpatory evidence and conclude by admitting that we found no smoking gun linking Courtney Love to her husband's death. One of America's most respected publications, *The New Yorker*, praised the objectivity of the book, describing it as a "judicious presentation of explosive material."

Thus, by the time I set out to indict Michael Jackson on film, I believed I was capable of also being as fair as possible in examining the evidence for and against his guilt. Nevertheless, I assumed that the viewers would come to a verdict different from that of the jurors. Until I actually began to examine the evidence.

Over the next three years, I was forced to juggle my Michael Jackson film amongst several other projects, including a book and another documentary already in progress. I hired a team of researchers to track down witnesses and I devoted much of my spare time to pursuing my mission of bringing Jackson to justice. During this period, I had also started a pop culture blog that was receiving a lot of attention and which I occasionally used to reveal a nugget or two about my Jackson findings.

Much of what I discovered did not present Jackson in a positive light, especially dealing with the period between the first molestation accusation in 1993 and the 2005 trial, when the beleaguered star engaged in behavior that was even stranger and more disturbing than what the world had come to expect. Some of it was positively creepy. But my progress in finding evidence of molestation was not as smooth as I had anticipated. In fact, the more I delved, the less convinced I became. Occasionally, the thought crossed my mind that Jackson himself was the victim. Still, the circumstantial evidence was highly suspicious. I believed it was just a matter of time before I found the smoking gun I needed.

Meanwhile, as the result of my blog and a documentary where I had posed as an actor to uncover the secrets of Hollywood and Scientology, I was traveling frequently in the sphere of celebrity journalism. I was encountering and corresponding with some of the world's top entertainment journalists, many of whom had covered Michael Jackson for years. In my frequent discussions, many of them appeared resolutely convinced that he was a pedophile. Whenever I confided that I was having trouble finding evidence proving he was guilty, they usually rolled their eyes and treated me as a naive bumpkin. "If you say in your film that he's not a child molester, you'll be a laughingstock," said one internationally known broadcaster. "He's a sick pedophile and everybody knows it." Another warned me not to let myself be "used" by Michael. "Don't fall for his act," he told me.

I assumed that their certainty was based on sources they had cultivated over the years or evidence that they were not allowed to publish. So I got excited. These people had already done the legwork. Surely they'd be all too glad to point me at the evidence. Yet time and time again when I asked them for some proof or credible sources, they were vague or noncommittal. "Read the trial transcript," said one. "It's all there."

And then when I was still trying to track down the story, I inadvertently became the story.

During the course of my investigation, I had cultivated a fairly impressive array of sources, even if none of them had been able to furnish me with the kind of evidence I was looking for. Some were disgruntled former employees, so their revelations had to be taken with a grain of salt; some were friends or hangers-on; and some still worked for him. At one point, I discovered that I had once dated one of the most trusted members of Jackson's staff, somebody who saw him almost every day and who was eventually fired when she revealed that she knew me.

My blog, ianundercover.com, was among the fastest-growing celebrity blogs in the United States and had gained a loyal following of fans, entertainment journalists and fellow bloggers, including Perez Hilton. On the rare occasion that I revealed something about Michael Jackson, I would invariable be contacted by a source offering new information about the reclusive oddball, sometimes specious, sometimes reliable.

When in December 2008 I shared on my blog an intriguing piece of medical information that I had confirmed with two sources, the world went crazy. I had revealed that Jackson suffered from a potentially fatal genetic condition and that he could barely walk. Within hours, paparazzi were camped outside my Manhattan apartment building. The story only intensified when a British newspaper added new details about his medical condition, seemingly confirming what I had written, and published photos of Jackson being pushed in a wheelchair and wearing a surgical mask.

The next day I was contacted by one of the most important players in the Michael Jackson saga, the Court TV broadcaster Diane Dimond, the woman who was perhaps most responsible for convincing the world that Jackson was a serial molester of young boys. She had some choice words of advice for me: "Don't let Michael manipulate you." She seemed convinced that it was Jackson who had fed me the story about his illness to garner sympathy.

Her warning reminded me of something told to me by one of Jackson's acquaintances who, strangely enough, was also one of his most ardent defenders. "Whenever he tells a particularly egregious lie, he explains to us that you've got to 'razzle-dazzle' them," said the longtime friend, explaining that Jackson was obsessed with the character Billy Flynn in the musical *Chicago*, who had patented that expression while continuously pulling the wool over everybody's eyes.

Was I simply allowing myself to become the victim of Jackson's razzle-dazzle?

Dimond told me that if I wanted to discover the truth about the King of Pop, I had to start with Jordan Chandler. I took her advice.

ONE

As Michael Jackson stepped onto the stage on January 19, 1993, for President Bill Clinton's inauguration gala, he was seemingly on top of the world. Media accounts hardly needed hyperbole to capture just how big a superstar he had become at this point in his career. They merely needed to quote the entries devoted to Jackson in *The Guinness Book of World Records*: "most successful entertainer of all time; highest-grossing live performer in history; best-selling album of all time; youngest vocalist to top the U.S. singles chart; first vocalist to enter the U.S. singles chart at number one; longest number of weeks at the top of the U.S. album charts; most successful music video; and highest-paid entertainer of all time."

His very presence could spark a mob scene reminiscent of Beatlemania. In fact, I was once stuck in a London bus for nearly an hour on Oxford Street because word had spread that Jackson was shopping inside an HMV record store. The crowds that gathered as a result shut down traffic for half a mile in all directions.

Nevertheless, the public found Jackson decidedly odd. Tabloid stories abounded about his strange behavior. It was said that he wanted to buy the bones of the Elephant Man and that he slept in a hyperbaric chamber to stay young. His ever-changing facial features were apparently sparked by his obsession to look like Diana Ross, his Motown mentor. Then, after he fell out with her, he decided to mold himself in the image of another Diana, the Princess of Wales. Despite his protests that such stories were absurd, his denials didn't assuage public skepticism. They had watched him turn from a dark-skinned youth to a bizarrely androgynous pale-skinned male before their eyes over the nearly quarter of a century that he had been in the public spotlight. Yet, rather than dampening his popularity, such behavior only seemed to elevate it. The worst adjective the media could usually summon to describe the singer was "eccentric." It helped that Jackson had never really been associated with the bad behavior often connected with other celebrities of his era, especially in the music business, where drugs and excess were the norm.

On the contrary, by January 1993, he was becoming almost as well known for his humanitarian efforts as he was for his music. During the eighties, he had befriended a teenager named Ryan White, a hemophiliac. Ryan became the national poster child for HIV and AIDS after contracting the infection through a blood transfusion. White helped shift the American perception that AIDS was a disease confined to homosexuals. He was instrumental in convincing President Ronald Reagan to address the crisis for the first time. Jackson's friendship with White helped him gain prominence as an advocate for HIV/AIDS research, cementing his reputation as a compassionate celebrity. At White's funeral in 1990, Jackson delivered a particularly touching eulogy, declaring, "Good-bye, Ryan White, you taught us how to stand and fight."

In 1992, explaining that he wanted "to improve [living] conditions for children throughout the world," Jackson founded the Heal the World Foundation to provide medicine to children and fight world hunger, homelessness, child exploitation, and abuse. The foundation also brought hundreds of low-income and minority children to visit Neverland, the spectacular 2,700-acre ranch he had purchased in 1988 in Santa Ynez, California, which came complete with a zoo and amusement park. In 1992, Jackson donated all the profits from his *Dangerous World Tour*—tens of millions of dollars—to the Foundation.

And so it was not a surprise when Jackson was invited to perform at President Bill Clinton's inaugural gala in 1992. He seemed a natural symbol for the new progressive era that Clinton represented after twelve long dark years of right-wing American presidents.

As Jackson bounded onto the stage to thunderous applause from the audience, including the new president and first lady, he dedicated a song to "all the children of the world." The next day, glowing media reports lauded his performance of "Heal the World" as a tribute to Jackson's "love of children." A few months later, those words would have a very different meaning and it would be Jackson's world that needed healing as it came crashing down around him.

The collapse of Michael Jackson's unprecedented reign as the world's most beloved and popular entertainer may have been triggered by a faulty spark plug. In May 1992, Jackson was alone driving his van down Wilshire Boulevard in Los Angeles when the vehicle suddenly broke down in heavy traffic. Without a cellular phone to call for help, Jackson got out of the van at a loss for what to do. Wearing mirrored sunglasses, a black turban and a scarf covering his face, he was immediately recognized by an employee of a nearby rental car agency on her way to work. She approached Jackson and offered to bring him to her agency to hire a vehicle. She then made a phone call to her boss, David Schwartz, owner of the rental agency. When Schwartz heard that Michael Jackson was on his way, he knew what he had to do. He immediately called his wife, June Chandler Schwartz, and told her to bring her twelve-year-old son—his stepson Jordan—to the office. He knew that Jordie had idolized Michael Jackson ever since the day he had bumped into him at a Los Angeles restaurant called the Golden Temple seven years earlier. From that moment on, he was obsessed with the star. He bought every Jackson album, knew the words to all his songs and imitated Jackson's dance moves in front of the mirror.

It was later reported that Jordie had sent Jackson a get-well card, enclosing his photo and phone number, after the singer's hair got singed in a Pepsi commercial. Michael thanked him personally by phone the same day. But this would have been impossible because Jordan was only four years old at the time of the 1984 Pepsi incident. There are also unconfirmed reports that Jordie once auditioned for a part in a commercial featuring Jackson, but was turned down.

Nevertheless, Jordie was very excited to meet his hero face-to-face. He was a little shy and didn't do much talking, but his starstruck mother, June, more than made up for it. She gushed about how thrilled they were to meet him, reminding Jackson that he had met the boy once before. Before Jackson drove off in a beat-up rental car from David Schwartz, June insisted on giving Jackson her son's phone number. Jackson pocketed the slip of paper she gave him, shook Jordie's hand and promised to call.

A few days later, the phone rang at the Schwartzes' home in Santa Monica. June was stunned to hear the unmistakable falsetto voice asking to speak to Jordie. She later claimed that Jackson asked if Jordie would like to visit him at his Century City condominium, but she had said that she would not permit it because her son was in the middle of his final exams. Jordan was finishing seventh grade at the time. People close to her, however, claim that she would never have turned down such an invitation, a claim that rings true given her subsequent behavior. Michael was about to embark on his Dangerous World Tour and the two didn't meet again until almost a year later. Meanwhile, Jackson phoned Jordie several times from the road, talking for hours at a time, and a friendship developed. When asked about these phone conversations, Jordie said Michael talked frequently about Neverland and how much fun it was for kids. He looked forward to the day when the boy could visit and see the amusement park, the video games, the water fort, and the zoo for himself.

A month after the Clinton inaugural gala, Jackson had completed the first leg of his world tour and was back in California. That's when Jordie finally got to visit Neverland for the first time. In early February, Jackson sent a limo to fetch Jordie, his mother and his five-year-old half sister, Lily. The family spent the weekend in Michael's guesthouse and had the time of their lives. The highlight was a shopping spree at a nearby Toys "R" Us store, which was kept open after hours so that Jordan and his sister could pick out as many toys as they wanted.

A few days after they returned home, Jackson invited them back the following weekend, promising to send a car for them on Friday afternoon. At the appointed time, the family was excited to discover that Jackson himself had come personally to fetch them. They were a little taken aback, however, when they stepped into the stretch limo to discover that he was not alone. Sitting on his lap was an eleven-year-old boy named Brett. Jordie later admitted how the sight made him jealous.

By the time Jordan Chandler met Michael Jackson, it was no secret that Jackson had a number of "special friends." The most famous of these friends were the pint-sized former *Webster* TV star Emmanuel Lewis and *Home Alone* child actor Macaulay Culkin. They always seemed to be at his side throughout the eighties, accompanying him to awards shows, movie premieres, and other events.

When Jackson purchased his sprawling ranch in 1988, he explained the name by describing his fascination with J. M. Barrie's Peter Pan stories featuring Neverland, an island where Peter Pan's gang, nicknamed the "Lost Boys," and children never have to grow up. He frequently described his own "lost" childhood, in which he was thrust into show business at an early age and never had a chance to do all the things other children his age did.

In a 1993 TV interview, talk show queen Oprah Winfrey asked him about this:

> Well, you don't get to do things that other children get to do, having friends and slumber parties and buddies. There [was] none of that for me. I didn't have friends when I was little. My brothers were my friends. And that is why I think because I didn't have it then, I compensate for that. People wonder why I always have children around. It's because I find the thing that I never had through them—you know, Disneyland, amusement parks, arcade games. I adore all that stuff because when I was little it was always work, work, work from one concert to the next. If it wasn't a concert it was the recording studio, if it wasn't that, it was TV shows or picture sessions. There was always something to do. . . . I loved show business and I still love show business, but then there are times you just want to play and have some fun and that part

did make me sad. I remember one time we were getting ready to go to South America and everything was packed up and in the car ready to go and I hid and I was crying because I really did not want to go, I wanted to play. I did not want to go.

In the same interview, Jackson vividly described being abused by his father, who frequently told him he was ugly and beat him. "I used not to look at myself. I'd hide my face in the dark, I wouldn't want to look in the mirror and my father teased me and I just hated it and I cried every day," he recalled.

After these experiences, Jackson explained that all he wanted out of life besides his music was to recapture that lost childhood. He said that's why he surrounded himself with kids and created Neverland as a place where he could live like a child. "I'm only happy when I'm with children," he once told a group of kids visiting Neverland.

Before the Jordan Chandler allegations surfaced, the media almost never questioned this aspect of Jackson's strange life. Previously, his friendship with children was always portrayed as innocent and charming. But forever afterward, it took on a sinister aspect. Suddenly, the public remembered some of his more famous "friends" and became suspicious. Perhaps these encounters had not been so innocent after all.

Probably the most famous of these child celebrity friendships was Jackson's longtime relationship with Macaulay Culkin. It had begun shortly after Culkin's debut hit, *Home Alone*, which made him a superstar at the age of ten.

Thirsty for an insight into Jackson's relationship with children, I met up with Culkin at a Los Angeles café. The first thing he told me was that I could never understand what makes Jackson tick. "I can describe our friendship and I can explain Michael's bond with children," he said, "but no matter what I say you can never understand. Unless you've been through what Michael and I have been through, you just can't comprehend what it's like."

That's what drew the two together and forged their friendship, he explained. "We understood each other because we've both been there."

Culkin acknowledged people's suspicions about Jackson and children. "I've heard all the stories. All the accusations. But you have to know Michael. It's impossible to understand the situation if you don't know him. He's not like anybody else. There's this expression about how somebody's a big kid. It's always just an expression. But with Michael, he *is* one. Not all the time. He can be talking about his music, what he calls his art, or business and he's a sophisticated adult. But then he just transforms. It's remarkable. He becomes a kid. He's not pretending. I remember thinking that he's not like any other adult I [had] ever met. He was just like me."

What did they do together?

"We had pillow fights, we goofed around, we rode on the rides. We played the arcade games. That was my favorite thing to do. Keep in mind that it wasn't just me. There were often other kids around too."

Did they ever sleep in the same bed? I wondered.

"Sure," he says matter-of-factly. "But it's not like

you think. First of all, it's a huge bed. There's always people, staff, servants, advisers, coming in and out of the room. The door is always open and my family was always invited. They were always around. It was like a giant slumber party. Sometimes there were other kids as well. We were always in pajamas and nothing the least unusual ever happened. It was just clean fun. I know it sounds weird to somebody who doesn't know that scene. Looking back, I guess it was a bit weird. But at the time, it just seemed so harmless, so normal. Michael is just Michael, and if you really knew him, you would know just how stupid the accusations are."

Were they still friends? I wondered.

"Sort of," he says. "But as I got older, Michael was not as interested in getting together. He's only really comfortable around children. That's when he can be a kid. I could sense at some point that I was getting too old. Plus, as I got older, Neverland didn't seem as amazing anymore. It was a place for kids and I was this cool teenager."

The boy sitting on Jackson's lap when he picked up Jordan Chandler that day was Brett Barnes, a young Australian who had come to the attention of the singer when he wrote him a fan letter in 1991. Along with another Australian boy, named Wade Robson, Barnes had become the latest of Jackson's special friends. He frequently accompanied Jackson on tour and became a routine visitor at Neverland along with his mother and sister.

Culkin told me that he remembered hanging out

with Barnes and Robson during those years. "There were often a few of us there," he recalls. "We had a blast together."

Jordie had now become the latest friend to be added to the entourage. Along with his family, he became a regular at Neverland and would often go on outings to Disneyland or other fun spots with Jackson. In March, the singer invited Jordie and his family to accompany him to Las Vegas, where he had a permanent suite at the Mirage Hotel. He booked a room at the hotel for June and Lily and a room for Jordan. That night, according to an account that would later become part of the official record, Michael and Jordie watched the graphic horror classic *The Exorcist* together. When the boy understandably became frightened, Jackson allegedly told him that he could stay over with him. So that night they slept in the same bed for the first time. Nothing untoward happened. But the next morning when his mother woke up and went to find Jordie, his bed was made and he later told her that he had slept in Jackson's bed. June was a little alarmed and told him to never do it again.

When Jackson found out about June's edict, he confronted her and wanted to know why she was upset. She later recalled that during this conversation, Jackson started to cry and told her, "It's about family, truth, honesty, and love."

She later recalled that his words made her feel guilty for thinking negative thoughts about Jackson. She then said she had no objection to the two sharing a bed as long as Jordie was okay with it.

By the time Michael Jackson entered Jordan's life,

the boy's mother and father were long divorced. His birth father, a dentist named Evan Chandler, was also an aspiring screenwriter who cowrote the semi-successful Mel Brooks comedy *Robin Hood: Men in Tights* a year earlier. Evan later claimed that he had actually collaborated on the script with Jordie and had two other screenplays— *Sleazoids* and *Bunnies*—in the works with his son. But there is little evidence to back up this claim and Jordan was never given a credit for writing the Brooks film. June had full custody of the boy, but he did spend some weekends and most holidays with his father and Evan's second wife, Nathalie, at their Brentwood home along with Jordan's half siblings, Nikki and Emmanuelle.

Aside from an artistic bent, Evan Chandler may have had other motivations to change professions and become a full-time screenwriter. His career as a dentist was somewhat clouded. In 1978, for example, he did restoration work for one of his patients on sixteen teeth in a single visit. When the Board of Dental Examiners looked at the results, they concluded that Chandler's work showed "gross ignorance and/or inefficiency" in his profession and revoked his license. They eventually changed the revocation to a ninety-day suspension and put him on probation for two and a half years. His wife, June, eventually left him, citing his temper, and was granted full custody of their young son Jordie.

As somebody hoping to make it big in Hollywood, Evan Chandler was quite excited when his son was befriended by the man who epitomized success in show business. At first, by most accounts, he encouraged his son's relationship with Jackson, captured one day for the world to see by the *National Enquirer*, which ran a photo of Jackson, Jordie, June, and Lily at June's Santa Monica home with the headline: "Jacko's New Family." Jackson had taken to staying at their home frequently whenever he was in Los Angeles, and it did seem to many that he had supplanted both Evan Chandler and June's new husband, David Schwartz, as a father figure in the boy's life. Yet this didn't seem to bother Evan very much at the time.

According to a 1994 investigation by Mary Fischer in GQ magazine, Evan Chandler often bragged to friends and associates about his son's friendship with Jackson. In fact, Chandler actually encouraged Jackson to spend *more* time with his son at the Santa Monica house. Fischer's sources told her that Chandler even suggested that Jackson build an annex to the house so the singer could stay there. "But after calling the zoning department and discovering it couldn't be done," she writes, "Evan made another suggestion—that Jackson just build him a new home." Evan often had long telephone conversations with the singer where he asked him for advice about Hollywood, about possible connections he may have, and other things. Moreover, Jackson often stayed at Evan's Brentwood home at Jordie's request.

Later, however, Evan would release his "diary" from this period. It allegedly revealed that he was starting to have serious doubts about Jackson's relationship with Jordie. At one point, he claims in this diary, which he later gave Diane Dimond, he asked Jackson straight out, "Are you fucking Jordie?" To this question, Jackson supposedly "giggled" and said, "I never use that word."

In her book, *Be Careful Who You Love*, Dimond recounts that Evan was not satisfied with this answer and pressed Jackson for more details, writing in his diary his account of the conversation that followed:

> "What exactly is the nature of your relationship?"
>
> Michael said, "It's cosmic. I don't understand it myself. I just know we were meant to be together."
>
> I asked him, "Well, what if someday you decide you don't want to be with him anymore? He'd be really hurt."
>
> Michael assured me, "I'll always be with Jordie. I could never hurt him."
>
> I believed him.

Then, on Memorial Day weekend in 1993, with Michael Jackson staying at the Brentwood house, Evan Chandler claimed he entered his son's bedroom to say good night and found Michael and Jordan fast asleep on the lower bunk bed fully clothed, but curled up in a fetal position with Michael spooning his son from behind and his hands resting on Jordan's crotch.

"I was very disturbed," Evan claims he wrote in his diary. "I thought Jordie might be gay."

Yet Evan didn't say anything. He continued to be friendly with the singer until Jackson gradually began to distance himself from Evan, allegedly sensing an "opportunist" more interested in furthering his own career than in his son. This did not sit well with Evan Chandler, who later claimed this distancing had nothing to do with his later actions.

If Evan had doubts about his son's relationship with Michael Jackson and suspected molestation, the appropriate course of action would have been to contact the California Department of Social Services, Children and Family Services Division. Instead he contacted a lawyer named Barry Rothman with a reputation of playing hardball for cash. Rothman was a key player in the events to come. Evan also started making threats against June and Jordie. He threatened to block Jordie from going out of the country with Michael on tour in June.

Evan had always had a cordial relationship with June's second husband, David Schwartz, and they talked frequently. Alarmed at Evan's increasing belligerence, Schwartz decided one day to tape a conversation he had with Evan about Jordie and Jackson. During this conversation, Evan described June as "cold and heartless." He claims that when he tried to talk to his ex-wife about his suspicions over Jackson, she told him, "Go fuck yourself."

At this point in the tape, Evan drops the first hint that he is angry that Jackson stopped communicating with him:

Evan: I had a good communication with Michael. We were friends. I liked him and I respected him and everything else for what he is. There was no reason why he had to stop calling me. I sat in the room one day and talked to Michael and told him exactly what

I want [*sic*] out of this whole relationship. What I want [*sic*]. I've been rehearsed [*sic*] about what to say and what not to say.

Schwartz: What has Jackson done that made you so upset?

Evan: He broke up the family. The boy has been seduced by this guy's power and money.

Evan: I am prepared to move against Michael Jackson. It's already set. There are other people involved that are waiting for my phone call that are in certain positions. I've paid them to do it. Everything's going according to a certain plan that isn't just mine. Once I make that phone call, this guy is going to destroy everybody in sight in any devious, nasty, cruel way that he can do it. And I've given him full authority to do that.

At another point, Evan makes it clear that he is looking for money and that his new lawyer, Barry Rothman, is readying to demand a financial settlement:

Chandler: And if I go through with this, I win bigtime. There's no way I lose. I've checked that inside out. I will get everything I want and they will be destroyed forever. June will lose [custody] and Michael's career will be over.

Schwartz: Does that help [Jordie]?

Chandler: That's irrelevant to me. It's going to be big-

ger than all of us put together. The whole
thing is going to crash down on everybody
and destroy everybody in sight. It will be
a massacre if I don't get what I want. This
attorney I found, I picked the nastiest son
of a bitch I could find. All he wants to do is
get this out in the public as fast as he can,
as big as he can, and humiliate as many
people as he can. He's nasty, he's mean,
he's very smart, and he's hungry for the
publicity.

TWO

When Schwartz relayed the gist of his conversation with Evan Chandler to Jackson, with whom he was still friendly, the singer immediately contacted his longtime entertainment lawyer Bert Fields.

Fields was a legend in the field of entertainment law and was long used to helping celebrities deal with their problems. Among the many well-known clients that Fields helped get out of one jam or another during his nearly half-century career were the Beatles, Tom Cruise, George Lucas, Warren Beatty, and John Travolta. As was the case with all defense attorneys, these legal jams occasionally necessitated contracting the services of a private investigator. Although Fields used a number of PIs to deal with various problems, one that had proven particularly effective in delicate matters was a soon-to-be-notorious character named Anthony Pellicano. At the time, he was known as *the* PI to the stars because of the work he did for many Hollywood celebrities. The Pelican, as his many friends and enemies called him, had acquired a reputation of doing anything to protect his powerful clients. Tactics that he was known to employ regularly included illegal wiretaps, a practice that would later see him sent to prison for 76 counts of racketeering and witness tampering. But Pellicano had established a solid reputation as a master of damage control, which is why Fields often hired him for high-profile cases.

On July 9, 1993, at Bert Fields' request, June and David Schwartz played the Pelican the tape of David's telephone conversation with Evan Chandler.

"After listening to the tape for ten minutes, I knew it was about extortion," Pellicano later told GQ writer Mary Fischer. As professionals bound by ethical guidelines, lawyers are often better off not knowing whether their client is guilty. This is why they hire individuals like Anthony Pellicano. But the first thing a PI who specializes in damage control needs to determine is the truth about what happened. Depending on what they learn, they can then decide how much has to be kept from becoming public and what the most effective method of containing the potential public fallout is.

Of course, Pellicano had no way of knowing whether Michael Jackson was a child molester or not. Given the notorious private investigator's reputation, innocence or guilt was likely not much of a consideration. But he needed to know how big a problem he was dealing with, and he needed to know fast. Less than an hour after hearing the tape, he drove to Jackson's Century City condominium where Jordan Chandler and his half sister, Lily, were visiting. Jackson was not there. After introducing himself and expressing concern for the boy's welfare, Pellicano claims he "made eye contact" with Jordie and asked him some "pointed questions" using the same protocols employed by social workers providing child welfare services.

The answers Jordan gave to those questions that day have never been disputed. "Has Michael ever touched you?" he was asked. "Have you ever seen him naked in bed?"

The answer to both questions was an emphatic no. Jordie insisted that Jackson had done nothing improper. Pellicano apparently left that day convinced that there was nothing to the allegations.

In the taped conversation with Schwartz, Evan Chandler made it clear he had a plan. It was now time to put it into action.

When June divorced Evan years before, she had been granted full custody. According to California state law, this made her Jordan's legal guardian. Evan was determined to change that, and he had just the person to help him do it.

The plan started with a simple request. Evan asked June if Jordie could stay with him for a week, beginning July 12. Unaware that her ex-husband had no intention of returning his son at the end of the agreed visitation period, June accepted the request with the understanding that Jordie would return home on July 18.

Instead, Evan turned to Barry Rothman, the lawyer who had vowed to "destroy everybody in sight in any devious, nasty, cruel way that he can do it." Chandler's choice of Rothman was something of a surprise. Although he was an entertainment industry lawyer,

Rothman had little experience in family law. More significantly, his reputation was far from stellar. According to an investigation by GQ magazine, his career "reveals a pattern of manipulation and deceit." At the time Chandler retained him, he already had more than twenty lawsuits filed against him and had been disciplined by California's state bar three times. A year earlier, in fact, his legal license was suspended for twelve months before. Rothman had the suspension stayed and was placed on probation instead. His legal secretary described an encounter with the diminutive lawyer as "like meeting a real-life demon straight out of the pits of hell." His ex-wife told her lawyer that she was surprised nobody had "done him in" because he had created so many enemies. After reviewing his credit file during one of the lawsuits launched against him, an investigator named Ed Marcus concluded in his report to California's Superior Court that "[h]e appears to be a professional deadbeat . . . He pays almost no one."

At the time he was retained by Evan Chandler, Rothman's firm had filed for bankruptcy and his career was in disarray. He was strapped for cash and running from one creditor after another. Meanwhile, Michael Jackson was worth half a billion dollars.

On July 13, 1993, the day after Jordie arrived at his father's for his one-week "visit," Rothman and Chandler swung into action. First, Evan made it clear to June that he had unilaterally taken over custody of their thirteen-year-old son. He presented her with a written demand prepared by Rothman prohibiting two things: taking Jordan outside of Los Angeles County and letting the boy have any contact with Michael Jackson. It allowed June two days of visitation per week. If she refused to sign, he made it clear that he was prepared to cause a lot of trouble. She later claimed that she signed the document under duress, because Evan had threatened that the boy would otherwise never be returned to her.

Next, Rothman arranged an appointment for Evan with a Beverly Hills psychiatrist named Mathis Abrams, a specialist in adolescent behavior. Evan proceeded to outline a "hypothetical" case of a twelve-year-old boy sleeping in the same bed with a celebrity while disguising details about what had been going on with Jordie and Jackson. Of course, if Evan had mentioned the name of his son or the celebrity involved, it would have immediately required reporting as a case of child abuse under California law.

According to Evan Chandler's account of what happened next, Dr. Abrams concluded that a thirty-four-year-old man consistently sleeping in the same bed with a thirteen-year-old boy when other beds were available constituted "lewd and lascivious conduct."

The psychiatrist suggested bringing his son in for an interview, but Evan declined, explaining that his son still loved the celebrity and that if he kept them apart, he might lose his son.

"You already lost him," responded Dr. Abrams.

Evan has always claimed that it was this conversation that changed his "suspicion into belief." But he needed proof.

At this point, Evan Chandler was the only person accusing Jackson of an act of molestation. Jordie himself had vehemently denied that anything improper had taken place. With these repeated denials, Evan Chandler's case was weak.

Then one day Dr. Evan Chandler, the dentist, decided his son needed his last baby tooth removed. Because the boy was afraid of needles, Evan asked anesthesiologist Mark Torbiner to assist with "conscious sedation," administering the boy gas so that his tooth could be pulled out.

By the time Jordan Chandler left his father's dental office that day, Michael Jackson's life and career would never be the same.

Diane Dimond quotes Evan Chandler's official account of the extraction in her book about the case:

> When Jordie came out of the sedation, I asked him to tell me about Michael and him. I [falsely told] him that I had bugged his bedroom and I knew everything anyway and that I just wanted to hear it from him . . . I told him not to be embarrassed . . . 'I know about the kissing and the jerking off and the blow jobs.' This isn't about me finding anything out. It's about lying—if you lie, then I'm going to take him [Jackson] down.

After an hour during which time Jordan remained silent, Evan resumed his interrogation.

Evan: I'm going to make it very easy for you. I'm going to ask you one question. All you have to do is say yes or no.

Jordie (speaking his first words): Promise.

Evan: Jord, did I ever lie to you in your whole life?

Jordie: No.

Evan: I never will.

Jordie: You won't hurt Michael, right?

Evan: I promise.

Jordie: I don't want anyone else ever to know. Promise me you won't ever tell anyone.

Evan: I promise.

Jordie: What's the question?

Evan: Did Michael Jackson ever touch your penis?

Unbelievably, Jordie still hesitated. Evan later described this as the longest couple of seconds of his life. Then finally Jordie answered in an almost inaudible whisper, "Yes."

Having just received proof that his son had been molested, a father would normally call the police or child protection authorities. Instead, Evan Chandler called Barry Rothman.

On August 4, Chandler arranged a face-to-face meeting with Jackson and Anthony Pellicano at a suite in L.A.'s Westwood Marquis Hotel to discuss the situation. He brought Jordie along. When they were all seated, Evan didn't mention the conversation with his son in the dental chair, but instead took out a copy of Dr. Abrams' letter and began reading it from the beginning. When he finished, he pointed his finger at Jackson and warned, "I'm going to ruin you."

Five days later, Anthony Pellicano arrived at Barry

Rothman's office at the latter's request. For weeks, the PI had been waiting for the financial demand he sensed was coming ever since he first heard the tape and suspected the case was about extortion. But Rothman was too smart to come right out and ask for money. He had a better idea. He was an entertainment lawyer and his client was a screenwriter. It seemed only natural to ask Michael Jackson to arrange some work for Evan Chandler. The whole mess could be made to go away, if only Jackson brokered a deal to purchase four screenplays from Evan at $5 million each. Total cost: $20 million.

Pellicano was furious. "No way, that's extortion," he responded as he stormed out of the office. A series of phone discussions followed over the next few days. Finally Pellicano responded to Rothman's request by fax.

Jackson had done nothing wrong, he declared, and would not consider paying the $20 million requested. However, to resolve the custody dispute and allow Evan to spend more time with Jordan by working on a screenplay together with his son as they had previously on the Robin Hood film, Jackson would be prepared to offer a screenwriting deal of $350,000.

On August 13, 1993, Rothman made a counter-offer. Chandler wanted three screenplay deals instead of one. Pellicano stood firm at one. (Chandler would later claim that it was Jackson who had originally proposed three screenplays and then changed his mind.)

"I almost had a $20 million deal," a disappointed Chandler told Rothman, according to a legal secretary who overheard the conversation.

• • • •

When I first discovered that Anthony Pellicano had offered Evan Chandler a screenplay deal to shut up and go away, my normal instinct would have been to interpret the gesture as a bribe. But as it turns out, I was once offered a similar deal by one of Pellicano's confreres who coincidentally also worked for Michael Jackson doing damage control on the Jordan Chandler case. And so I had some insight about how these things work.

In 1996, I was in the middle of my investigation and book about the mysterious death of Kurt Cobain when I came home one day to find a large bearded man waiting in the courtyard of my Montreal apartment building. The man introduced himself as a private investigator from San Francisco who had been hired by Courtney Love. "I want to talk to you about your book," he said. "Let's go out to dinner, anywhere you want to go."

Bemused but curious, I accepted his invitation. Then over a four-hour dinner at a fancy Italian restaurant, Pellicano proceeded to charm, cajole, and intimidate me, saying I could get in "big trouble" if I didn't show him my manuscript. In between the threats, he told me stories about his impressive roster of clients, which included Patty Hearst, Snoop Doggy Dogg, and John DeLorean.

At the time, he failed to mention another of his prominent clients, Bill Clinton, whose campaign had hired him to contain "bimbo eruptions" during Clinton's 1992 presidential campaign. Pellicano, in fact, figured prominently in the subsequent impeachment hearings, though he was never accused of any wrongdoing.

Halfway through the dinner, the investigator reached into his briefcase and pulled out a thick dossier on my life, covering past jobs, old girlfriends, and so forth. Fortunately, I had nothing to hide. Otherwise, I might have caved at this intimidation tactic.

When he failed to get what he was after, Pellicano had one more trick up his sleeve. Knowing that I was an aspiring musician, he mentioned his many music industry contacts, including Michael Jackson, and suggested that he could help me get a recording contract. The implication was clear. Or was it? I made it clear I wasn't interested, so I never found out whether the offer was an outright bribe designed to get me to drop my investigation. But at the time I believed it was damaging enough to cast serious doubt on Pellicano's client, Courtney Love, who I assumed had orchestrated the offer. Why would she offer me a recording contract if she had nothing to hide? I wondered. Until I did my homework.

After consulting a number of entertainment lawyers and other industry professionals, I discovered that my dinner with Pellicano and his implied offer were merely par for the course. According to one veteran Hollywood publicist, "That kind of thing happens every day. There are billions of dollars at stake in this town in safeguarding people's reputations and image."

Most high-profile actors and musicians, my contact explained, are constant victims of "vultures and sleazebags trying to get a piece of their fortunes." Apparently, much of the time, she said, these people were merely crackpots and easily dismissed. Others would threaten to spill all a star's secrets if they were not appeased.

"Those are the easiest cases to dispose of. Usually they'll either just ignore them or turn them over to the police for investigation."

And sometimes, according to the publicist, the claimant would have some provable link to the star in question.

"Those are trickier," she explained. "If the person has some connection—for example, a former employee—then they can do more public damage. Sometimes they really do have some genuine dirt. That's when you have to do risk assessment and determine just how much damage they can cause either by selling their story to a tabloid or by filing a lawsuit."

Almost every star, she divulged, had a lawyer on retainer for only such cases, and these lawyers in turn had a stable of private detectives who they could call on to dig up the goods.

Depending on the case, she says, the accuser would be treated in a number of different ways.

Sometimes they are paid off. I've seen other cases where a high-paying job is arranged through a third party for themselves or a member of their family. And every once in a while the client will call their bluff because the demands are too outrageous. Of course that just applies to the cases when the star actually did something illegal or embarrassing. Then there are all the times when they are victims of extortion, somebody threatening to publicly accuse them of something they didn't do. That's much messier and much harder to deal with.

As a publicist, I can tell you that all my clients go through it to some degree. It's agonizing. They spend years building up a reputation only to see it jeopardized by some greedy bastard. I think a lot of them live in fear to a degree, though it helps that most people don't believe what they read in the tabloids anymore, so the risk isn't as great as it once was even if somebody sells a phony story. Still, my job is to keep bad stories out of the papers or to minimize the damage if something leaks.

She, however, made it clear that she didn't believe Pellicano's offer of a recording contract could be classified as a bribe. "He was just doing standard damage control, and he went as far as he could go without crossing the line. You do what you have to do to protect your client, and in this case, she was being accused of murder. That counts as something that might need to be contained."

Evidently, Anthony Pellicano still counts Michael Jackson as a client. I received a call from Pellicano's office in January 2009 demanding to know what I planned to reveal about Jackson in my upcoming book and film. To this day, I'm not sure if it was actually him. His voice sounded an octave higher than I remember. Perhaps it was someone from Jackson's camp pretending to be him in an attempt to intimidate me into disclosing key information. Naturally my lips were sealed. "I can't reveal anything until the tome is published," I told the voice on the other end of the phone. "No need to be alarmed, it will be very fair." In fact, my investigation seems to have drawn the attention of Jackson's entire damage control team because at least one American publisher received a communiqué from Anthony Pellicano himself about my book.

"Stay away from Halperin. He's not credible," Pellicano warned a U.S. publisher from the federal prison where he is currently serving his fifteen-year sentence.

On August 16, 1993, June Chandler filed a California Superior Court motion demanding that her son be returned to her custody. A hearing was scheduled for the next day, at which a judge was expected to order Jordie to be given back to his mother. A week earlier, June had told Evan that she believed Jordie had been coerced into making the molestation allegations against Jackson. She simply did not believe it was possible.

When Evan received notice of the hearing, he was taken aback. After consulting Barry Rothman, he made a phone call that would unleash a hurricane.

Chandler telephoned Dr. Abrams, the psychiatrist, and filled in the names and details of the hypothetical child abuse case. The doctor insisted he bring Jordie to see him the next morning, when he talked to the boy for nearly three hours.

That night, an investigator from the Los Angeles County Department of Children and Family Services, accompanied by two Los Angeles police department officers, paid a visit to Evan Chandler's home asking to speak to Jordan.

Four days later, unaware that the Department of Children and Family Services had got involved, Michael

Jackson boarded a plane to Thailand to begin the next phase of his *Dangerous* world tour.

It was left up to his personal maid to greet the authorities when they raided Neverland in the early hours of August 23, 1993.

THREE

By the time the police finished rifling through Jackson's closets, seizing books, video, clothing, and other assorted paraphernalia, local radio stations were already reporting that a raid was under way at Neverland. But details were still sketchy. When the raid was completed and authorities carted away boxes of the singer's personal effects, a police spokesperson confirmed that Jackson was the target of a criminal investigation resulting from a complaint filed with the Los Angeles Police Department several days earlier.

The world was still not aware of what had prompted the investigation, but Anthony Pellicano figured it was only a matter of time before somebody leaked the details, so he decided to launch a preemptive strike.

The PI revealed that the investigation had been prompted by "an extortion gone awry," in an interview with Los Angeles TV station KNBC.

"Besides all the damage this is going to do, Michael will prevail," Pellicano said. "These people tried to extort Michael for a lot of money. When we would not pay, a phone call was made to Child and Family Services, which started this investigation."

He did not elaborate, but later that day, a New York station reported that a woman had accused Jackson of abusing her child during a visit to Neverland and perhaps at his Century City condominium as well. Shortly afterward, a source who had seen confidential police documents in the case told the Associated Press that the thirteen-year-old son of a Beverly Hills dentist had confided to his therapist that he had been fondled by Jackson.

The media had a field day, fans around the world were stunned, and Jackson's camp was in disarray, not least because the singer was halfway around the world preparing to go onstage in Thailand when the allegations were made public.

As the press descended on the Bangkok arena where he had just heard the news, one of Jackson's aides dismissed the allegations: "We are very confident that if any charges are ever filed they will not be in [Jackson's] direction. People can be nasty about Michael simply because he likes kids. He is a very gentle guy."

Meanwhile, his friend and longtime defender Elizabeth Taylor was stunned, along with the rest of the world, to hear what Jackson had been accused of. In the 20 years that she had known him and repeatedly witnessed his interaction with his "special friends," the aging screen legend was convinced he was incapable of such a crime. As a onetime child star who felt she too had been robbed of her childhood, Taylor sensed a special bond with Jackson. She too had been the victim of countless allegations made against her over the years as well as a number of extortion attempts. She knew the game all too well. Taylor immediately made plans to fly to Asia and show her support for her friend during his darkest hour.

Ironically, the public charges of child molestation didn't stop Jackson from surrounding himself onstage that evening with forty children at the end of his concert, the proceeds of which were being donated to various children's charities. Nor did it stop adoring fans from flocking to the show as a sign of support. Scalpers were getting as much as $400 a ticket because of the publicity, an enormous sum in a country like Thailand.

Back in the States, the tabloids were feasting on the news. The *New York Post* ran a headline "Peter Pan or Pervert?" that summed up what a lot of people were thinking. Still, most Americans doubted the claims. The TV show *A Current Affair* conducted a poll which revealed that 80 percent of its viewers didn't believe the allegations against Jackson. At this point, however, they had still not heard the details.

This changed on September 14, 1993, when Jordan Chandler went to court. Shortly after the Neverland raid, Barry Rothman hired his own lawyer, Robert Shapiro, who would come to fame by defending O. J. Simpson a year later. Rothman knew that the Jackson camp was threatening to charge both him and Evan Chandler for extortion and he wanted to be prepared.

Around the same time, Evan had convinced June that she would be seen as the enabler if she continued to defend Jackson against her son's allegations. She had, after all, willingly consented to the questionable sleeping arrangements at the heart of Jordan's case. If she didn't want to be seen as the villain, it was time to get on board.

His argument was effective. June agreed to join with her ex-husband in hiring an attorney to press forward with a lawsuit. The first lawyer they retained was the high-profile women's rights activist Gloria Allred, but they were uncomfortable with her initial strategy of taking the case to the media and allowing the public to vilify Jackson. Shapiro argued that such a tactic would back the singer into a corner and prevent him from settling, lest it be seen by the public as an admission of guilt. He recommended a skilled civil lawyer named Larry Feldman, whom the couple retained in early September.

Less than two weeks later, Feldman appeared at the Superior Court of California in Los Angeles County to file a civil suit against Michael Jackson on behalf of Jordan Chandler. The complaint pulled no punches, alleging "sexual battery; seduction; wilful misconduct; intentional infliction of emotional distress; fraud, and negligence." Among the more colorful details, the complaint alleges that Jackson engaged in a number of "sexually offensive contacts," including "defendant Michael Jackson orally copulating the plaintiff, defendant Michael Jackson masturbating [the] plaintiff, and defendant Michael Jackson eating the semen of [the] plaintiff."

Along with the formal complaint, Feldman in-

cluded a four-page affidavit, where for the first time
Jordan's claims were laid out for all to see in graphic
detail. They were highly disturbing. The affidavit begins
by describing Jordan's initial meeting with Jackson at a
Rent-a-Wreck outlet in May 1992, followed by a long
series of telephone calls from various locations around
the world until February 1993, when he spent his first
weekend at Neverland.

In March 1993, Jordan recalls, his mother and Lily
were flown on a private jet to Las Vegas as Jackson's
guests at the Mirage Hotel:

> One night, Michael Jackson and I watched *The
> Exorcist* in his bedroom. When the movie was
> over, I was scared. Michael Jackson suggested
> that I spend the night with him, which I did. Al-
> though we slept in the same bed, there was no
> physical contact.

From then, whenever they were together, they slept
in the same bed, he adds. They slept in the same bed
together for two or three more nights in Las Vegas, but
again there was no physical contact. The sexual contact,
he states, increased gradually.

> The first step was simply Michael Jackson hugging
> me. The next step was for him to give me a brief
> kiss on the cheek. He then started kissing me on
> the lips, first briefly and then for a longer period
> of time. He would kiss me while we were in bed
> together.

The next step happened when Jackson put his tongue in the boy's mouth:

> I told him I did not like that. Michael Jackson started crying. He said there was nothing wrong with it. He said that just because most people believe something is wrong, doesn't make it so.

At that point, Jordan claims, Jackson cited another of his "young friends" who would allow him to put his tongue in his mouth. "Michael Jackson said that I did not love him as much as this other friend." In May, Jordie accompanied Jackson to Monaco along with his mother and his half sister, Lily. That was "when the situation really got out of hand," he said. "We took a bath together. That was the first time we had seen each other naked. Michael Jackson named certain of his children [sic] friends [who] had masturbated in front of him."

At that point, Jordan states, Jackson masturbated in front of him.

> He told me that when I was ready, he would do it for me. While we were in bed, Michael Jackson put his hand underneath my underpants. He then masturbated me to a climax. After that Michael Jackson masturbated me many times both with his hand and with his mouth.

On another occasion when the two were in bed together, he says Jackson grabbed his buttock and kissed him, putting his tongue in his ear. "I told him I didn't like that. Michael Jackson started to cry. [He] told me that I should not tell anyone what had happened. He said this was a secret."

By the time I had finished reading Jordan Chandler's affidavit for the first time, I was convinced beyond a shadow of a doubt that Michael Jackson was a sick pedophile. Children don't make that kind of thing up. I immediately vowed to redouble my efforts to prove his guilt.

That was before I had ever heard of sodium amytal.

FOUR

If the story Jordan Chandler first told his father while having a tooth extracted on July 12, 1993, was true, the case against Michael Jackson was sealed. He was a predatory pedophile who deserved to go to prison for his crimes. It is hard to believe that a twelve-year-old boy would make up such a story. But in May 1994, long after the case had faded from the headlines, a reporter from a local Los Angeles TV station, KCBS, obtained new information that could potentially shed some light on Jordan's allegations. According to the report, the boy had been administered a drug called sodium amytal, and under its effects, had told his father about the alleged molestation.

Sodium amytal is a barbiturate that puts people into a hypnotic state. It is rarely used for dental procedures. The drug's documented effects include drowsiness, feelings of inebriation, relaxation, a sense of well-being, and a willingness to discuss things one usually would not discuss with strangers. Once believed to be a truth serum effective in the interrogation of prisoners, it has become associated in recent years with something far more sinister—false memory syndrome.

During the 1980s, as the number of reported child sexual abuse cases soared, therapists began to report something called repressed memory. It involved adults reporting cases of sexual abuse and incest from their past that they had long buried in their subconscious. The concept of repressed memory actually dates back to Sigmund Freud and his landmark nineteenth-century study *The Etiology of Hysteria*, in which he argued that child sexual abuse was the single greatest cause of adult "hysteria." After a backlash from the psychoanalytic community, Freud later abandoned his seduction theory. But papers unearthed later in his archives indicated that he did so only to save his reputation, not because he doubted the theory.

In 1992, a new backlash began when the term *false memory syndrome* (FMS) was coined to describe a theory that many of those with belated memories of sexual abuse had them falsely implanted during something called recovered memory therapy. FMS implied that therapists had inadvertently elicited false memories of sexual abuse in an attempt to summon repressed traumatic memories from their patients. In order to evoke buried traumatic memories, the practitioners of this therapy commonly used a number of techniques, such as hypnosis, guided visualization, age regression, and drug-assisted interviewing with barbiturates like sodium amytal.

There have been a number of high-profile cases in which patients under the influence of these techniques, which in some cases have proven quite effective, have recalled events that couldn't possibly have occurred. In one notorious example, Nadean Cool, a nurse's aide in Wisconsin, was convinced by a psychiatrist that she had repressed memories of having been in a satanic cult, of eating babies, of being raped, of having sex with animals, and of being forced to watch the murder of her eight-year-old friend.

In another case, a therapist helped a Missouri woman named Beth Rutherford "remember" that her father, a clergyman, had regularly raped her between the ages of seven and fourteen and that her mother sometimes helped him by holding her down. Under her therapist's guidance, Rutherford remembered her father impregnating her and forcing her to abort the fetus herself with a coat hanger. When the allegations became public, her father was forced to resign his church post in disgrace. However, a later medical examination of the daughter revealed that she was still a virgin at age twenty-two and had never been pregnant. The daughter sued the therapist and received a $1 million settlement in 1996.

And then there's the case of Elizabeth Carlson, the Minnesota woman whose battle with depression led her to sodium amytal, the same drug that may have induced Jordan Chandler to accuse Michael Jackson of heinous acts. When Carlson was thirty-five years old, she encountered a respected psychiatrist at the United Hospital in St. Paul, who assured her of help. On a highway, did Carlson ever miss an exit because she was thinking about something else? "Of course," she said. The diagnosis: Carlson wasn't depressed. Instead, she had multiple personality disorder (MPD). Before long, the same psychiatrist was employing a number of supposedly proven techniques to help the patient overcome her disorder. First came guided imagery, then came hypnosis, and then came the drugs. One day the psychiatrist injected Carlson with sodium amytal, which she described as a "truth serum." Before long, her patient was transformed into her "demonic alter ego, growling and spitting as in *The Exorcist.*" She became convinced that her parents had brutalized her as part of a satanic cult. After five hospitalizations, she formed a group of other MPD sufferers. They all soon discovered that they had identical memories drawn from the same movies and books. Carlson sued the therapist and was awarded $2.5 million by a jury.

The highest-profile case involving sodium amytal involved a nineteen-year-old Napa, California, woman named Holly Ramona. During the course of her treatment for depression and bulimia, Holly suddenly recalled that her father had repeatedly violated her during childhood after the therapist told her that bulimia was usually caused by incest and other sexual molestation. When Holly confronted him and the case became public, her father lost his $400,000-a-year position as a senior sales executive at a winery. His wife divorced him, he was shunned by the community, and his daughter launched a lawsuit against him.

During the subsequent civil legal proceedings, in which the father countersued, it emerged that Holly's recall of the molestation came only after she was administered sodium amytal, what her therapist told her was a truth serum. A variety of experts were called. Each discredited the drug and suggested that it could easily be used to plant false memories in an individual.

One of the most compelling experts was a University of Pennsylvania psychiatrist named Martin Orne, a pioneer in the use of sodium amytal and hypnosis in his own practice. Orne testified that the drug is "not useful in ascertaining truth." The patient becomes sensitive and receptive to suggestions due to the context and to the comments of the interviewers. "Amytal," he added, "is even more problematic than hypnosis in its effects of producing false memories and confabulations." The jury ruled in favor of the father and awarded him $500,000 in damages, concluding that the therapist had indeed planted the memories in Holly's head. Just as important, it brought sodium amytal, more widely known by its trade name Amytal, and similar treatments under increased scrutiny.

The American Medical Association's Council on Scientific Affairs concluded that such treatments "not only fail to be more accurate but actually appear to be generally less reliable" than other methods. In 1994, Dr. August Piper, a Seattle-based psychiatrist and researcher, reviewed more than twenty medical studies on the use of sodium amytal as a means to recover memories of childhood sexual abuse in patients. "Nearly all the investigations reviewed indicate that under Amytal, patients often distort reality," he concluded. "This distortion causes a serious difficulty for those who believe barbiturate-facilitated interviews have a role in discovering 'truth.' Because people may produce grossly distorted or even frankly psychotic material after administration of intravenous Amytal, claims made by those who are under the influence of the drug cannot be assumed to be literal and accurate representations of something that actually happened to those individuals." Therapist interviews facilitated by Amytal, he concluded, "may be worse than useless, because they may encourage patients' beliefs in completely mythical events."

Elizabeth Loftus, a professor of psychology at the University of Washington, is considered one of the world's leading experts in the field of false memory syndrome. Loftus has conducted over 200 experiments involving more than 20,000 individuals that document how easily false memories can be implanted.

She often uses large groups of people to demonstrate how anyone can be convinced that they remember something in their past that could not have happened. One of her most famous experiments involved a group of 120 people split into four groups. After the group was exposed to a Disneyland advertisement featuring Bugs Bunny, 30 percent of the participants recalled meeting Bugs when they visited Disneyland. They vividly remembered shaking his hand and even stroking his fur. Of course, the scenario is impossible because Bugs Bunny is a Warner Bros. character and would never have been present at Disneyland. These kinds of findings, Loftus explains, "confirm earlier studies that many individuals can be led to construct complex, vivid and detailed false memories via a rather simple procedure. Hypnosis clearly is not necessary."

Loftus maintains that if memories can be implanted

this easily without artificial means, the use of drugs is especially dangerous. Drugs could help implant a false memory to the point of brainwashing. Clearly, the use of sodium amytal in the Jordan Chandler case calls into question the accuracy of the allegations he made after he was given the drug by his father. The entire case, in fact, would seem to collapse under the weight of the drug's dubious history. But by the time KCBS revealed the role of the drug in the Michael Jackson case, it was too late to make much of a difference, except in public perception.

There was, however, one woman who would not let the story of a drug-induced confession exonerate Michael Jackson, even in the public mind.

For more than a decade, Diane Dimond has been the archenemy of the legions of Michael Jackson fans who will never believe their hero is capable of harming a child.

Dimond was once a mainstream radio and TV journalist who cut her teeth in journalism as a Washington correspondent for National Public Radio's flagship news show, *All Things Considered*. For years, she reported from the halls of Congress and the White House press room, gaining a reputation as a solid reporter. But in 1992, the big bucks beckoned and Dimond jumped to a new tabloid TV show called *Hard Copy*, featuring hard-hitting reports about celebrities.

Less than a year after she joined the show, her producer told her that the Los Angeles Police Department had just raided two homes owned by Michael Jackson.

Later the same day, a "confidential source" approached *Hard Copy* and asked to meet with a reporter to share a few documents. When Dimond met the source at an Italian restaurant in Santa Monica, she was shown a file containing allegations that Michael Jackson had repeatedly molested a twelve-year-old boy. With the documents in hand, Dimond became the first newscaster to break the news about Jordan Chandler. She has remained obsessed with the case ever since and, for better or worse, is probably the reporter most associated with the story in the public eye, at least in America.

From my first meeting with Dimond, I was impressed with her journalistic integrity. I was working on my investigation of Kurt Cobain when a Los Angeles musician named Eldon Hoke approached *Hard Copy* with the news that Courtney Love had offered him $100,000 to kill her husband four months before his death. I was flown to Los Angeles by the show to discuss the case and to address Hoke's allegations. Before she would air the segment, Diane Dimond insisted that Hoke's claim be verified. This was not the sort of diligence I had expected from a program such as *Hard Copy*, which had already gained a somewhat sleazy reputation in media circles for its questionable tactics. The show decided it would have Hoke undergo a polygraph examination. But the person hired to do the test was not just any fly-by-night private detective with a cheap lie detector kit. It was Edward Gelb, at the time acknowledged as America's leading polygraph examiner. He taught an advanced polygraph course for the FBI.

Hoke passed the test with flying colors, according

to Gelb, scoring a 99.9 percent certainty that he was telling the truth. However, I never learned whether the meticulous fact-checking employed by the program was the result of Dimond's journalistic standards or whether it was done at the insistence of the show's lawyers, nervous about airing an accusation that a celebrity had attempted to have her husband murdered.

In the years since she first broke the news of Jackson's accuser, Dimond has made no secret of the fact that she thinks he is a child molester. Her reporting on the case, in fact, has verged on being zealous. Jackson's press representative has described it as "loathsome," and his fans have targeted her with abuse and even threats.

When she ventures out in public, she is often dogged by Jackson fans shouting, "Michael's innocent!" or "Leave him alone!" At one point, Paramount, the producers of *Hard Copy*, assigned a security detail to escort Dimond to and from work every day.

Not long after Dimond broke the story, she claimed to have heard a series of suspicious clicks on her phone line. Knowing that Jackson's PI, Anthony Pellicano, had a reputation for wiretapping, she immediately suspected that he was up to his old tricks. To test her theory, she had her husband call her office line to discuss a fictional "Pellicano documentary" that she was preparing. Twenty minutes later, a member of the Paramount legal team called asking about the so-called documentary. Dimond replied that she was working on no such documentary and asked where they had heard about it. The lawyer announced that they had just received a call from the office of one of Michael Jackson's attorneys.

The Jackson camp had good reason to be nervous.

In some ways, I can sympathize with Dimond's relentless attempts to portray Jackson as a child molester. Believing he is guilty of a terrible crime, she has taken it upon herself to expose him and alert the public that a serial predator is on the loose. I can identify with and even understand her attitude. In many ways, I had exactly the same motivation when I first embarked on my own investigation. Unfortunately, it seems that Dimond has taken her crusade to the point where occasionally the facts get in the way of the truth.

One of the most striking examples of this phenomenon revolves around her reporting on sodium amytal. For more than a decade, its association with false memory syndrome has been a thorn for those who, like Dimond, are convinced that Jordan Chandler is merely the tip of the iceberg in Michael Jackson's long career of allegedly abusing children. If Chandler's accusations are true, then they could certainly form a pattern of behavior, when and if other boys come forward claiming molestation. If, however, accusations were being falsely induced under a powerful drug, then it helps support Jackson's claim that he is a victim of ruthless extortionists determined to separate him from his vast fortune.

In 2005, Dimond wrote a book, *Be Careful Who You Love*, about Jackson's decade-long battle against the abuse charges. The book goes into great length about Jordie's sodium amytal episode.

Indeed, Dimond acknowledges that if the allegations were correct that Jordie was administered the drug, then his charges against Jackson "would have to be viewed as unreliable, if not highly questionable."

She even quotes a Cleveland psychiatrist named Phillip Resnick who admits that false memories can be easily implanted under the influence of sodium amytal: "It's quite possible to implant an idea through the mere asking of a question." "The idea can become part of their memory, and studies have shown that even when you tell them the truth, they will swear on a stack of Bibles that it happened." That's when Dimond drops the other shoe. Ten years after the story of sodium amytal was first reported, she reveals that she obtained information from "confidential sources, the boy's uncle, Raymond Chandler, and documents, including the anesthesiologist's own report, that show Jordan Chandler was not, in fact, given sodium amytal that day."

She goes on to claim that, according to the anesthesiologist's records, there is "no reference to the barbiturate sodium amytal." Furthermore, she writes, "The purchase of sodium amytal requires the filing of specific forms with the Drug Enforcement Administration (DEA). No such forms were ever located by anyone in law enforcement or the media."

If Dimond's revelations were true, the credibility of Jordan Chandler's claims remained intact. But she appeared to have missed some crucial facts.

In October 1994, a senior reporter for GQ magazine named Mary Fischer published the results of a months-long investigation with the headline: "Was Michael Jackson Framed?" Among the figures Fischer probed at length for her piece was the anesthesiologist, Mark Torbiner, whom Evan Chandler had called on to administer whatever drug he used to extract his son's tooth that day. Torbiner was an anesthesiologist for hire. According to a former patient, Nylla Jones, he boasted that he had $100 a month in overheads and an income of $40,000 a month by providing services to various dental offices around Los Angeles on a freelance basis.

Four years before he treated Jordan Chandler, according to GQ, Torbiner got "caught in a lie and was asked to leave UCLA, where he was an assistant professor of dentistry."

At the time of Fischer's article, he was being probed by the U.S. Drug Enforcement Administration for administering drugs, such as morphine and Demerol, to patients for pain unrelated to dental work. This would violate his license with the Dental Board of California, which limited his practice to dental procedures only.

In fact, it was Torbiner's nondental practice that brought him to the attention of Evan Chandler. He was introduced to the anesthesiologist by Barry Rothman, who had hired Torbiner at least eight times to apply a general anesthetic during hair transplant procedures. Dr. James De Yarman, the doctor who performed these hair transplants, told Fischer that he was "amazed" to learn Torbiner was not a medical doctor as he believed. So the fact that he failed to keep meticulous records of his use of sodium amytal and that he violated normal procedures may have been in keeping with his character. Nevertheless, it doesn't prove that Torbiner administered the drug to Jordan Chandler.

In Dimond's book, she writes that "questions about

whether Dr. Chandler implanted the molestation in Jordie's subconscious while the boy was under the influence of anesthesia first surfaced in a story that ran in GQ magazine."

Dimond may be unaware that in fact the allegations were first reported not by Fischer, but by a newsman for KCBS-TV five months earlier.

She may also be unaware that the reporter asked Evan Chandler whether he had used the drug on his son. Rather than denying sodium amytal was involved, Chandler claimed he had used a drug only to pull his son's tooth out and that while under that drug's influence, the boy came out with the allegations. This admission is notable for two reasons. First, the drug's effects on Jordie appear to be consistent with the use of sodium amytal. Equally important, experts in the use of this barbiturate claim that the drug is not customarily used in dental extractions.

"It's unusual for it to be used [for pulling out a tooth]," explained Dr. John Yagiela, director of the Dental Anesthesiology Residency Program at the UCLA School of Dentistry. "It makes no sense when better, safer alternatives are available." Fischer, however, was not content to rely on the KCBS-TV report. She preferred to go straight to the source and ask Mark Torbiner whether he used sodium amytal during Jordan Chandler's procedure. Rather than deny it, he told Fischer, "If I used it, it was for dental purposes."

FIVE

As damning as the sodium amytal revelations are to the case against Michael Jackson, Jordan Chandler also revealed details that his father couldn't have possibly have known about and therefore could not have implanted under the influence of drugs. When the police questioned the boy shortly after searching Neverland, he told them much the same story as was contained in his affidavit. But this time he added a bizarre detail.

According to a later affidavit sworn by Deborah Linden, the officer who questioned him, Jordan provided a detailed description of Jackson's naked body to prove his claim that sexual activity had occurred. The singer, he claimed, had distinctive "splotches" on his buttocks and one on his penis, " which [were] a light color similar to the color of his face."

Jordie even drew a picture of Jackson's genital area. Beside it, he wrote, "Michael is circumcised. He has short pubic hair. His testicles are marked with pink and brown marks. Like a cow, not white, but pink color. He has brown patches on [his] ass, on his left gut."

There was a swimming pool at Neverland where Jordie often swam and Jackson had already admitted that the two often slept in the same bedroom. It was quite possible that the boy had seen Jackson undress for bed or in the locker room when he was changing into his trunks. Linden was searching for details that the boy couldn't have simply spotted during these routine periods of nudity.

So Jordan described where the splotch lay on the singer's penis when he was erect.

Prosecutor Tom Sneddon has always claimed that he was at home watching a college football game when the Los Angeles Police Department searched Michael Jackson's houses on August 23. When the BBC called him to ask why Neverland was being raided, he truthfully told them he didn't know. After a few phone calls, the Los Angeles police authorities clued him in. As district attorney for Santa Barbara, the county where Neverland was located, Sneddon was well aware of the implications of the accusations leveled against the famous superstar who lived in his jurisdiction. To his detractors, his subsequent actions reeked of political ambition. What better launching pad for a run at attorney general, maybe even governor, than to go after the world's biggest superstar? To his defenders, he was a tireless crusader whose single-minded quest has been to protect children from a monster.

Whatever his motives, it didn't take Sneddon long to seize the case as his own.

The raids themselves had failed to turn up much incriminating evidence. The initial warrant made it clear what the authorities had been looking for under a section "Items to be seized":

1. Any photographs, slides, negatives, or video recordings of male juveniles, dressed, nude and/or in sexually explicit poses. Any undeveloped film.
2. Diaries, telephone books, address books, correspondence or other writings tending to identify juveniles who have been victims of sexual abuse.
3. To photograph the interior and exterior of the location for identifying purposes and to corroborate witness statements and descriptions.

Police ended up confiscating a total of fifty boxes filled with photographs, notebooks, files, and documents and broke into a safe belonging to the star. In later years, much was made of the seizure of a picture book called *A Boy: A Photographic Essay*. The critically acclaimed book, published in 1963, features more than 400 candid photographs of boys in various poses, mostly innocent. There are also a few photos containing full frontal nudity, which were taken on location during the shooting of the 1963 film *The Lord of the Flies*. Because of these photos, and its connection to the case, the book was frequently described in media accounts as "child pornography" or "child erotica." Even if such a case can be made, police discounted the value of the find when they discovered that it hadn't been purchased by Jackson, but had been sent to him by a fan. Inside was the inscription "To Michael, from your fan. Kiss, kiss, kiss, hug, hug, hug, RhONda."

The police had reached a dead end in their investigation. They had failed to turn up any evidence to corroborate Jordan Chandler's claims. But when Tom Sneddon read Jordie's detailed description of Jackson's genitalia, he was convinced that he had found the smoking gun he was missing. Now he just needed to confirm whether the description was accurate. This was no easy task, given Jackson's high-priced legal team.

At the suggestion of Bert Fields, the singer had retained a well-respected criminal defense attorney named Johnnie Cochran, who would achieve worldwide notoriety a year later when he successfully defended O. J. Simpson against what appeared to be an open-and-shut case of murdering his wife. When Cochran learned that Tom Sneddon wanted to photograph Michael Jackson naked, he went ballistic. "Over my dead body," he railed when he first heard about the district attorney's unusual request. But Sneddon was nothing if not persistent. After being rebuffed twice, Sneddon convinced a superior court judge to issue a "body search warrant" to photograph Jackson's genitals and determine whether they matched Jordan's description. Because of the sensitive nature of the request, the D.A. was instructed to work out the details with Jackson's legal team beforehand to ensure that the search was handled as delicately as possible.

Jackson himself was still out of the country on tour, but Cochran managed to wangle a number of concessions from Sneddon's office. Among these, the singer would be able to choose the location of the exam—Neverland. He could have his own doctor and photographer present. Only one detective could attend and no females were allowed in the vicinity. Above all, the whole procedure would have to be conducted in strict secrecy. During the negotiations, Jackson's team was never told exactly what the investigators were looking for.

At the appointed time, the afternoon of December 20, 1993, a law enforcement team swooped in with a warrant authorizing them to examine and photograph every inch of Jackson's body, including his penis, testicles, and buttocks.

Jackson had flown back to the States ten days earlier to prepare for the most humiliating and painful ordeal he had ever experienced. In November, the singer had abruptly canceled the remainder of his *Dangerous* tour after Elizabeth Taylor arrived in Mexico City with her husband, Larry Fortensky, to fetch Jackson in her private jet. Taylor was deeply worried about her friend. Reports had been filtering back to her from members of Michael's entourage of his unstable behavior. Jackson had developed a dependency on painkillers years earlier after his scalp was badly burned in a freak accident during the filming of a Pepsi commercial in 1984. The stress of the Chandler case was starting to take a severe toll and, according to one of his aides, "Michael was popping pills like candy." Ativan, Valium, and Xanax were his drugs of choice, and they were causing him to lose weight to the point where he looked so sickly that even his full-time makeup artist couldn't hide his deteriorating appearance. Taylor was enlisted to convince her friend to enter rehab to deal with his addiction. On November 12, 1993, she flew him to Europe.

Taylor's 727 made stops in Canada and Iceland before landing at Luton airport near London. After a brief stay with Elton John's manager in the English countryside, Taylor took off again, heading for Geneva, where a limo was waiting to bring the star to her chalet in Gstaad, Switzerland. Nearby was a private Swiss clinic that gave celebrities a place to dry out in total privacy.

Aside from the toll on Jackson's health, the Chandler allegations were already beginning to affect him financially. He had recently been barred from appearing at two November concerts in Dubai. Anonymous pamphlets had been circulated urging a boycott of the concerts and of Jackson's longtime sponsor, Pepsi-Cola. The emirate said its ban was "in line with the traditions, values, culture and habits of the Arab society in the United Arab Emirates."

Meanwhile, fearing a backlash against its public image by the molestation allegations, Pepsi also moved to sever its relationship with the celebrity who had become closely associated with their product. Nine years earlier, Jackson had signed an endorsement deal with the soft drink maker, paying him $6 million. At the time, this was a record for any celebrity endorsement. Since then, Pepsi had sponsored all three of his concert tours, paying him fees of more than $20 million. Over the same period, Pepsi reportedly picked up two market share points on its archrival Coca-Cola—a jump that analysts estimated to be worth about half a billion dollars in annual sales.

• • • •

It was time to face the music. Jackson was nearly cata-tonic about the humiliation he was about to endure. For days, he had told Johnnie Cochran he wouldn't allow it, but his savvy lawyer reminded him about the headlines that would follow if he refused to cooperate. "They'd say you have something to hide," Cochran told him convin-cingly. "You'd be playing right into Sneddon's hands."

The investigative team arrived just before 5:00 p.m. in a limousine designed to hide their presence from the paparazzi who had descended on the ranch in swarms since Jackson's return from Europe ten days earlier. Overhead, news helicopters hovered over Neverland, sensing something was up.

Accompanying Sneddon that day were two detec-tives, one from the Santa Barbara Police Department and one from the Los Angeles Police Department, re-flecting the competing jurisdictions resulting from Jack-son's multiple residences. Also in attendance were a police photographer and a dermatologist, Dr. Richard Strick, who had been assigned to study and report on the distinctive skin markings Jordie described. Jackson stalled the team as long as he could but finally, after a long wait, Sneddon became impatient and ordered the exam to begin.

The team was brought to the Neverland security office, where they were introduced to Jackson's two personal doctors, including his own dermatologist, Dr. Arnold Klein. Jackson's personal photographer and his chief of security were also present. The investiga-tive team was ushered to a room upstairs where Jackson waited nervously on a couch wearing a light-colored bathrobe. The Santa Barbara detective, Russ Birchim, and the Los Angeles detective, Frederico Sicard, introduced themselves and expressed their desire to make the procedure as painless as possible.

"Thank you" was Jackson's reply as one of his lawyers, Howard Weitzman, accepted the search warrant and began to look it over with alarm. The warrant made it clear that the district attorney was particularly interested in Jordie's descriptions of the blotches on Jackson's skin. Over the years, the singer's appearance had become increasingly more bizarre as his skin lightened. One journalist described the evolution as a transformation "from a normal-looking black boy into a white woman." A few months earlier, Jackson had addressed these changes during his televised interview with Oprah Winfrey, explaining that he was suffering from a condition called vitiligo. It results in a loss of pigment, thereby producing white patches. Oprah started the discussion by asking him about the rumors that he bleached his skin:

Michael: Number one, as I know of, there is no such thing as skin bleaching, I have never seen it, I don't know what it is.

Oprah: Well, they used to have those products, I remember growing up always hearing always use bleach and glow, but you have to have about 300,000 gallons.

Michael: Okay, but number one, this is the situation. I have a skin disorder that destroys the pigmentation of the skin, it's something that I cannot help. Okay. But when people make up stories that I don't want to be who I am, it hurts me.

Oprah: So it is . . .

Michael: It's a problem for me that I can't control, but what about all the millions of people who sits [sic] out in the sun, to become darker, to become other than what they are, no one says nothing about that.

Oprah: So when did this start, when did your . . . when did the color of your skin start to change?

Michael: Oh boy, I don't . . . some time after *Thriller*, around *Off the Wall*, *Thriller*, around some time then.

Oprah: But what did you think?

Michael: It's in my family, my father said it's on his side. I can't control it. I don't understand, I mean, it makes me very sad. I don't want to go into my medical history because that is private, but that's the situation here.

Oprah: So okay, I just want to get this straight, you are not taking anything to change the color of your skin . . .

Michael: Oh, God, no, we tried to control it and using makeup evens it out because it makes blotches on my skin. I have to even out my skin. But you know what's funny, why is that so important? That's not important to me. I'm a great fan of art. I love Michelangelo, if I had the chance to talk to him or read about him I would want to know what inspired him to become who he is, the anatomy of his craftsmanship, not about who he went out with last night . . . I mean, that's what is important to me.

If Jordan Chandler or his father had seen the Oprah interview, it would have required little effort to look up vitiligo in a medical dictionary and discover that it resulted in skin splotches, the description that Jordan gave in his statement to the Los Angeles Police Department. But Sneddon was convinced that the photographs would reveal characteristics that Jordan could not have possibly known about without engaging in the type of intimate activities the boy had described.

When Jackson's lawyer read the warrant and realized for the first time what the authorities were searching for, he whispered in Jackson's ear. Suddenly the calm was shattered as the flustered singer began to order the officers to leave.

"Get out! Get out!" he sobbed, lashing out. As both his doctor and lawyer sought to restrain him, Jackson was almost uncontrollable. Johnnie Cochran was summoned from downstairs where he was conversing with Tom Sneddon, who had been prohibited from watching the exam.

Cochran huddled with Jackson and Weitzman and then went back downstairs and asked Sneddon for a favor. Jackson was willing to cooperate fully with the examination and submit to as many photos as was required, but he didn't want the detectives to be present because it would make him feel like a criminal.

After considerable back and forth, Sneddon agreed to the request and the exam began.

In his declaration to the court, Detective Birchim described what happened next.

> At approximately 18:08 hours the door suddenly burst open and I saw Jackson in the doorway struggling to leave the room and being physically restrained by Dr. Klein. Dr. Klein was pleading with Jackson to settle down and he told him, "Michael, you can wear your shorts." Jackson, struggling with Dr. Klein several feet from me and Detective Sicard, pointed at me and yelled, "I want pictures of you two next." Dr. Klein was successful in pulling Jackson back into the room and the door was once again closed.

According to the sheriff's photographer, Sergeant Gary Spiegel, Jackson's demeanor was "a combination of hostility and anger" as he lowered the gray swimming trunks he was wearing under the robe, sobbing softly.

As every eye in the room focused on his genital area, the doctor, holding Jordan Chandler's description, immediately asked, "Is the subject circumcised?"

As everybody went in for a closer look, the answer became apparent.

"Well, the subject is clearly *not* circumcised," the doctor stated.

He did have patchy-colored skin on his buttocks, as the boy described, and he did have short pubic hair.

"I then took photographs of Jackson's penis,"

recalled Spiegel. "First the right side, then the left. When I was photographing the left, the D.A.'s doctor told Michael Jackson to lift up his penis. He didn't want to, so there was a lot of discussion about that. Finally he did it. Then he angrily jumped off the platform. 'That's it,' Jackson said. 'That's enough.'"

As he stormed out of the room, he turned to his head of security, Bill Bray, and said, "Don't you ever let that happen again."

Tom Sneddon had what he came for. If the exam could confirm Jordan's description, then he had the smoking gun that he needed to seek an indictment. Nevertheless, the District Attorney's office remained silent.

It was left up to Jackson to speak first about what had occurred, and on December 22, two days after the ordeal, he purchased satellite time to tell his side of the story. That day, speaking from Neverland, he looked into the cameras wearing a red shirt and white makeup and issued an emotional statement:

I am doing well and I am strong. As you may already know, after my tour ended I remained out of the country undergoing treatment for a dependency on pain medication. This medication was initially prescribed to soothe the excruciating pain that I was suffering after recent reconstructive surgery on my scalp. There have been many disgusting statements made recently concerning allegations of improper conduct on my part. These statements about me are totally false.

As I have maintained from the very beginning, I am hoping for a speedy end to this horrifying experience to which I have been subjected. I shall not in this statement respond to all the false allegations being made against me since my lawyers have advised me that this is not the proper forum in which to do that. I will say I am particularly upset by the handling of this matter by the incredible, terrible mass media. At every opportunity, the media has dissected and manipulated these allegations to reach their own conclusions. I ask all of you to wait to hear the truth before you label or condemn me. Don't treat me like a criminal, because I am innocent. I have been forced to submit to a dehumanizing and humiliating examination by the Santa Barbara County Sheriff's Department and the Los Angeles Police Department earlier this week. They served a search warrant on me, which allowed them to view and photograph my body, including my penis, my buttocks, my lower torso, thighs, and any other areas that they wanted. They were supposedly looking for any discoloration, spotting or other evidence of a skin color disorder called vitiligo which I have previously spoken about. The warrant also directed me to cooperate in any examination of my body by their physician to determine the condition of my skin, including whether I have vitiligo or any other skin disorder. The warrant further stated that I had no right to refuse the examination or photographs and if I failed to cooperate with them they would introduce that refusal at any trial as an indication of my guilt. It was the most humiliating ordeal of my life, one that no person should ever have to suffer. And even after experiencing the indignity of this search, the parties involved were still not satisfied and wanted to take even more pictures. It was a nightmare, a horrifying nightmare. But if this is what I have to endure to prove my innocence, my complete innocence, so be it. Throughout my life, I have only tried to help thousands upon thousands of children to live happy lives. It brings tears to my eyes when I see any child who suffers. I am not guilty of these allegations. But if I am guilty of anything it is of giving all that I have to give to help children all over the world. It is of loving children of all ages and races, it is of gaining sheer joy from seeing children with their innocent and smiling faces. It is of enjoying through them the childhood that I missed myself. If I am guilty of anything, it is of believing what God said about children, "Suffer little children to come unto me and forbid them not, for such is the kingdom of heaven." In no way do I think that I am God, but I do try to be God-like in my heart. I am totally innocent of any wrongdoing and I know these terrible allegations will all be proven false. Again, to my friends and fans, thank you very much for all of your support. Together we will see this through to the very end. I love you very much and may God bless you all. I love you. Good-bye.

By this time, a number of tabloid accounts had already reported that the exam confirmed Jordan's description. Diane Dimond later disclosed that sources told her the dark patch on Jackson's genitals "was found exactly where young Jordan Chandler said they could find such a mark."

But in January 1994, USA Today and Reuters cited law enforcement sources confirming that "photos of Michael Jackson's genitalia do not match descriptions given by the boy who accused the singer of sexual misconduct."

SIX

If the strip search had turned up the evidence Tom Sneddon was looking for, it's likely that he would have gone to a grand jury seeking an indictment. By December 1993, as many as twelve investigators from Santa Barbara and Los Angeles were working full time on the case. They had the sworn statement from the alleged victim and now they had visual evidence to go with his claims. Nevertheless, Sneddon hesitated.

By this time, the team had already spent more than $2 million on the investigation. They had interviewed more than 200 witnesses, including scores of children who had slept with Jackson at Neverland. They had scoured every inch of his home and they had examined his genitals. Yet by most accounts, Sneddon had still failed to find the evidence he needed to go forward.

What he needed was an eyewitness who had seen Jackson molest a child. But much to the frustration of the investigators, no such witness had yet turned up. Moreover, they still had not found a single credible piece of evidence to confirm this. The team had apparently reached a dead end.

And then they caught a break from 8,000 miles away.

Shortly after Jordan Chandler's accusations were made public, a Filipino man named Mark Quindoy called a press conference in Manila to confirm that he had witnessed Jackson molesting children when he and his wife, Faye, worked as housekeeper and cook, respectively, at Neverland between 1989 and 1991. The couple had either quit or been fired in a dispute over overtime pay, claiming Jackson owed them almost $280,000. But now Mark Quindoy, who said he was writing a book about the singer, claimed that they had actually quit because they could not stomach what they had witnessed between Michael and the young children that he shepherded through the ranch on a daily basis.

He claimed that seventy-five boys visited the Jackson estate during his two years there and that he had recorded the names and addresses of the visitors. Moreover, he kept a diary of events along with 200 photographs. He also indicated that he had made detailed notations of what he saw every day at Neverland. Stars on the pages, he said, meant instances of abuse. Asked why they had kept quiet for so long and hadn't gone to the authorities to report what they saw, Quindoy claimed he was afraid of "threats by Jackson's associates." He added, "Michael is such a big man. I was trying to protect him, but it lingered in my mind that it was a civic duty to tell the truth."

Then he dropped the bombshell. Jackson, he declared, was a "gay pedophile."

Elaborating on this accusation, he said that "whatever a gay man does to his partner during sex, Michael does to a child."

He described a scene he had allegedly witnessed involving Jackson and one of his "special friends" as an example. "I swear I saw Michael Jackson fondling the little kid, his hands traveling on the kid's thighs, legs, around his body. And during all this, the kid was playing with his toys."

Another time, Quindoy recalled, he was driving Michael and a seven-year-old friend to a nearby town when he looked back and discovered the spectacle of Jackson kissing the boy "like a lover." The boy wasn't protesting at all, but rather sitting there unmoved. "It was just like a boy kissing a girl in the backseat," he said. "I was utterly stunned—appalled that he could do that to a seven-year-old boy."

Before long, Quindoy was appearing on the tabloid TV show, *A Current Affair*, where he took his accusations a step further, saying that he saw Jackson putting his hands down a boy's underwear.

"Michael Jackson, I think, is uncompassionate. He is insensitive. He is a scheming person. He is a pedophile and I was taken aback when I saw him on television declare that he is innocent, that he has not committed any crime. I think Michael Jackson is guilty as hell."

Tom Sneddon and his team were ecstatic when the Quindoys surfaced with the evidence they needed to move against the singer.

Two investigators—Detective Fred Sicard of the Los Angeles child abuse unit and Sergeant Deborah

Linden of the Santa Barbara Sheriff's Department—immediately flew to Manila to question Mark Quindoy for three hours. After the session, Quindoy contacted reporters. This was becoming a habit.

"I indicated my intentions to go [to the U.S.] if I was asked," he said. He was never asked.

When the Quindoys first surfaced, Anthony Pellicano had described them as "cockroaches" and "extortionists." Now the district attorney was not going to debate the point since his investigators had concluded that their testimony was worthless and the credibility of their claims highly questionable.

It later emerged that the Quindoys had shopped their story around to the highest bidder—a story that changed constantly depending on how much money was on offer. At one point, they were asking $900,000 for the story until Rupert Murdoch's London-based tabloid, *The News of the World*, gained the story for free based on a previous $25,000 agreement with the couple to provide a full and frank account of life with the Jacksons.

Four years later, Mark Quindoy hired a book agent and attempted to sell his so-called diary for the staggering sum of £15 million, promising to expose his "intimate insight" into the singer's sexual preferences through his book, *Malice in Neverland*. Among the purported highlights of the book was his claim that Jackson had flown to London where surgeons removed distinguishing marks from his penis. There were no offers.

The tabloids were salivating. As the allegations against Jackson started to come out in dribs and drabs, they sensed an unprecedented opportunity. Caroline Graham of the world's largest English-language tabloid published out of London, *The Sun*, summed up the mood. The Jackson saga, she wrote, was "probably one of the great stories of the century." Their sales were booming with each juicy headline. And the tabloids were willing to pay for it.

Nobody knew better just how much money they were willing to pay than Paul Barresi. The former gay porn star—best known for his roles in such films as *Men of the Midway* and *What the Big Boys Eat*—had established a lucrative new career brokering sensational stories to American supermarket tabloids such as the *National Enquirer* and the *Globe*, who were known to pay six-figure sums for the right stories.

Barresi had once dated a French woman named Stella LeMarque, a woman who managed Michael Jackson's Neverland household with her husband, Philippe, after the Quindoys left. Now Barresi approached his tabloid contacts promising that the LeMarques had a juicy story to tell—if the price was right.

Philippe was willing to go public with a claim that he had seen Jackson groping his young friend Macaulay Culkin at Neverland in the early morning hours. The *National Enquirer* wanted the LeMarque story badly. They already had the headline to be splashed on the cover of the next edition picked out: "I Saw M.J. Molesting the Culkin Kid." A year earlier, Barresi had sold a story to the *Enquirer* for $100,000. He convinced the LeMarques that he could get more for their story.

In fact, the couple already had a relationship with the notorious supermarket tabloid, having taken money in October 1991 to sneak some *Enquirer* reporters into the ranch to witness Elizabeth Taylor's wedding to her seventh husband, Larry Fortensky. Not long afterward, they were fired from their posts.

"My interest in helping them was that they promised me a percentage of what they got," Barresi confided later. "I was not on any kind of crusade to bring anyone to justice. And whether Michael was guilty or innocent at that point was inconsequential. My interest was strictly for the money, as was their interest too, I might add."

Soon the bidding was up to $150,000 and Barresi thought he had a deal. His cut would be 10 percent.

But then the LeMarques got greedy. They had been approached by a Beverly Hills lawyer named Arnold Kessler, who told them he could get them at least $500,000 for their story. When they tossed Barresi aside and went with Kessler, Barresi hit the roof. It was then that Barresi figured out a way to cash in without their cooperation. He decided to surreptitiously tape their story and sell it himself.

The story, as they later told it, was that one night at Neverland, at about 3:00 a.m., LeMarque received a call that "Silver Fox wanted some French fries" Silver Fox, he said, was Jackson's Neverland code name.

LeMarque said he prepared the late-night snack and delivered it to the arcade room, where he found Jackson and Culkin playing a game based on the singer's *Thriller* album.

"He was holding the kid because the kid was small and couldn't reach the controls. His right hand was holding the kid, maybe midwaist. And the left hand was down into his pants."

"I almost dropped the French fries," he recalled.

His wife, Stella, added details about an Australian boy whom Jackson groped in the dark at a Neverland movie theater as the boy's mother sat nearby.

"In the cinema, he did the same thing. And the mother was two or three rows in front. They were like lovers. That's not normal." Stella also claimed that the singer had a bedroom within his bedroom where he would take his "special friends." In those rooms, she said, he would watch porn movies with the kids all night long.

In another instance, according to Philippe, the local fire department arrived at Neverland when an alarm was sounded at the ranch. "When the chief fireman arrived, Stella and I were there, and Jackson came downstairs," he said. "The fireman was trying to account for everyone, and he asked where Macaulay was sleeping. Michael snapped at him, 'What does that matter? What has that got to do with you? Why are you asking me that?'"

"Everyone always says, 'Oh, Michael, he loves children,'" Stella said. "I say that's bullshit."

"Everybody knows what's going on at the ranch," her husband added. "Everybody knows, but nobody talks."

In the secretly taped conversation, the couple told Barresi that Jackson's relationship with children deeply troubled his good friend Marlon Brando.

"The only one who ever said something was Marlon Brando," Stella related. "He would come to the ranch and always see Michael playing, [and] disappear with the children. Michael would never spend time with the adults who came to the ranch. He was the only one. He said, 'What the hell is Michael doing with those kids?'"

To get even with the LeMarques for what he called their double-crossing, Barresi turned the tapes over to Anthony Pellicano, who would use their inconsistencies to discredit the couple and ensure nobody would buy their story.

"They didn't make a dime, the c***suckers."

He also turned their tapes over to the district attorney, at which point the illegally taped conversations became legal under California laws because they were now part of the case record.

Barresi would later give a number of interviews demonstrating how the LeMarques changed their story after they first contacted him.

"Every time they told the story, they would add a little more," he says. "[Jackson's] hand went from outside the kid's pants to inside the kid's pants. It was outside the kid's pants when their asking price was fifty grand, and inside the kid's pants when their asking price went up to a hundred thousand."

Still, Tom Sneddon was intrigued enough by their account that he brought the couple before the two separate grand juries he had convened to address the charges against Jackson.

Evidently the jurors didn't find their story all that credible, even though at the time they had no idea that the couple had repeatedly attempted to sell it to the highest bidder. If the LeMarques had ever gone to court to testify against Jackson, the cross-examination would have focused on more than simply their tabloid sales attempts.

There was at least one other factor weighing on the couple's credibility. It seems that some time after they had tried and failed to sell their lurid story about Michael Jackson, they had also launched a hard-core pornographic website called Virtual Sin, billed as the "most sinful site on the Internet." Visitors to the site were greeted by a friendly welcome: "Welcome Beaver Hunters." Surfing the large gallery of photos and videos, one could find a number of enticing captions, depending on the category: "c*** ***kin' is licking gooood!" or "We will give you a big lick on your big one or small one."

Another page promised the "search for the perfect PUSSY" as well as Mr. LeMarque's ruminations, such as "Why I love whores." In this list, he outlined what he considered were the leading virtues of prostitutes:

- Whores are musicians [who] can play the skin flute.
- Whores know how to share with others, even their most private parts!
- Whores are excellent calcium therapists, they can make an 8-inch boner out of nothing.

Virtual Sin wasn't the couple's only entrepreneurial venture. Another site, Galaxy 2001, offered a tutorial to would-be online porn merchants. "Selling SEX is not difficult if you know how to manage your boat through the intricacies of the Internet," the site declared. It also contained a flashing link to another porn site promising "TEENS, TEENS, TEENS." Mr. LeMarque claimed that Galaxy 2001 doubled as a web host and housed "hundred[s] of adult website[s]" on its servers.

After these sites went under, Philippe and Stella again tried their hand at cashing in on their association with Jackson. On a site they started about the California food and wine scene, Philippe describes a book he wrote about the couple's tenure at Neverland Ranch, "especially Michael's behavior which at times puzzles the public."

The book, he adds, covers "the most hush-hush topic at the ranch that barely anyone has ever unveiled—the 'Ghosts of Never[l]and Valley.'" For $4.95, visitors could download "the Complete Chapter of our stay at Michael Jackson's Never[l]and Valley."

With dubious witnesses such as the LeMarques and the Quindoys, Tom Sneddon knew he had hit a dead end. He still didn't have a single credible eyewitness capable of convincing a grand jury.

And then suddenly he got a break, thanks to a reporter who was fast becoming the D.A.'s greatest asset.

On December 15, 1993, as Tom Sneddon was getting ready to serve his body search warrant on Michael Jackson, the tabloid TV show *Hard Copy* aired a special segment hosted by Diane Dimond called "The Bedroom Maid's Painful Secret." In a potentially devastating interview, Jackson's former maid Blanca Francia, an illegal immigrant from El Salvador who had worked five years for Jackson beginning in 1986, told Dimond that she saw Jackson bathing naked with at least two young boys in the Neverland shower and Jacuzzi. She claimed that Jackson once asked her opinion of what she saw.

"I said it was none of my business," she said. "He liked that." Occasionally, she revealed, "I would get some reward. Money, or a gift . . . I would keep my mouth shut to keep my job."

She also claimed that she frequently saw Jackson sleeping in the same sleeping bag as young boys. In addition, she said, he kept a secret apartment at Neverland specifically for entertaining his young friends.

She claimed that Jackson would often have young boys stay with him for weeks at a time and that he always gave them the same nickname—Rubba.

"I saw little things like rubbing a boy against his body," she said. "He had boys sitting in his lap and rubbing them." That, she speculated, was the explanation behind the unusual nickname.

Among the most bizarre allegations she made was her claim that Jackson would often be too lazy to go to the bathroom, so he would simply relieve himself in his pants.

"Don't be surprised if you see any dirty underwear," she recalled him saying. "Sometimes I can't hold it, so I just go in my underwear." On the subject of toilet habits, she says he also went through entire days speaking in "doo-doo," calling himself and everybody around him "doo-doo head."

The most contestable part of the interview, however, was Francia's implication that Jackson molested her young son, Jason.

"Our conversation about exactly what happened to her son was confusing," Dimond admitted years later. "At some points she said she didn't think anything happened. But in the next breath she would be in tears, worried that she would never be able to reach or heal her damaged son."

Francia claimed she didn't want her son to become one of his "special friends."

"I know about these special friends that he has," she said. "He will drop one and get another one and drop another one and get another one . . . I think he was planning to keep my son as his special friend."

When Dimond asked her straight out whether she thought Jackson had actually molested her son, she replied, "I don't think I gave him the chance to do it," adding she is unsure because [her son] Jason was "so quiet and angry."

Eventually, she said, she finally quit in disgust when she found Jason sitting on Jackson's lap. When she questioned them about it, she received what she called "vague answers."

The next evening, Jackson's mother, Katherine, gave an interview to Black Entertainment Television to trash the maid's story and come to her son's defense. She called Francia a "sacked, disgruntled employee," adding, "[m]ost of the time when people are sacked they always try to get back at Michael."

Whether or not Francia quit, as she claimed, or was

fired, as Katherine Jackson maintained, most people wanted to know why she had told her story for the first time to a tabloid TV show instead of informing the authorities, especially if she suspected her own son may have been abused.

That's not the only question critics were asking in the wake of Dimond's explosive interview. *Hard Copy* had acquired a reputation of paying its sources. Had Francia been paid to tell her story to the program?

This topic became the subject of a testy exchange when she appeared a week later on CNN's respected media issues program, *Reliable Sources*. Her answer only raised more suspicions. On the program, the moderator, Bernard Kalb, hosted a panel featuring Dimond, *People* columnist Mitchell Fink, and senior *Newsweek* correspondent Jonathan Alter to discuss the media's coverage of the Jackson abuse allegations. Alter, in particular, was clearly annoyed at the way the case had been dominating the news lately:

Alter: We put Michael Jackson on the cover in early September when a lot of other people were ignoring the story, and I thought then that it was the right decision. You had at that point his defenders setting aside the criminal allegations, you had his own defenders sitting in Neverland, his estate, saying that this thirty-five-year-old man slept in the same bed with preteens. So right there, setting aside whether any charges have been leveled against him, right there, his own defenders have turned this into some kind of a story. The question is what kind of a story, how big, and what I'm looking for here is just some sense of perspective, not fastidious[ly] the way the *New York Times* won't touch this, it's above that. This is a big story. He's the biggest star in the world. But it doesn't deserve to dominate *Hard Copy* every single night with new paid accusers on every single night.

Dimond: Well, wait a minute. Wait a minute.

Kalb: Yeah, Diane. Speaking of that . . .

Dimond: Wait a minute. Wait a minute. Wait a minute.

Kalb: Money?

Dimond: Every single person in this story—and *Hard Copy* broke this story. Pat ourselves on the back for that. Every single person in this story has a money motivation, from the very high paid lawyers, from the very high paid private detectives on both sides. Everybody's got their hand out on this thing, and everybody is making money.

Kalb: Yeah, but the question . . .

Dimond: Now I know the question is going to be . . .

Kalb: Diane, that I'm going to ask you—everybody may have their hand out, but who is filling it? For example, what did *Hard Copy* give the personal maid to Michael Jackson for that long interview that you did?

Dimond: You know, I'll tell you, everybody has said

to me, "Well, she only came forward because she paid her." Wrong. She came forward because I spent seven weeks . . .

Kalb: Did you pay her?

Dimond: . . . I spent seven weeks trying to find her. I'm not going to comment on whether we paid her or not . . .

Alter: Oh, of course.

Dimond: . . . because, if I did, then every single interview that we did, I'd have to answer that question.

Alter: Well, what's wrong with answering it?

Dimond: That's not the point.

Alter: Why not disclose? If you're going to pay them, fine.

Dimond: The point is . . .

Alter: If you want to defend that . . . but then say what you paid them. Then we can judge this—we can then assess these accusers in a better way. It's fine, if you want to say you're going to pay them, to put them on and say, "We . . ."

Dimond: If you want to judge these accusers . . .

Alter: ". . . pay them," and then we could factor that in . . .

Dimond: If you want to judge these accusers . . .

Alter: But you don't ever say you pay them when you introduce them. This . . .

Dimond: If you want to judge these accusers . . .

Kalb: Excuse me, Diane. Please, Jonathan, hang on. Diane—let Diane—she's in the witness chair for the moment, so to speak. Diane, yours.

Dimond: If you want to judge the veracity of these witnesses, you talk to the district attorney, you talk to the Los Angeles police, the Santa Barbara police, you talk to the attorney for the thirteen-year-old boy, and you're talking about the maid we just put on recently, Blanca Francia. They say that she is a very significant witness and I found her, and I put her on the air, and . . .

Fink: I'm not trying to defend Michael Jackson now.

Dimond: I think part of this . . .

Fink: Diane . . .

Dimond: I think part of this is professional jealousy because *Hard Copy*, whether you like our show or not, has been out on front on this story.

Fink: Nobody—

Kalb: Diane, let someone else . . .

Fink: Excuse me. Nobody is jealous of *Hard Copy*. This story is not about who gets paid and who doesn't.

Dimond: That's exactly right.

Fink: This story is about Michael Jackson and what he has done at each step in this story, and had Michael Jackson come forward and returned to the United States when these allegations first surfaced, this might have been a completely different story, but

Michael Jackson stayed out of the lime-light, I mean, even went—before he left for London amid the supposed drug de-pendency—when he left, he was in Mexico City. He was sequestered in a hotel room.

Kalb: Mitchell, I don't want to go through the entire itinerary. I just . . .

Fink: But you've got to understand, Bernie,that it's his behavior that has dictated how this story has gone.

Alter: Of course, his behavior has dictated it, but the journalist[ic] question is, if you're going to pay, we deserve to know that you've paid. In other words, at the beginning of each of those *Hard Copy* episodes—and some of them have broken some very im-portant developments in this story. I think Diane has done a good job, but if you're going to introduce new elements of the story and you have paid them, in the inter-est of full disclosure, you should introduce each one of those accusers with a caveat that says, "You should, you the viewer, should understand this person has been paid." That doesn't mean they're not tell-ing the truth, but "You should understand that [. . .] money is involved." The motive is very important to understanding this.

Dimond's refusal to answer the question about whether Francia was paid to tell her story made the Jackson legal team curious. The team quickly discovered that *Hard Copy* had in fact paid the maid $20,000 for her interview. Dimond later claimed that the sum was paid by her employer, Paramount Pictures, as part of a "corporate decision."

"Just because somebody gets money doesn't mean they're lying," said Dimond.

Indeed, the fact that *Hard Copy* paid Francia for an interview does not by itself disqualify the validity of her story, though it certainly provided a welcome opportunity for the defense to discredit her credibility. It also sparked a heated debate in the American media about the ethics and implications of paying sources.

"I think what money presents is the inducement to tell the worst, most salacious story—maybe even make it up," wrote *Los Angeles Times* media critic Tom Rosenstiel.

"Anybody who doesn't pay money, it's like cavalry riding into machine-gun fire. It's anachronistic," said Stuart White of the London *News of the World*, which has long had a reputation for paying sources. "Journalism cannot be done today at our level without, at some point, somebody getting a cheque out and going to one of the principals—who will be demanding this money—and hopefully presenting him with the best offer."

A year after the Chandler civil suit was filed, *Hard Copy*'s willingness to pay its sources—and the resulting blow to the paid witness's credibility—was cited as one of the most important factors in the acquittal of O. J. Simpson. A woman named Jill Shively was the only eyewitness to put Simpson near the scene of his wife's murder when she saw him driving a white Ford Bronco with its lights out around the same time that his ex-wife and Ronald Goldman were stabbed to death. But prosecutors declined to call Shively to the witness stand when they learned that she had accepted $5,000 to tell her story to *Hard Copy*.

Michael Jackson biographer J. Randy Taraborrelli, who was working on his book, *The Magic and the Madness*, at the time when Jordan Chandler's accusations were made public, ended up being highly suspicious of the allegations, precisely because of the sheer number of "witnesses" asking for money.

"I've seen so many extortion attempts against the Jackson camp and they never turn out to be worth anything," Taraborrelli told *Time* magazine, lamenting that during the course of his research, "[e]very damn butler, housekeeper, chauffeur and chef wanted $100,000 for their insights into his private life. I've written about Diana Ross, Cher, Carol Burnett, and Roseanne Arnold, but I never had that experience with any of my other books. And that was just me, a biographer. You can imagine what it's like for him with his millions."

In the end, it wasn't necessarily Blanca Francia's acceptance of $20,000 that damaged her credibility as a witness. Instead, it was her deposition taken by Jackson's legal team in which she admitted embellishing her story to *Hard Copy*. Under oath, she admitted that she had never actually seen Jackson shower with anyone or naked with boys in his jacuzzi. They always had their swimming trunks on, contrary to the story she had told Diane Dimond.

In addition, *Hard Copy* may not have been the only media source to have paid her for her story. In 1997, a longtime *National Enquirer* reporter named Jim Mitteager died, bequeathing a large collection of tapes he had compiled to Paul Barresi.

On one of the tapes, Barresi discovered that a *National Enquirer* reporter named Lydia Encinas was with Blanca Francia when the police came to question her about Michael Jackson in early 1994. Encinas, it turned out, acted as the interpreter, translating Francia's account from Spanish to English for the police.

On a tape, dated March 23, 1994, *Enquirer* editor David Perel is heard telling Mitteager: "The reason why Lydia Encinas is involved is because she speaks Spanish and she's got a pretty good relationship going with Blanca. The cops took Lydia yesterday to Blanca's house. [Blanca has] only got a sixth-grade education, so there is a problem there. Blanca is very distrustful . . . The cops are looking for copies of agreements between Jackson and parents."

At one point on the tapes, Perel is heard giving instructions to Mitteager. It provides considerable insight into the lengths the tabloids were willing to go to get new dirt on Jackson:

Jim, when you go in on these deals, talk big money and don't back off. I mean, talk fifty grand. We need [Jackson's former manager] Frank DiLeo telling all, at $100,000, if we can get him. We need all of Jackson's celebrity pals. Anything they said. Every kid that has ever been with Jacko, we want to know who he is . . . where he's coming from . . . any pictures available. We want to put big offers to any member of the family. We need to go with the big money. The big offers. It's the biggest story since [Elvis] Presley's death.

Meanwhile, two other former Neverland housekeepers came forward to discredit Francia's allegations, telling CNN that the stories were made up.

"I think it's ridiculous," declared Shanda Lujan, who worked at Neverland for almost a year. "I mean, there's just no way that Michael could do that. Michael's just not that type of person."

Francin Orosco worked for Jackson for two years and also said Jackson was incapable of the kind of behavior he was being accused of. "I think it's pure lies. I think it's just pure lies. It's disgusting what they—what they could accuse somebody of for, and I think it's just all for money. Michael could never do something like that. Never, ever."

Both Orosco and Lujan claimed that Francia had actually been fired because of a bad attitude and was obsessed with the pop superstar.

"You could tell a lot that she had a little crush on him. And very jealous of the other housekeepers and didn't want no one close to Michael. There was . . . there's a lot of jealousy there," said Orosco.

"He was great with kids," added Lujan. "I mean, you know, if . . . I think he would be a very good father. I mean, he's just wonderful with them." The former maids said their ranch chores involved entering Jackson's room at times, but that they had never seen anything suspicious.

Most notable about their statements was that at the time of their interviews, each of the two women were no longer on Jackson's payroll and were not paid for their interviews, and therefore had no incentive to lie.

The scene in Tom Sneddon's office was one of despair. For weeks, the D.A. had hit one roadblock after another in his quest to indict Jackson. Witness after witness was questioned by his investigators, one boy after another. Each told the same story. Nothing improper had occurred. Their parents said the same thing. The search of Jackson's Century City condo had turned up nothing of value. They had gone through Neverland with a fine-tooth comb. Still nothing. But Sneddon refused to give up. He was certain a witness would come forward with the smoking gun.

In an effort to turn up such a witness, investigators had become increasingly aggressive, perhaps to the point of desperation.

Parents of Jackson's former special friends began to complain to Jackson's lawyer Bert Fields of officers coming to their homes telling them that their children had been molested by the singer, despite the children's continuing denials that anything improper had ever taken place.

Outraged, Fields went so far as to draft a letter to Los Angeles police chief Willie Williams complaining about his officers' tactics.

"I am advised," Fields wrote, "that your officers have

told frightened youngsters outrageous lies, such as 'we have nude photos of you' in order to push them into making accusations against Mr. Jackson. There are, of course, no such photos of these youngsters and they have no truthful accusations to make . . . I urge you to put an end to these abuses. Investigate these accusations as thoroughly as possible, but do it in a manner more consistent with honest, common decency, and the high standards that once made me proud of the [Los Angeles Police Department]."

One officer, Federico Sicard, later admitted to Jackson's attorney, Michael Freeman, that he had lied to the children he'd interviewed by telling them that he himself had been molested as a child.

Even with these questionable tactics, however, not a single youngster had even hinted that Jackson had harmed them.

But as Sneddon watched a breaking news report on CNN, he believed he had finally found what he had been waiting for. In a press conference held at a Tel Aviv hotel, Jackson's elder sister, La Toya, had just accused her brother of molesting children.

"I can no longer remain a silent collaborator in Michael's crimes against small, innocent children," she told the assembled reporters.

La Toya, who had just arrived in Israel with her husband/manager, Jack Gordon, was scathing in her remarks.

"If I remain silent, then that means that I feel the guilt and humiliation that these children are feeling and I think it's very wrong," she declared.

She also said she had seen "proof" of Michael's illicit involvement with children. "I have seen checks payable to the parents of these children," La Toya said.

It didn't take long for the rest of the Jackson family to weigh in. "La Toya is lying and I'll tell her to her face she's lying. And she knows it," mother Katherine Jackson responded angrily in an interview with a Los Angeles TV station, KCBS.

"She lies all the time," Michael's father, Joe Jackson, piped in. "This is how they [La Toya and her husband] make their living, by lying."

They both accused La Toya's husband, Jack Gordon, of putting her up to the accusations in an attempt to cash in.

Katherine called Gordon a con man and a thug and accused him of beating and brainwashing her daughter.

La Toya had become something of an outcast since she married her brutish manager in 1989. She immediately distanced herself from the rest of the family, and shortly after her marriage she posed nude for *Playboy*, resulting in one of the highest-selling issues in the magazine's history.

Around the same time, La Toya announced she planned to write a book that would tell "the whole truth about my dysfunctional family." Behind the scenes, she intimated to the family that she would write about Michael being molested as a child. Meanwhile, Jack Gordon allegedly offered to cancel the book project if her parents paid her $5 million.

Now, with Jackson's sister finally ready to spill the beans, Tom Sneddon immediately made plans to depose

La Toya, convinced her compelling testimony would impress a grand jury. But she had already changed her mind before he had a chance to make the arrangements. She announced that she had said what she did about her brother only under threat of violence from her husband. Indeed, a number of news outlets, including CNN, reported that Gordon had been shopping La Toya's story about Michael's abuse for a minimum of $250,000.

Still, the sudden retraction was hard to swallow. Had Michael's people got to her? Had they paid her to change her story?

The first hints of the torment La Toya had been suffering for years at the hands of Jack Gordon came when she briefly left her husband in 1994. While she was separated, she appeared on a London talk show hosted by Frank Skinner, who asked her about her sudden about-face. At first she said she was contractually obligated not to discuss it, but then she concluded that this obligation was valid only in the United States. Without mentioning Gordon by name, she opened up for the first time:

> I was under the control of this individual where if I didn't do or say what he said, he threatened many times to not only kill me, but he would kill my brother and he would kill my sister. As strange as this may sound, I believed this man because I had seen things before and I'd seen the things that can happen. I didn't have a choice . . . [My siblings said] that's not her, she wouldn't say that, someone's controlling her. However, no one

really stepped forward to try and stop him all the way. They did, but he would cut them off each time, keeping them away from me. And it came to that point that I knew he was going to kill me. So I phoned one of my brothers and said, "You've got to come get me. I'm tired of this control. I'm tired of this." That's basically what happened, he came, he rescued me. He knocked on the door and he said "Let's go" and we ran and we caught the plane and I just left. I was afraid that if he caught me in the act, I knew he would kill me. He promised me he would kill me. He promised me if I didn't say certain things, he would kill my brother, my sister. So what do you do in a case like that? Do you say, "I don't care, go kill them." Or do you say, "well, let me just do this now and I'll explain it to them later."

Inexplicably, La Toya ended up getting back together with Gordon for a brief period until she finally walked out on him for good when he attempted to force her to dance at a Cleveland strip club in 1996. When she refused to do so, the audience greeted her with boos and catcalls, causing her to flee the club. When she returned home that evening, she was severely beaten.

The divorce proceedings that followed provide a telling glimpse into the couple's marriage and appear to support La Toya's claims that her husband forced her to make up stories about Michael. What started as a productive business relationship had quickly degenerated into a pattern of severe emotional and physical abuse.

Gordon was in fact arrested twice during the marriage for assaulting his wife. In her autobiography, La Toya also claimed that the wedding itself was both unplanned and against her will. Gordon, she claimed, "tricked" her into the marriage by brainwashing her into believing that her family was going to attempt to kidnap her.

Despite her brief reconciliation with Jack Gordon, she continued to disavow her comments about Michael, which she maintains were literally "scripted" by her ex-husband. La Toya's reversal, of course, meant that Tom Sneddon had been thwarted once again.

SEVEN

Like Tom Sneddon, I spent a lot of time attempting to track down Michael Jackson's "special friends." The more I read about the district attorney's unsuccessful attempts to find good witnesses, the more I wondered if it was the goon-like tactics of his investigators that scared away potential sources. Perhaps, I thought, a kinder and gentler approach would produce better results.

Poring over contemporary media accounts and interviewing friends and former staff, we were able to locate more than 40 people who had slept over at Neverland at least once as children. It was a far cry from the 200 that Sneddon's team had identified with their vast financial resources. But like him, I couldn't find a single person who even hinted that Jackson had acted improperly. Each of the 42 people we interviewed were now adults, most with professional careers, for the most part living in California.

Yet none would agree to go on camera and defend him for my documentary, except a single person who would agree to appear only if his voice and face were disguised. This young man, named Joseph, in his early thirties, explained his reluctance. "It's embarrassing," he explained. "Most people assume that something perverted went on, no matter how hard I swear it was all innocent. It's ironic because at the time I did a lot of bragging about it and all my friends were jealous."

Looking back, he admits, "The whole thing was surreal. Here was this mega mega star taking us shopping, having bubble battles, watching movies, and playing video games and all I could think of at the time is how cool it was. I never even thought for a second that there was anything strange about it. Neither did my mom or dad. Later on, when all this stuff started to come out, my dad kept asking me over and over again if he did anything to me. He even wanted to know if maybe during a tickle fight or something, he might have 'accidentally' slipped his hands in my pj's. There was nothing like that. Michael was just this big oversized goofy kid."

Joseph says his only regret about his time with Jackson is that it was hard to accept that it had to come to an end.

"He sort of just stopped sending for us at some point, and I remember being very sad for a long time, kind of like withdrawal, though he sent great presents for my birthday for a couple of years afterwards."

I had already met with one of Jackson's more famous special friends, Macaulay Culkin, but when I was doing research to track down the children, I realized that I just happened to know another one.

I was working on an unrelated project with Sean Lennon when I came across a plethora of newspaper articles from the period when he and Michael were inseparable. Lennon, in fact, appeared in Jackson's *Moonwalker* film when he was thirteen years old, though he had been hanging out with Jackson since he was eight. I wasn't sure how he would respond if I brought up the subject, but Sean's eyes lit up when I mentioned Jackson. At his sprawling SoHo loft, where I was working on a video project for his then girlfriend, I casually asked him about those days.

"We used to have a blast," he told me.

I was reluctant to bring up the topic of child molestation, but it was in fact Sean who ended up broaching the subject.

"It's funny," he said. "People who think Michael's a diddler always assume that he bought off the families of the kids he molested. You hear it all the time. They say he must have just written a million-dollar check to all the kids who threatened to come forward. But look at me. I was one of those kids that he befriended at a young age. I may have spent more time with him than almost anybody else. I've seen all kinds of people publicly speculate that he abused me. But I think my family is actually richer than he is. So it would be quite the trick to buy me and my mother off. It's ridiculous. No way is Mike a child abuser. Take it from me. I knew the kids he knew. I would have known if anything funny was going on."

It wasn't much different from what Culkin had said to me, but Lennon did tell me one thing that I had never heard before.

"It wasn't just boys, you know. There were girls around too, and not just the sisters."

This threw me for a loop. One of the recurring

themes in the coverage of the allegations against Jackson was that he chose only boys to be his special friends. Time and again, people questioned why he never had friends who were girls. I remember always being a little suspicious of that myself.

"He's a gay pedophile," said Mark Quindoy at his Manila press conference. "He always surrounded himself with boys."

And shortly after La Toya leveled her accusations against Michael, her husband, Jack Gordon, gave an interview to CNN where he also accused his brother-in-law of being a homosexual pedophile.

"I saw little boys constantly going through the house," said Gordon. "I never saw little girls. I used to ask the question: 'Why are there little boys here and there are no little girls?' I never got an answer."

In her scathing 1995 article for *Vanity Fair*, "The Jackson Jive," Maureen Orth also notes the absence of girls in Jackson's life. "Investigators who contacted approximately 400 witnesses say that no one has found a single little girl who was invited to bed with Jackson. He slept only with little boys," writes Orth, who would regularly eviscerate Jackson in print.

According to Lennon, Jackson was very shy around girls, like an "awkward teenager." But every once in a while, he would hit it off with one and would invite her to his home for sleepovers.

During the course of my investigation, I found four of these girls. One of them, Allison V. Smith, is now a world-renowned photographer who has shot photos for *The New York Times*, *Esquire*, and *The New Yorker*, among others. She is also an heiress to the Neiman Marcus luxury department store fortune as the granddaughter of the late retail legend, Stanley Marcus.

"During the [2005 child molestation] trial, they kept talking about all the boys who slept in his bed. Well, I'm a girl and I slept in his bed when I was a kid. The prosecutor must know that there were girls around, but he never mentioned it," she says, adding that her friendship with Jackson was "a lot of fun" but that she doesn't like talking about it publicly.

"I was tempted to offer myself up as a defense witness," she recalls, "but I didn't relish the media circus."

In 1993, as the Jordan Chandler case dominated the headlines, U.S. talk show host Geraldo Rivera staged his own nationally televised mock trial where real witnesses were called to present the case for and against Michael Jackson in front of a jury. Among the most poignant moments of the trial was the testimony of a seventeen-year-old girl name Mandy Porter, who had been a "special friend" of Jackson since she was eleven. The defense attorney was prominent New York lawyer Raoul Felder. He had just called Mandy's mother, Carol Nilwicki, to appear jointly with her daughter on the stand:

Rivera: (Voiceover) When last we spoke, the counselor for the defense of Michael Jackson called a Saint Louis housewife, Carol Nilwicki. Carol is here in court with Mandy, her daughter. Counselor?

Mr. Felder: Carol, you're Mandy's mother, right?

Mrs. Carol Nilwicki (Saint Louis, Missouri): Yes.

Mr. Felder: Let me cast your mind back to six years ago, Saint Louis, a very cold day. Do you remember?

Mrs. Nilwicki: I remember.

Mr. Felder: Twenty-two degrees below zero. What were you doing on that day?

Mrs. Nilwicki: I was standing in line waiting to get Michael Jackson tickets.

Mr. Felder: And did you get any tickets?

Mrs. Nilwicki: No.

Mr. Felder: Okay. Now, let's leave you right there and could we have Mandy come up? 'Cause she comes into this story.

Rivera: OK. Mandy Porter. Mandy, Carol's teenage daughter, is a young lady who suffers from a disease—don't know the Latin name—but the net effect is that Mandy is losing her vision, I believe, in both eyes. It was a condition that Michael Jackson was made aware of. Counselor?

Mr. Felder: Carol, so you couldn't get the tickets. What happened after that?

Mrs. Nilwicki: I came home and she was standing at the top of the stairs all excited. "Did you get my tickets?"

Mr. Felder: Yes.

Mrs. Nilwicki: And I was like, "No." And she said, "Well, if Michael found out about all this, he'd be really upset."

Mr. Felder: What—what did she do?

Mrs. Nilwicki: I have a friend that was at the house at

the time, and he made a video recording. Three days went by. I went ahead and went to church that evening. And came back home to find her standing at the top of the stairs going, "My friend Mikey called." And I was like, "Well that's nice, honey." And my husband was standing there. He said, "Michael Jackson was calling, leaving a message for us—for Amanda on the answering machine." And they got to be friends. They started talking on the phone. He talked to my husband and myself to gain permission.

Mr. Felder: He asked your permission whether to talk to your daughter?

Mrs. Nilwicki: Michael is always respectful.

Mr. Felder: Your daughter has some medical problems. Did Michael ever help out?

Mrs. Nilwicki: Yes, Michael's helped out with her medical bills.

Mr. Felder: Okay. She's still friendly with Michael?

Mrs. Nilwicki: Oh, yeah.

Mr. Felder: Before I ask her a couple of questions, you have a little boy, too, don't you?

Mrs. Nilwicki: Yes, I do.

Mr. Felder: How old is that boy?

Mrs. Nilwicki: Seven.

Mr. Felder: Would you have any problem about letting Michael take care of that boy or go out with that boy?

Mrs. Nilwicki: I would trust Michael Jackson with my son's life.

Mr. Felder: Okay. Thank you. Mandy, can I ask you . . . (Applause). Mandy, you've known Michael a long time now.

Ms. Mandy Porter (Friend of Michael Jackson): Yeah.

Mr. Felder: You're buddies with him?

Ms. Mandy Porter: Yeah.

Mr. Felder: What sorts of things do you with him?

Ms. Mandy Porter: Well, basically, anything else that anybody else would do with their child or their friends. As teenagers go out, and they like to go out shopping and looking around. That's what me and Michael like to do. We like to talk about—and catch up on things that we haven't caught up with from the previous time that we talked.

Mr. Felder: Did he ever do anything that upset you or . . .

Ms. Mandy Porter: No.

Mr. Felder: . . . we'll say was improper? Never, never, never?

Ms. Mandy Porter: Never.

Mr. Felder: Okay. I have no further questions.

Hon. Becker: Ms. Walden, do you wish to inquire?

Ms. Walden: Please. It's Mrs. Porter?

Mrs. Nilwicki: Nilwicki. Mrs. Nilwicki.

Ms. Walden: Nilwicki, I'm sorry. Mrs. Nilwicki, how old is your daughter?

Mrs. Nilwicki: She will be seventeen in December.

Ms. Walden: And she's known Michael Jackson how long?

Mrs. Nilwicki: Since she was about eleven.

Ms. Walden: Eleven. Would you, by any chance, know how old Mr. Jackson is?

Mrs. Nilwicki: Yes, ma'am, I'm well aware of his age.

Ms. Walden: Would you tell the jury and the audience?

Mrs. Nilwicki: He's thirty-five.

Ms. Walden: Now if this was any other thirty-five-year-old man, would you let your daughter go off with him?

Mrs. Nilwicki: You must realize something. We sought Michael Jackson out. He did not seek my daughter out.

Ms. Walden: You have a seventeen-year-old daughter, Mrs. Nilwicki. If another thirty-five-year-old man approached you and said he wanted a friendship with your daughter, would you allow it?

Mrs. Nilwicki: The situation would depend. I'll be honest with you.

Ms. Walden: Elaborate for us.

Mrs. Nilwicki: We have family friends. You have to understand. You're talking about going out. Are you talking about going out in a dating situation?

Ms. Walden: I'm talking about any thirty-five-year-old man taking your seventeen-year-old daughter anywhere?

Mrs. Nilwicki: Well, that leaves a lot of room for speculation. It really does.

Ms. Walden: Amanda?

Ms. Mandy Porter: Yes.

Ms. Walden: You and Michael Jackson are still very good friends?

Ms. Mandy Porter: Yes, we are.

Ms. Walden: He's a special friend?

Ms. Mandy Porter: Yes, he is.

Ms. Walden: You love him very much?

Ms. Mandy Porter: Yes, I do.

Ms. Walden: You consider yourself lucky and privileged to have him as a friend.

Ms. Mandy Porter: Yes.

Ms. Walden: You would do nothing or say anything that would harm or hinder or perhaps sever that friendship, would you?

Ms. Mandy Porter: If it was the truth, yes, I would.

Ms. Walden: Do you have any other thirty-five-year-old male friends?

Ms. Mandy Porter: Yes, I do. And I have some that are older than that.

(Applause)

Ms. Mandy Porter: It's not the age. It is not the age that matters.

At the end of the broadcast, the jury found Jackson not guilty.

In August 1993, two Los Angeles police officers met with June Chandler Schwartz to discuss her son's allegations against Jackson. She still believed Jackson was innocent of the charges because she had never seen anything the slightest bit suspicious during all the time Jackson and Jordie were together. She changed her mind after listening to what the officers told her that afternoon.

According to her attorney, Michael Freeman, who was present at the meeting, "[the officers] admitted they only had one boy, but they said, 'We're convinced Michael Jackson molested this boy because he fits the classic profile of a pedophile perfectly.'"

"There's no such thing as a classic profile. They made a completely foolish and illogical error," claims Dr. Ralph Underwager, a Minneapolis psychiatrist who has treated pedophiles and victims of incest since 1953. Michael Jackson "got nailed" because of "misconceptions like these that have been allowed to parade as fact in an era of hysteria," Underwager told GQ magazine.

"I found the case suspicious, precisely because the only evidence came from one boy. That would be highly unlikely. Actual pedophiles have an average of 240 victims in their lifetime. It's a progressive disorder. They're never satisfied."

Indeed, I have found studies claiming that the number of victims of the average pedophile who abuses boys is more than 280, though others put the figure at 150. But with the vast access Jackson had to young children, surely that number would have been much higher in his case.

Why hadn't Tom Sneddon or I been able to find a single other victim? Why weren't they coming out of the woodwork the way the victims of Roman Catholic priests were after the Church's sex abuse scandal hit?

For her 2005 book about the case, Diane Dimond

interviewed an FBI agent named Ken Lanning, who wrote the bureau's guide called *Child Molesters: A Behavioral Analysis*. She asked him how a multiple molester could be assured they would all be quiet and Lanning responded:

> On any given day the pedophile is attempting to do four things: he is recruiting, seducing, molesting, and—to put it very bluntly—dumping. In other words, he recruits the kid, he seduces the kid, he molests the kid, and then at some point the kid gets too old so he wants the kid to move on . . . to get to his next victim. The hard part is when you finish with the child and the child begins to sense that the only reason the guy was nice to me and did all these wonderful things for me is because I was a child . . . And as soon as I lost that child-like appearance and characteristic he is not interested in me anymore. And here is where the threats, the blackmail, the violence, the threat of violence may come into play, as part of their effort to now keep this child quiet.

As Dimond no doubt intended by quoting Lanning's description, some of that sounded like what I already knew about Jackson's modus operandi with his special friends. He certainly had a habit of dumping these friends when they got too old. But again I wondered why they didn't later come after him, smelling a giant payday, when they reached adulthood and realized that they had been used in the manner the FBI agent describes.

Did Jackson really fit the rest of the profile if one could be said to exist?

The U.S. Department of Justice has identified twenty-five behavioral characteristics and indicators of a pedophile:

1. Usually an adult male, but some women also sexually abuse children
2. Often a child molestation victim themselves
3. Seeks out children of the age group they were when victimized
4. Usually married and hard-working
5. Employed within a wide range of occupations
6. Usually well-liked and respected community members
7. Often well-educated and regular churchgoers
8. Relates better with children than adults
9. Some prefer boys, some prefer girls
10. Usually prefers a specific age group of children
11. Takes and collects photographs of victims while dressed, nude, or in sexual poses
12. Collects child-adult pornography
13. Seeks to lower inhibitions of potential victims
14. Regularly attends children's events in the community
15. Volunteers in youth organizations
16. Coaches children's sports
17. Chaperones camping or overnight trips
18. Frequents video arcades, playgrounds, or shopping malls
19. Offers babysitting services

20. Seeks jobs where children are easily accessible
21. Befriends parents, especially single mothers, to gain access to children
22. Participates in internet gaming with children
23. Joins social networking websites, such as MySpace, Facebook, and other social media
24. Become foster parents
25. Seeks job opportunities where children are easily accessible

And while Jackson may fit into only a handful of those categories, experts in pedophilia also identify the ways child molesters lure children into their world. It is this category that seems to apply more closely to Jackson.

"Child molesters are professional con artists, manipulating children with various 'grooming methods,' in order to create a special bond of warmth and trust," writes Lin Burress. "This may involve lavish attention and gifts, money, alcohol or drugs, playful touching or tickling, all in an effort to create an atmosphere of secret keeping. It is important to note that most victims of child sexual abuse do not tell they were sexually abused, even when directly asked by a parent or other authority figures."

Responding to whether Michael Jackson himself fits the profile, clinical psychologist Nicholas Groth stated, "What we see in the pattern of a fixated offender is that he seems to get along well with people significantly older than him and those who are younger. He has a significant absence of peers. He lives more in the world of childhood than the adult world."

And when the sex is gay, says Groth, coauthor of

the book *Sexual Assault of Children and Adolescents*, the offender is often homophobic. "Rather than seeing a boy as gay, he has a narcissistic identification. But even if the allegations against Michael Jackson are true, it doesn't mean all of his good deeds for children were motivated simply to seduce them. He surely has a genuine love of children that goes beyond any sexual interest."

In building his case against Jackson, Tom Sneddon could not rely on these kinds of very subjective studies about what constitutes a child molester. But he knew that the defense would undoubtedly call upon studies of their own choosing. In her somewhat one-sided 1994 article for GQ magazine, "Was Michael Jackson Framed?," Mary Fischer quotes a U.S. Department of Health and Human Services study that shows many child abuse allegations—48 percent of those filed in 1990—proved to be unfounded.

As the father of a young child myself, I find quoting this kind of statistic troubling for two reasons. First, it may result in people doubting children when they come forward claiming they were abused. Child abuse is a serious crime and children should be taken seriously when they are brave enough to report it. Second, I find it hard to believe that the numbers are that high.

On the other hand, accused molesters have legitimate rights and have to be protected against false claims of abuse when they occur. I decided to do some research. What I found is that fathers' rights groups have for years made a habit of intentionally misrepresenting the incidence of false child abuse claims. Often this involves taking the rate of "unsubstantiated" claims and interpreting them as false, which is not the same thing at all. In fact, it is often very difficult to prove child abuse occurred, absent physical evidence.

There is no question that false claims of child abuse do occur, especially in divorce and custody hearings, where one parent coerces a child to level a false claim of child abuse against the other. But according to the most credible studies I have reviewed, the actual rate of false claims is somewhere between 2 and 10 percent, depending on the methodology and the jurisdiction. I never located the actual study that Fischer refers to in her article, but I am certain that the reported level of false claims is inaccurate.

Some groups like to quote a 1999 Canadian study by two Queens University researchers that looked at Canadian family law judgments over a ten-year period that dealt with sexual and physical abuse allegations in the context of parental separation.

In 46 of the 196 cases considered (23 percent of all cases), judges found on the "balance of probabilities" (the civil standard of proof) that abuse had occurred. However, in 89 separate cases, the judge made a finding that the allegation was unfounded, while in 61 cases there was evidence of abuse, but no finding that abuse had occurred. In 45 of the 150 cases where abuse was not proven (30 percent of cases), the judge considered the allegation to be intentionally false.

But in a more comprehensive 2003 Canadian study cited by the same researchers, reports were collected from child welfare workers about the characteristics of children and families investigated by their agencies. Studying all reports of child abuse and neglect made to child protection agencies—11,562 altogether—49 percent were regarded as substantiated by the worker undertaking the investigation, 13 percent were suspected, 27 percent were unsubstantiated but made in good faith, and only 4 percent were considered to be intentionally false. These and countless other studies unmask the myth that a high percentage of false child abuse claims exist.

Nevertheless, knowing how easily statistics can be manipulated and used to argue any point, Tom Sneddon wanted to cover all his bases. In consultation with the Chandlers' lawyer, Larry Feldman, Sneddon arranged for Jordan to fly to New York to be interviewed by Dr. Richard Gardner, considered one of America's leading authorities on false child abuse claims.

Gardner, a clinical professor of psychiatry at Columbia University, sat Jordan down for a lengthy taped interview. The dialogue on that tape, which was later leaked by Jordan's uncle and which I recently obtained, is intriguing and revealing. At one point, after a lengthy conversation about the details of the abuse, Gardner wants to know what motivated Jordan to come forward:

Gardner: How did your parents learn about this?

Jordan: I guess, after we had—Michael and I had stayed that night.

Gardner: Where?

Jordan: At my father's, during the finals. He saw that, like, it wasn't a healthy relationship for me.

Gardner:	What did he observe directly in terms of the sexual activities?
Jordan:	No sexual activities.
Gardner:	He didn't observe sexual activities? But there were sexual activities?
Jordan:	There was, but he didn't observe them.
Gardner:	What did he observe?
Jordan:	He observed Michael and I having almost the same personality, the same interests, the same way of speech.
Gardner:	When you say similar personality . . .
Jordan:	Like, I would act like him.
Gardner:	Did you find yourself consciously doing that?
Jordan:	No.
Gardner:	Did you make a decision or it just happened?
Jordan:	It just sort of happened. Like, the more we hung out together, his personality and his way of speech and everything else would rub off on me. And so he . . . Dad saw me alone one time at Cody's, his pre-school graduation, and he told me 'You and Michael have lied to me,' and it seemed like he knew what was going on, without actually saying what was going on.
Gardner:	So your father suspected. Is that what you're saying?
Jordan:	Yeah. And he said it in a stern, serious voice, not yelling.
Gardner:	Was he speaking to you alone, or . . .

Jordan:	Alone.
Gardner:	When did this happen?
Jordan:	I, like, right before my school graduation.
Gardner:	That's May or June?
Jordan:	June.
Gardner:	So what did you say then?
Jordan:	I didn't. He didn't ask me what did you and Michael do together.
Gardner:	By the way, going back, did he say, "It's a secret"?
Jordan:	Michael?
Gardner:	Yeah. In terms of did he make any threats?
Jordan:	I think he may have said, like, if you tell— if people say "Don't worry, just tell us, Michael will go to jail and nothing will happen to me . . . you." He said that wasn't true, and I could, like, go to juvenile hall or something.
Gardner:	That he could go to jail but you'd go to juvenile hall?
Jordan:	Something like that.
Gardner:	That he himself could go to jail?
Jordan:	I don't specifically remember. I'm almost positive, though, what he said about juvenile hall. I'm almost positive he said that, but I do indeed remember that he said that he would go to jail, and that, like, I wouldn't get off scot-free.
Gardner:	Did you believe that?
Jordan:	Well, I didn't really believe it at the time, and I definitely don't now. But at the time

I didn't really believe it, but I said, okay, whatever, and just went along with it.

Gardner: Now let's see. When your father confronted you at first, what did you say?

Jordan: Well, um, it was an intimidating circumstance, where he was talking to me, and he said, "You've lied to me, as well as Michael." And I said . . . I was like, fairly nervous. And he said, "What would you do if I said that I don't want you to go on the tour?" Because I was supposed to be on tour with him now. He's on the tour.

Gardner: Uh-huh.

Jordan: We were planning on going on the tour. And I said, like, "I probably would go anyway because I don't know of any valid reason you have," I said to my dad.

Gardner: You still wanted to go on the tour?

Jordan: Yes, at the time.

Gardner: Why is that?

Jordan: Because I was having fun. At the time, the things Michael was doing to me, they didn't affect me. Like, I didn't think anything was totally wrong with what he was doing since he was my friend, and he kept on telling me that he would never hurt me. But presently I see that he was obviously lying.

Gardner: You're saying you didn't realize it could hurt you? Is that what you're saying?

Jordan: I didn't see anything wrong with it.

Gardner:	Do you see the wrong in it now?
Jordan:	Of course.
Gardner:	What is wrong as you see it?
Jordan:	Because he's a grown-up and he's using his experience, of his age in manipulating and coercing younger people who don't have as much experience as him, and don't have the ability to say no to someone powerful like that. He's using his power, his experience, his age—his overwhelmingness—to get what he wants.
Gardner:	All right, so, you finally did tell your father. Who was the first adult you told?
Jordan:	My father.
Gardner:	How many times did he have to ask you before you told him?
Jordan:	Once.
Gardner:	The first time he asked, you told him?
Jordan:	Well, see, at the graduation he said, "You guys are lying to me," and that was it, he didn't ask me any questions.
Gardner:	And what did you say?
Jordan:	I just said, "Huh?" like, "I didn't know."
Gardner:	You made believe you didn't know what he was talking about?
Jordan:	Right. And then he demanded me over to his house, because he knew that the circumstances were wrong. And he, like, I was with my mom and Michael, and he demanded me over to his house. So I went to his house, and he said just for a week and

then you can go back. And I really started liking it there. And he had to pull my tooth out one time, like, while I was there. And I don't like pain, so I said could you put me to sleep? And he said sure. So his friend put me to sleep; he's an anaesthetist. And um, when I woke up my tooth was out, and I was all right—a little out of it but conscious. And my dad said—and his friend was gone, it was just him and me—and my dad said, "I just want you to let me know, did anything happen between you and Michael?" And I said "Yes," and he gave me a big hug and that was it.

Gardner: And you never gave him the details?

Jordan: No.

Gardner: Now you divulged this when? When did you tell him? In what month?

Jordan: July. I believe July. I remember that because it was very close to my sister's birthday, which is July.

Listening to the entire conversation in detail [see Appendix], it is difficult to believe that Evan Chandler could have implanted so many details into his son's memory while under the influence of sodium amytal.

What intrigued me, however, is how much Jordan's account to the psychiatrist differs from his father's own account of the same dental chair incident. Jordan told Dr. Gardner that his father merely asked him when he awoke from his sedation whether anything had ever happened between him and Michael. But according to Evan Chandler's own account, there was much more to the conversation:

> When Jordie came out of the sedation I asked him to tell me about Michael and him. I [falsely told him] that I had bugged his bedroom and I knew everything anyway and that I just wanted to hear it from him. I told him not to be embarrassed. "I know about the kissing and the jerking off and the blow jobs. This isn't about me finding anything out. It's about lying—If you lie then I'm going to take him [Jackson] down."

According to Evan, Jordie didn't respond for more than an hour, during which he sat contemplating his father's words in silence. Then Evan resumed the interrogation:

Evan: I'm going to make it very easy for you. I'm going to ask you one question. All you have to do is say yes or no . . .

Jordie: Promise.

Evan: Jord, did I ever lie to you in your whole life?

Jordie: No.

Evan: Well, I never will.

Jordie: You won't hurt Michael, right?

Evan: I promise.

Jordie: I don't want anyone else to ever know. Promise you won't ever tell anyone.

Evan: I promise.

Jordie: What's the question?

Evan: Did Michael Jackson ever touch your penis?

Jordie (*still hesitating*): Yes.

At the end of his interview with Jordan, Dr. Gardner—who died in 2003—concluded that the boy was telling the truth, though it's uncertain whether he would have come to the same conclusion if he had known about sodium amytal.

EIGHT

On November 23, 1993, Jackson's lawyer Bert Fields engaged in an unusual move of brinksmanship. He went before a Los Angeles County judge and sought a delay in Jordan Chandler's civil suit by claiming that a Santa Barbara grand jury was about to indict Jackson on criminal charges. Fields argued that since a criminal action appeared imminent, the civil case should be postponed because Jackson risked incriminating himself during the trial.

"Your honor, you've got a district attorney sitting up in Santa Barbara, about to indict. You can't get too much closer to an indictment than to have a grand jury sitting there," he said.

In fact, no such indictment was in the works because neither Tom Sneddon nor Los Angeles District Attorney Gil Garcetti had yet uncovered enough evidence to back up Jordan's story.

But the Jackson team had no way of knowing that at the time.

Later that day, another Jackson attorney, Howard

Weitzman, backtracked, telling reporters that he had heard a rumor that subpoenas were being issued, but he evidently was misinformed.

"I think Mr. Fields really misspoke himself, because I perhaps delivered the message too quickly," Weitzman said. "I have no idea whether a grand jury has in fact been impaneled and is going to consider evidence. What I was told is that subpoenas have been issued."

The same week, Jackson's legal troubles mounted when five former security guards who worked at his family's estate, Hayvenhurst, filed a lawsuit against him claiming that they were fired because they had knowledge of his "nighttime visits with young boys."

Curiously, the group of guards launched their wrongful termination lawsuit after the Jordan Chandler case became public even though they had all been fired in February 1993, months earlier.

In their lawsuit, they claimed they were fired by Jackson's longtime administrative assistant, Norma Staikos, and that after they left they were intimidated into silence by the strong-arm tactics of Anthony Pellicano and Jackson's lawyers, who attempted to "obstruct, impede, and if possible prevent any investigation or inquiry dealing with allegations that Jackson had sexually molested any young boys."

The guards claimed that during their time at Hayvenhurst, they had seen Jackson bring more than thirty boys for sleepovers in his private quarters, sometimes in the middle of the night.

"They would spend the night there. Most of them do spend the night. Some of them leave . . . I've never seen a grown person, a woman or man, that stays over all night," said one of the guards, Leroy Thomas, implying that the five were fired because they knew too much about these sleepovers.

But even Diane Dimond later acknowledged the unusual timing of their lawsuit, writing, "Nearly a year after they were let go, the guards were alleging their termination had something to do with a scandal that had not even erupted yet." This didn't stop Dimond from splashing their story all over *Hard Copy* and featuring interviews with Thomas and his former supervisor, Morris Williams.

"I've never really seen Michael abuse a kid, understand?" Thomas said on the program. "And I'm saying I've never been in his room with him and a kid, so I don't know what goes on in his room. And . . . but as far as when you look at a grown man with a young kid, in a Jacuzzi, sitting down, it will make you think, like, why would you want to do that?"

Thomas claimed that Jackson often enlisted the guards' help in keeping the children away from the sight of Jackson's parents, who also lived at Hayvenhurst. "[Jackson] instructed us that we should keep the kid in the guard house until [Jackson's] parents or brothers would leave. He then asked us if they were already retired to bed and if his brother had left and I told him, 'yes,' . . . then he called and asked . . . to bring the kid up to his room."

Williams said that Jackson "maybe felt that his family was critical of him hanging around kids and maybe he just got tired of hearing it. That could be one of the reasons that he would call ahead and make sure no one was there."

Although most of their account was laced with innuendo, Thomas took the accusations a step further when he claimed that Jackson had once asked him to remove a Polaroid photograph of a naked young boy from the singer's bathroom and destroy it.

According to the guard's account, he asked Jackson one night if there was any chore he could help with. "He said, 'Okay. I want you to [do] something for me.' He said, 'I want you to go upstairs,' and I had a cordless phone. I went upstairs and he said, 'Are you up?' And I said, 'Yes, I am upstairs.' He said, 'I want you to look on the bottom of the fridge. There is a key.' I want you to go to the bathroom which is on your right.' I walked up to the bathroom. He said, 'I want you to take this picture down.' There's a picture there, I want you to take it down."

Thomas claimed the photo in question was a profile shot of a completely naked prepubescent blond-haired boy. The photo "was on the mirror," he said. "So I took it down and looked at it and I was, like, 'Oh well.' He said, 'Do you have it?' I said, 'Yes.' He said, 'I want you to destroy it.'" However, Polaroids cannot be torn.

"Well, you know, I ripped the back of the picture, the front was soft," he recalled. "So yes I destroyed the picture and he told me to put the key back and lock the door. He was talking to me all that time on the phone. At the time I didn't see anything wrong with it. When you're from a country like I am from, things like that don't strike you to be illegal or bad. In my country a naked person or a naked kid is nothing new. Kids run around Jamaica until they're ten or eleven without clothes. It's one of the natural things."

For a lot of people, Thomas's story was far-fetched. Besides the ludicrous and completely inaccurate description of the Jamaican attitude toward nude children (six different Jamaicans whom I asked said nothing could be further from the truth about their country), why would Jackson be reckless and stupid enough to alert a security guard to the existence of such a photo when he could have easily destroyed it himself?

When it emerged that the group of guards had been paid as much as $100,000 to $200,000 by *Hard Copy* for their stories, their credibility took a further hit, although Dimond claimed the negotiations over price took place without her and she never knew exactly how much they received for their stories.

The guards' lawsuit was later thrown out of court because they had signed an agreement forfeiting their right to sue, although the merit of the claims was never decided in a court of law.

Meanwhile, behind the scenes with Jackson's defense team, a battle was brewing. Shortly after Bert Fields erroneously announced that an indictment was forthcoming, he resigned from the case. Ever since Howard Weitzman had joined the team, discussions about legal strategy had taken a different tone.

Fields, along with his investigator, Pellicano, wanted to fight the allegations tooth and nail. They were determined to go on the offensive and portray

Chandler as an extortionist and Jackson as a victim. Weitzman argued that they needed to get Jackson front and center to show that he was willing to stand up and face the charges for which he was falsely accused. From the moment he entered the case, Weitzman was talking settlement.

When Fields and Pellicano left the case, they made it clear that they didn't agree with the direction Weitzman was pursuing. They were convinced Jackson would be exonerated in court and that a settlement would be tantamount to an admission of guilt in the public mind. What would it do to his career?

With Fields out of the way, it was Weitzman—now in complete charge of the defense—who brought in Johnnie Cochran, with an eye to a potential criminal trial.

Despite repeated maneuvers, the Jackson team had been unable to delay the civil trial scheduled to go before a judge in March 1994. The overwhelming majority of civil suits are settled out of court. It often made good legal and financial sense for both sides. But this wasn't just any civil case. And the person being sued wasn't just any defendant. Neither Weitzman nor Cochran particularly relished the idea of settling.

They had good reason to be apprehensive.

"Never. I didn't do anything wrong," Jackson wailed when Weitzman first mentioned that a settlement might be the smart way to end the case. "They'll say I did it."

In 2008, I met with a former assistant to Jackson's best friend, Elizabeth Taylor. He was working with Taylor at the time of the Chandler negotiations and was privy to much of what went on.

"Michael was always a drama queen," recalled the aide. "But he was a complete basket case during that time. He kept asking, 'Why are they doing this to me? I never hurt anyone.' The lawyers were using Miss Taylor as a go-between. She was practically the only person he trusted. I remember before he came back to the States, and after the allegations had hit the headlines, he was traveling with these two boys, I forget their names. A boy and his younger brother. Miss Taylor at one point mentioned that he might want to send them home for the sake of appearances and Michael said, 'Why should I? They're having fun. I'm not going to let those bad people ruin their trip.'"

After the body search, he says, Taylor joined the lawyers in convincing Jackson that a settlement made sense.

"It was like an intervention," Taylor's aide recalls. "They told him it would be his word against a child and you never know who a jury might believe. The kid would be coached on what to say, he'd paint Michael as a monster. Even if he won the case, the public would hear all this sordid stuff. His image would be destroyed. But he just kept saying, 'No, no, no, no,' over and over. He didn't want to hear about a settlement. Miss Taylor kept working on him, and in the end she might have had some influence, but I never saw him cave for a minute. To be honest, I was surprised when I heard he settled. I thought he'd fight it, I really did. He would have won." In the end, he may not have had much of a choice.

On January 24, 1994, the media reported the first rumors that an out-of-court settlement was in the offing.

Cindy Adams of the *New York Post* cited unnamed sources saying that the settlement would be $5 million, with $1 million going to the boy's father and the rest paid into a trust fund. *Time* magazine also reported the $5 million figure, while a London tabloid reported the settlement as closer to $40 million.

A day later, Johnnie Cochran and Jordan's lawyer, Larry Feldman, called a press conference outside the Santa Monica courthouse. To the assembled media throng, Feldman read a statement:

> We wish to jointly announce a mutual resolution of this lawsuit. As you are aware, the plaintiff has alleged certain acts of impropriety by Mr. Jackson and from the inception of those allegations Mr. Jackson has always maintained his innocence. However, the emotional trauma and strain on the respective parties have caused both parties to reflect on the wisdom of continuing with the litigation. The plaintiff has agreed that the lawsuit should be resolved and it will be dismissed in the near future. Mr. Jackson continues to maintain his innocence and withdraws any previous allegations of extortion. This will allow the parties to get on with their lives in a more positive and productive manner. Much of the suffering these parties have been put through has been caused by the publicity surrounding this case. We jointly request that members of the press allow the parties to close this chapter in their lives with dignity so that the healing process may begin.

While neither Feldman nor Cochran was allowed to disclose the terms of the settlement, the Associated Press cited close sources that revealed the boy would receive $15 million. Over the years, estimates would range as high as $30 million and most media accounts have used the figure of $20 million. In reality, the Associated Press was remarkably close. The final settlement was $15,331,250 to be held in trust for Jordan Chandler until he reaches the age of majority, plus $1.5 million for each of his parents and millions of dollars in legal fees.

The speculation began almost immediately. Why would Jackson have settled if he wasn't guilty? Diane Dimond correctly noted that the original civil suit cited the "negligence of defendant Michael Jackson." In the settlement, Jackson agreed to pay on the complaint of "negligence." This was "insurance company language" said a number of lawyers familiar with these agreements to Dimond.

"An insurance company will pay out if a policyholder has been 'negligent,' but not if he or she has committed a crime," Dimond writes. The implication is that it was Jackson's insurance company who paid the claim.

I recently obtained a court document which confirms this and appears to suggest that it was Jackson's insurance company that forced the settlement on him.

Buried among hundreds of thousands of court documents in Jackson's 2005 molestation trial is a motion filed by his attorney, Thomas Mesereau Jr., on March 22, 2005, entitled "Memo in support of objection to subpoena for settlement documents." In the motion, which argues that the defense had no obligation to reveal the confidential Chandler settlement in the unrelated criminal trial, there are some telling details about the original settlement:

> The [1994] settlement agreement was for global claims of negligence and the lawsuit was defended by Mr. Jackson's insurance carrier. The insurance carrier negotiated and paid the settlement, over the protests of Mr. Jackson and his personal legal counsel.

The motion proceeds to explain the role of insurance companies in these kinds of cases: "It is general practice for an insurer to be entitled to control settlement negotiations and the insured is precluded from any interference."

The document cites the 1971 appeals court ruling in *Shapiro v. Allstate Insurance Co.* and the landmark 1958 case *Ivy v. Pacific Automobile Insurance Co.*, which held that the insured is precluded from interfering with settlement procedures:

> Under the majority of contracts for liability insurance, the absolute control of the defense of the ma[tt]er is turned over to the insurance company and the insured is excluded from any interference in any negotiation for settlement or other legal proceedings. An insurance carrier has the right to settle claims covered by insurance when it decides settlement is expedient and the insured may not interfere with or prevent such settlements.

Even if Jackson's insurance company forced the settlement, doesn't it mean that they thought Jackson would lose?

"Not at all," explains insurance lawyer Lewis Kaplan. "Insurance companies almost always settle. That's what they do. It's not an admission of guilt. It's an attempt to avoid a long, costly legal process and one where there's always a risk. You never know what a jury might do. In this case, with the defendant worth hundreds of millions of dollars, settling is a no-brainer. Of course they would settle."

Following Feldman's statement at the new conference, it was Johnnie Cochran's turn to speak for Jackson:

> The past ten days, the rumors, the speculation surrounding this case have reached a fever[ed] pitch and by and large have been false and outrageous. As Mr. [Larry] Feldman [the boy's lawyer] has correctly indicated, Michael Jackson has maintained his innocence from the beginning of this matter and now this matter will soon be concluded. He still maintains that innocence.
>
> The resolution of this case is in no way an admission of guilt by Michael Jackson. In short, he is an innocent man who does not intend to have his career and his life destroyed by rumors and innuendos.
>
> Throughout this ordeal he has been subjected to an unprecedented media feeding frenzy, especially by the tabloid press. The tabloid press

has shown an insatiable thirst for anything negative and has paid huge sums of money to people who have little or no information and who barely knew Michael Jackson.

So today the time has come for Michael Jackson to move on to new business, to get on with his life, to start the healing process and to move his career forward to even greater heights.

This he intends to do. At the appropriate time, Michael Jackson will speak out publicly after the agony, torture, [and] pain he has had to suffer in the past six months.

Thank you very much.

In the fifteen years since Michael Jackson settled the civil suit with Jordan Chandler, a dangerous myth has grown—the myth that the settlement prevented Jordan Chandler from testifying against Jackson in a potential criminal case. In fact, there is not a word in the settlement documents that precludes Chandler from giving testimony against Jackson. Jordan's own lawyer, Larry Feldman, made that clear following the settlement.

"[The] plaintiff has agreed the lawsuit should be resolved," Feldman declared. "Nobody has bought anyone's silence. He is allowed to testify against Mr. Jackson in a criminal proceeding."

Yet there have been literally tens of thousands of media accounts implying that it was the settlement prevented a criminal prosecution.

Among the worst offenders in this regard is Diane Dimond, whose reporting encouraged this myth.

"It soon grew increasingly clear to both Los Angeles District Attorney Gil Garcetti and Santa Barbara County District Attorney Tom Sneddon that without the testimony of Jordan Chandler, or some other complainant, they could not win a case against Michael Jackson," she writes.

Either district attorney could have subpoenaed Jordan to testify. Jordan had already signed a lengthy affidavit detailing the abuse that had occurred. But the fact is that if Jordan had appeared in a criminal trial, he could have been cross-examined under oath, under threat of perjury. If justice was the object, and not money, why not testify?

It is a question that would arise again a decade later when another boy would level similar abuse charges against Michael Jackson. He badly needed Jordan Chandler to establish a pattern.

For now, Sneddon and Garcetti were getting increasingly desperate. Each had convened his own separate grand jury to hear evidence. But that evidence was getting sparse. They had both conducted their own thorough investigations into most of the so-called witnesses who claimed they could corroborate stories of Jackson's abuse. Although the ragtag assortment of disgruntled former employees made sensational guests on *Hard Copy*, the district attorneys had evidently discovered that their testimony and credibility were next to worthless.

There was one name that kept popping up time and again. Brett Barnes was an Australian boy who in the early nineties became one of Jackson's most prominent "special friends." In 1987, Barnes and his sister handed a fan letter to a member of Jackson's entourage during the singer's *Bad* tour. Four years later, Barnes and his family were invited to Neverland, and according to his sister, Brett ended up sleeping in Jackson's bedroom at least 365 times during their subsequent friendship.

Barnes was of particular interest to the district attorneys in California because they believed he could be the key to corroborating the accuser's story. He was the boy, in fact, who was sitting on Jackson's lap the first time he came to fetch Jordan's family to bring them to Neverland. And although Jackson's team didn't know it at the time, Jordan had told a psychiatrist that the singer had originally seduced him by claiming that Brett had been glad to perform sexual acts with him.

"[He told me] that if I didn't do it, then I didn't love him as much as Brett did," Jordan had told Dr. Gardner.

Ironically, Sneddon and Garcetti saw Jackson's multimillion-dollar settlement with Jordan Chandler as a mixed blessing. They were convinced that boys and their families would start crawling out of the woodwork in search of a huge payday: accuse Jackson of molestation and make a few million dollars. Of course they were not suborning perjury. Both district attorneys were absolutely convinced that Jackson was a serial pedophile with hundreds of victims capable of serving as witnesses. A lucrative out-of-court settlement could be all the inducement these victims needed to finally cooperate.

They were so sure that Barnes would finally come forward that five members of the investigative team, including Sneddon himself, flew to Melbourne in January to interview the thirteen-year-old boy and his family.

Once again, they came back empty-handed. Barnes's family were outraged at the suggestion and Brett continued to deny that Jackson had ever molested him.

For another five months after Jordan settled, two grand juries—one in Los Angeles, one in Santa Barbara—continued to hear evidence, sparse though it may have been.

For Garcetti's jury, that evidence was slim pickings. Grand jury testimony is secret, but among the witnesses called was Jackson's mother, Katherine, who presumably offered nothing of substance.

Sneddon called the former maid, Blanca Francia, some parents of Jackson's former "special friends," and Janet Jackson's former husband, James DeBarge.

Besides Francia, the only grand jury witnesses with the potential to inflict real damage were a group of security guards that had once worked for Jackson—later known as the Neverland Five. The five claimed to have damning information that could corroborate many of Jordan Chandler's claims. It's impossible to know what this group told the grand jury, but in later years, when the five former employees filed a lawsuit against Jackson, their credibility would be so tarnished that it's hardly surprising their stories made little impression on the jurors.

After another eight months and countless millions of dollars spent attempting to solidify the case against Jackson, Garcetti and Sneddon held a joint news conference on September 21, 1994. They announced that they wouldn't be filing criminal charges against the singer. In announcing the conclusion of the investigation, they failed to mention that they hadn't found a single piece of supporting evidence or credible witness to secure an indictment. Instead, Garcetti would once again perpetuate the myth that the case had stalled because Jordan wouldn't cooperate.

"After about thirteen or fourteen months of investigation, this is our conclusion," he told the assembled media. "We have a very important witness who has told us 'I'm sorry. I do not want to and will not testify.' And I'm telling you that if he steps forward a month from now, two months from now, and says, 'Now I want to testify,' we would reevaluate our case at that time."

Later the same day, Jackson issued his own statement: "I am thankful that the investigation has reached a conclusion. I've continually maintained my innocence. I am grateful to all of my family, friends, and fans who have stood by me and also believed in my innocence."

The case could have been closed and Jackson spared a criminal trial at that point. But many people chose to believe that where there's smoke there's fire. Countless talk shows and tabloid newspapers debated the question. Why else would he have agreed to pay out millions of dollars unless he was guilty?

Even the serious press emphasized the continued doubts. The headline in the *Los Angeles Times* the day after the investigation was halted said it all: "Jackson Not Charged, but Not Absolved."

Watching the coverage that week, one woman was doing a slow burn. Geraldine Hughes had to fight the urge to call her own press conference to tell her story. Or she could have sold it to a tabloid for considerably more than the $28,000 a year she was earning at her day job.

Instead, she chose not to risk her career and decided to keep her mouth shut.

Hughes had a unique perspective on the Chandler case. She happened to be working as a legal secretary for Barry Rothman at the time he was hired by Evan Chandler to go after Michael Jackson.

Rothman was the same attorney Evan Chandler referred to in his tape-recorded conversation with Jordan's stepfather, Dave Schwartz, when he said, "Once I make that phone call, this guy is going to destroy everybody in sight in any devious, nasty, cruel way that he can do it."

At the time she was hired to work for him, she had been working in the legal field for almost fifteen years, but she had never before encountered anybody like Rothman, whom she describes as "like meeting a real-life demon straight out of the pits of hell."

She says it wasn't long after Evan Chandler hired Rothman that she sensed something was wrong about the case. "Instead of the usual activities that happened during most cases," she recalls, "the Chandler case began to look more like scheming and plotting." Her suspicions prompted her to start keeping an annotated diary of what was occurring on a daily basis.

Before long, she began to conclude that Chandler and Rothman were conspiring to extort huge sums from Jackson. "Just the knowledge of typing letters and court documents that sparked the child molestation allegation was troublesome to me," recalls Hughes, who claims she knew early on that Jackson was an innocent victim of extortion.

She says Rothman ran his office like Fort Knox, with huge precautions to safeguard the secrets inside. Once Rothman arrived at the office, she notes, his presence would be immediately felt. "His arrival would immediately create a disturbing and hostile atmosphere of yelling, disgust, and anger." She said he would verbally abuse and attack his employees on a daily basis with a manner that was at once intimidating and physically threatening.

During the case, she said, many meetings took place at the offices: meetings between Rothman and Evan Chandler; meetings between Rothman and Anthony Pellicano; meetings with Evan Chandler, June Chandler, and David Schwartz. Jordan Chandler himself, she recalls, spent "an enormous amount of time" in the conference room after the allegations first surfaced.

Although Hughes says many of the meetings were conducted in the utmost secrecy, she was able to glean a lot of what was going on from typing pleadings and correspondence. She also reveals that she learned many of the inside details of the case from Rothman's associate attorney, who often confided in her. Hughes, however, is reluctant to reveal specific details of what she was told because "she was a practicing attorney under the code of confidentiality."

Hughes personally met Jordan Chandler twice while she was working for Rothman. "From all appearances, he seemed like a perfectly normal child interested in playing and listening to the music and was curious about everything," she recalls. As for Evan Chandler, she repeatedly cites the tape recorded conversation between him and Dave Schwartz, saying that everything he says on the tape happened exactly as he and Rothman planned it.

"Dr. Chandler admitted, in his own words, that he had been 'rehearsed about what to say,' [he] 'paid people to move against Michael' and that there was a 'plan,'" she notes. To her this was an admission of guilt and a harbinger of what was to come.

"Dr. Chandler further stated, 'It's going to be bigger than all of us put together. The whole thing is going to crash down on everybody and destroy everybody in sight. It will be a massacre if I don't get what I want.'"

Hughes says this conversation was a blueprint for extortion and that she was a witness as the scheme gradually unfolded exactly the way Chandler and Rothman had planned it.

At some point in the case, during which Hughes would report her suspicions to her elderly mother on a regular basis, she says her mother urged her to come forward and reveal what she knows. The mother then arranged a meeting between Hughes and Anthony Pellicano.

"At first when my mother told me of the scheduled meeting, I thought I was meeting with the investigators from the district attorney's office who were investigating the extortion allegations." At the meeting, Hughes says, she informed Pellicano about what had been going on. She also saw him frequently during his often stormy negotiations with Rothman.

In her diary, Hughes documents the last meeting

between the two men, which took place in Rothman's office on August 13, 1993. "Mr. Pellicano stormed out of the office saying, 'No way,'" she writes. "The following Tuesday, August 17, 1993, Dr. Chandler took his son to see the psychiatrist who reported the allegations."

"What if Michael Jackson had agreed to pay the twenty million dollars?" Hughes later asked herself. "Would Dr. Chandler not have taken the boy to the psychiatrist?"

On the subject of the psychiatrist, Hughes claims that one of the things that made her the most suspicious of Chandler's and Rothman's motives was something she observed her boss do around this time, which she recorded in her diary.

"Rothman advised the father how to report child abuse via a third party rather than going directly to the police," she said. "If it were any other case, you'd just pick up the phone and call the police."

After Bert Fields and Pellicano left the case in November, leaving Jackson's defense to Howard Weitzman, Hughes said she called the private investigator to ask him why he had quit. "He told me he did not agree with the direction in which Mr. Weitzman was taking the case. He vehemently disagreed with the idea of settling with Dr. Chandler. He was angry at the thought of the settlement and was fully convinced that if Michael Jackson would fight this out in court, he would be exonerated."

Years after Jackson settled with Jordan Chandler, she had still not talked publicly about this case. Having eventually been fired by Rothman, she did turn over her diaries anonymously to Mary Fischer, who used them when she was writing her article for GQ, "Was Michael Jackson Framed?" Meanwhile, her mother regularly implored her to write a book about the case to "expose the injustice that had been done to Michael Jackson." By this time, Hughes was working as a Christian missionary, tending to poor Latinos and African Americans in the Watts area of Los Angeles. In 1997, she began to draft the outline of a book, but kept it on a shelf.

Before her death, Hughes' mother approached a number of publishers, imploring them to put out her daughter's book. Finally she found a tiny publishing house in Virginia willing to do so, and in 2004, Geraldine Hughes's book about the case, *Redemption*, was published.

While Hughes was promoting the book that year, she appeared on a talk show and made a startling claim found nowhere in the book.

Discussing the original settlement negotiations between Pellicano, Evan Chandler, and Rothman, in which they discussed the idea of Jackson financing a screenplay as part of the original proposed settlement, Hughes says:

> They were trying to produce a movie. Initially they were negotiating for money for a movie deal. And you need to know that the little boy was a part of this, too. Him and his dad were very creative. The little boy was the one that came up with the idea for a movie that the [. . .] father took [. . .], so they were very creative. They were coming up with movie ideas. All they needed was the money to produce it.

Is it possible this revelation stems from something Hughes was told by Rothman's associate and inadvertently let slip on the air? Could Jordan Chandler have been in on the "plan"? Is this why he has always refused to testify against Jackson in a criminal trial where he would be subjected to cross-examination under penalty of perjury? Hughes has never elaborated on this startling claim.

Jordan Chandler received the final lump sum of his settlement money from Michael Jackson in 1999. With the money, he and his family bought a home in New Jersey, along with condos in Manhattan and Santa Barbara.

He appeared to be living a normal life until court documents surfaced revealing that in 2005, Jordan's father, Evan, viciously attacked him with what he described as "a life-threatening incident of physical abuse."

I have obtained the case records from a 2006 New Jersey appellate court revealing that on August 5, 2005, Jordan was granted a temporary restraining order against his father for an act of domestic violence when Evan "struck him on the head from behind with a twelve-and-one-half-pound weight and then sprayed his eyes with mace or pepper spray and tried to choke him." In granting the order, the judge ruled that the weight could cause serious bodily injury or death. At the time, the twenty-five-year-old Jordan was living together with his ex-dentist father at a house in New Jersey.

A year later, an appeals court judge refused to make the restraining order permanent, but both parties remained tight-lipped about the incident.

NINE

On May 26, 1994, as the grand juries were still hearing evidence, a news report out of the Dominican Republic shook the world—or so it seemed from the sheer number of front-page headlines it generated. It was, after all, a royal wedding.

Michael Jackson—the King of Pop—had just married Lisa Marie Presley, the daughter of the King of Rock and Roll—in a small civil ceremony on the tiny Caribbean island.

Hugo Alvarez Perez, the judge who married them, asked Jackson: "Do you take Lisa Marie to be your wife?"

Jackson replied, "Why not?"

After the wedding, the judge told reporters, "It was all very strange, but it is not my job to ask why people are getting married."

Nineteen days later, the newly married couple appeared on an ABC-TV prime-time special hosted by Diane Sawyer to answer that question directly. For weeks, the idea of Michael and Lisa Marie had been openly derided, mocked, and laughed at by reporters, late-night comedians, and everyday Americans. Most people, it seemed, could not fathom it.

On the special, watched by millions, the newlyweds begin by talking about how they first met:

Sawyer: Glad you're here. It occurs to me, looking at the two of you, I have got to start by asking how this marriage took place, how it began. Let me guess it wasn't over miniature golf and a . . . a hot dog or something. When did it start? What was the dating?

M.J.:   Well, we first met, she was seven years old and I was seventeen. This was in Las Vegas. She used to come and see my show. We had the only family show on the strip—*The Jackson 5*. And um, she used to come as a little girl and sit right up front. She came quite often. She came with a lot of bodyguards.

After Sawyer asks who proposed to whom and how it happened, the couple seem to get a little flustered:

M.J.:   I did.
Presley: He did.
Sawyer: When? Where?
M.J.:   When? Where?
Presley: On the telephone.
M.J.:   Oh yeah, oh yeah, on the telephone.
Presley: He first asked me. . . . We were going out four months, um . . . right? Four months?

M.J.:	I don't remember.
Presley:	Yeah, anyway we were spending a lot of time together. I don't know how it didn't manage to get in the press, because we weren't hiding it. I was in Las Vegas, we were in . . . everywhere. We were everywhere.
M.J.:	We went to bookstores . . .
Presley:	To bookstores. We were not hiding it.
Sawyer:	And you said yes right away?
Presley:	I was separated for four months and I said . . . he said what would you do if I asked you to marry me? And I said I would. Um . . .
M.J.:	A big "I would."

Sawyer has stressed to her audience that there were no ground rules imposed on her for the interview. She was free to ask about any topic. She then proceeded to ask about the subject that Jackson has still never discussed in detail.

Sawyer:	You have said that you would never harm a child. I want to be as specific as I can. Did you ever, as this boy said you did, did you ever sexually engage, fondle, have sexual contact with this child, or any other child?
M.J.:	Never ever. I could never harm a child, or anyone. It's not in my heart, it's not who I am, and it's not what I'm . . . I'm not even interested in that.

Sawyer: And what do you think should be done to
          someone who does that?

M.J.:   To someone who does that? What I think
          should be done? Gee . . . I think they need
          help . . . in some kind of way . . . you know.

Sawyer: How about the police photographs, though?
          How was there enough information from
          this boy about those kinds of things?

M.J.:   The police photographs?

Sawyer: The police photographs.

M.J.:   That they took of me?

Sawyer: Yeah.

M.J.:   There was nothing that matched me to
          those charges. There was nothing.

Presley: There was nothing they could connect to
          him.

M.J.:   That's why I'm sitting here talking to you
          today. There was not one iota of informa-
          tion that they found that could connect
          me . . .

Sawyer: So when we heard the charges . . .

M.J.:   There was nothing . . .

Sawyer: . . . markings of some kind?

M.J.:   No markings.

Sawyer: No markings?

M.J.:   No.

Sawyer: Why did you settle the . . .

M.J.:   Why am I still here then?

Presley: You're not going to ask me about them,
          are you? (Laughs) About the markings.
          (Laughs)

Sawyer:	If you volunteered . . .
Presley:	No, I'm just . . . The point is . . . is that when that finally got concluded there was no match-up. It was printed this big, as opposed to how big it was, what the match-up was supposed to be.
M.J.:	Because it isn't so!
Sawyer:	Why did you settle the case then?
M.J.:	The whole thing is a lie.
Sawyer:	Why did you settle the case, and, and it looks to everyone as if you paid a huge amount of money . . .
M.J.:	That's . . . that's . . . most of that's folklore. I talked to my lawyers and I said, "Can you guarantee me that justice will prevail?" and they said, "We cannot guarantee you that a judge or a jury will do anything." And with that I was like catatonic. I was outraged . . .
Sawyer:	How much money . . .
M.J.:	(totally outraged) So what I said . . . I have got to do something to get out from under this nightmare. All these lies and all these people coming forth to get paid and all these tabloid shows, just lies, lies, lies. So what I did—we got together again with my advisers and they advised me, it was hands down, a unanimous decision—resolve the case. This could be something that could go on for seven years.
Sawyer:	How much money was . . .
M.J.:	We said let's get it behind us.

Sawyer: Can you say how much?

M.J.: It's not what the tabloids have printed. It's not all this crazy outlandish money, no, it's not at all. I mean, the terms of the agreement are very confidential.

Sawyer: I want to ask . . .

Presley: He's been barred to discuss it.

Later in the show, Sawyer plays a clip of an interview she conducted with Jackson's friend Elizabeth Taylor about the molestation charges and Taylor's role in spiriting Jackson away from Singapore to a Swiss rehab center the previous November. The movie legend begins by talking about how few people know the real Michael Jackson.

Taylor: When he's on tour he goes to hospitals without the press following him. Without anyone knowing. He'll get up in a disguise and do it. Take his disguise off when he's there and kids know. "Wow! It's Michael Jackson."

Sawyer: Was there no point at which you said to yourself . . . reading everything everybody had been reading . . . "maybe this is true, maybe I completely didn't understand who he was."

Taylor: No way. Absolutely not.

Sawyer: Never?

Taylor: Never. I know Michael's heart. I know his mind and his soul. I'm . . . not that insensitive. Especially to him, or people I love.

Sawyer: How did you decide to go to Singapore?

Taylor: He was my friend. He was alone. He was to-
            tally alone. And he just . . . he needed help.
            Nothing in the world could have hurt him
            more. If it had been calculated. If they'd
            planned an assassination, they couldn't have
            done it any better. It almost . . . it almost
            broke his heart. He wasn't aware of what
            was happening. He was dulling his pain. But
            it really frightened me because I have been
            there and I know how easy it is to get there
            when you're in mental or physical pain.

Sawyer: And . . . he knew right away that he had
            to . . . deal with it, to . . .

Taylor: Not right away. Not right away . . . but he
            knew.

Sawyer: There were some reports during this period,
            Michael, that it was . . . such agony for you
            that you were actually suicidal. Is that true?

M.J.:   I was never suicidal. I love life too much to
            ever be suicidal. I'm resilient. I have rhi-
            noceros skin. Never, ever suicidal.

Sawyer: Did it leave you, though . . .

M.J.:   Heartbroken, but not suicidal.

Finally Sawyer brings up the subject that was on
most people's minds, the suspicion that their marriage is
a sham, designed to rehabilitate Jackson's image:

Sawyer: You said you don't sleep in separate bed-
            rooms and I'm gonna confess. Okay . . .

this is live TV and I'm copping out right here, because I didn't spend my life . . . as a serious journalist to ask these kinds of questions. But I'm not oblivious to the fact, that, your fans had one question they most wanted to ask . . . of you . . .

Presley: Do we have sex?

Sawyer: We have . . .

M.J.: (*Laughs*) Shh . . . she didn't ask!

(Presley laughs.)

M.J.: She didn't ask!

Presley: Okay, I won't ask.

M.J.: We don't know what it was gonna be.

Presley: Is that what you were gonna ask?

Sawyer: Let's play just a minute or two.

Presley: Sorry. (*Laughs*)

Sawyer: Let's play one or two.

(Sawyer plays clips.)

Person 1: We wanna know, if you've done "the thing"?

Person 2: Michael, I know this is an intimate question, but are you having sex together with Lisa Marie?

Person 3: Do you guys really love each other or are you just doing this to satisfy the media?

Person 4: Are you guys intimate?

(The clip ends.)

M.J.: I can't believe it!

Presley: Woooww!

Sawyer: But this is about . . . the suspicion.

Lisa Marie looks into the camera and answers the question: "Yes. Yes! Yes!"

Three months later, the couple opened the MTV Music Awards, striding on to the stage hand in hand to a standing ovation. Jackson turned to the audience and proclaimed, "And they thought this wouldn't last," before laying a passionate but awkward kiss on Lisa Marie's lips. As they were heading offstage the cameras caught her wiping her lips with the back of her hand as if in disgust.

The next day the kiss was treated with almost universal scorn by the media and by the public.

On his popular talk show, Geraldo Rivera showed a freeze-frame of the kiss and then asked his audience whether they think it was sincere. In unison, they shouted back, "No!"

Again, nobody believed the marriage was real. But why?

The answer, I suspect, lies in what virtually everybody who I've interviewed for this project told me about Michael Jackson: he's gay. Even those who are his most ardent defenders, people who maintain he is innocent of the molestation charges, insist that he is homosexually inclined.

While most won't say it on the record, Joe Franklin has no such reservations. Franklin is best known as the host of the world's first-ever TV talk show, which began in 1951 on New York's WJZ-TV and ran for more than forty-three years, earning him a place in the *Guinness Book of World Records* as the longest-running talk show host. During that time, he interviewed more than 10,000 guests and gave a number of future legends their first TV appearance, including Woody Allen, Barbra Streisand, and Julia Roberts. He also ghost-wrote a book for his friend and onetime lover, Marilyn Monroe. Needless to say, the eighty-three-year-old Franklin has been around the show business scene for a while.

"I had Michael and his brothers on my show many times," he told me in early 2009. "Take it from me, he's gay. There's no doubt about it. He likes men in their teens and early twenties." I ask him how he knows. Has he ever seen Jackson engaged in sexual activities or even kissing another man? The answer he gives is typical of the answers from the people who swear to me he's a child molester. "No, but I just know it. I'm very close to his family."

Indeed, I've been told by a number of sources that Jackson's mother, Katherine, has long suspected her son is gay, as do a number of his siblings. La Toya herself once said her mother calls Michael a "faggot." Their suspicions, however, are apparently based on his frequent associations with young boys, rather than any specific acts they've witnessed.

In 1979, Jackson's biographer J. Randy Taraborrelli asked him straight out: "Just for the record, are you or are you not gay?"

"No, I am not gay," he quotes as the singer's response. "I am not a homo. I'm not going to have a nervous breakdown because people think I like having sex with men. But I don't and that's that."

Taraborrelli claims a source told him that Jackson's sister Rebbie once disclosed an incident when Michael was fifteen and a member of his family decided he was old enough to have sex.

"This person then arranged the services of two hookers for Michael," the source told the author. "He told them to work him over, and then locked him in a room with them. Rebbie said this incident absolutely traumatized her brother. Whether Michael actually had sex with the hookers, she didn't say."

Some others told me they think he's actually asexual.

"I've known Michael since he was fifteen," said one musician I frequently jam with in New York. "I've never seen him with a girl in the romantic sense. Not even one in all the years I've known him. Nobody that I know has ever seen him with one either. But I've also never seen him with a man that way either unless you believe he's doing those kids he hangs around with. He doesn't give off a gay vibe at all to me, he gives off a no-sex vibe. It's like he's a preadolescent boy before they discover girls."

The well-known music producer Mark Ronson, brother of Lindsay Lohan's girlfriend Samantha Ronson, tells a story about the time he and Sean Lennon were hanging around Neverland with Jackson when they were kids:

"It's a weird story," he says. "We used to watch the porn channel because we were, like, ten and, 'Oh my God, tits!' So Michael was in bed. And me and Sean said, 'Michael, do you want to see something cool?' We turned the dial to the porn channel and there were strippers shaking their tits around. We were like, 'Michael, Michael, how cool is this?' We turned around and he was cringing, saying, 'Ooh, stop it, stop it, ooh, it's so silly.' We were like, 'Michael, you have to look, maybe you're not seeing it right, it's naked girls!' He was not down with the program whatsoever! I think he had really strong feminist views on porn."

Finally in late 2007 I saw the smoking gun that Michael was homosexual and that his taste was for young men—albeit not as young as Jordan Chandler or Gavin Arvizo. In the course of my undercover investigations on Jackson, I spoke to two of his gay lovers, one a Hollywood waiter, the other an aspiring actor. The waiter had remained friends—perhaps more—with the singer until his death. When he served Jackson at a restaurant, Jackson made his interest plain and the two slept together the following night. According to the waiter, Jackson fell in love. The actor, who has been given solid but uninspiring film parts, met Jackson in mid-2007. He told me they had spent nearly every night together during their affair—an easy claim to make, you might think. But this lover produced corroboration in the form of photographs of the two together, and a witness. When I asked the lover for copies of the photos to use for publication he completely lost it. "I would never betray Michael that way," he said. "I'll love him forever, even if he doesn't love me anymore. I'll always be there for him, no matter what he does."

"Lawrence" said Jackson was introduced to him by the sister of one of his aides. Their affair was short but "passionate" and took place almost every night for three weeks at the actor's home in the Hollywood Hills. "He was very shy," recalls the actor, "but when he started to have sex, he was insatiable. He was a bottom, but he was so thin, I worried that I would break him. The very first time he blew me, he said, 'The King of Pop's going to lick your lollipop.' I still laugh thinking about that." He also said Jackson liked to dress in women's clothing but "only occasionally, not every time." Lawrence showed me three separate photos of himself with Jackson, including one that appears to have been taken in a kitchen, and at one point introduced me to an eyewitness, his Colombian gardener, who met Jackson at Lawrence's house on two occasions, though he says he never "saw anything."

Before leaving, the lover admitted he had signed a confidentiality agreement with Jackson to never reveal details of their secret relationship. For Jackson, this was a common way of handling his affairs. He'd do the same to every employee he had, as well as family members and even his parents. "I know for a fact that Michael makes everyone he comes in contact with sign a confidentiality agreement," a close aide of Jackson said. "He's done that for decades. That's the way he operates."

Other witnesses speak of strings of young adult men visiting his house at all hours, even in the period of his decline. Some stayed overnight. When Michael moved to Las Vegas in 2007, to the upscale residential community Palomino Lane, it made a lot of parents in the community fume. He lived right down the street from the Wasden Elementary School. "We were all worried that he would prey on our children," said one local resident. "Until he moved out, we all lived in fear. Even though he was acquitted of being a pedophile, most of us believed he was guilty."

When he lived in Las Vegas, Jackson rarely left his residence. When he did, according to one of Jackson's closest confidents, it was to meet a male boyfriend at a run-down Las Vegas motel. "He met a guy who was a construction worker and fell madly in love with him," the source said. "Michael would leave the house in disguise, often dressed as a woman, and would go meet his boyfriend at a motel that was one of Vegas' grungiest dives. It was infested with rats and bugs. Michael was broke. He struggled to put food on the table for his children. That was all he could afford then."

A close aide of Jackson who confirmed the affair to me said he had no knowledge of what went on behind closed doors at the motel, but said that Jackson would dress as a woman after midnight to meet the burly half-Asian worker in his early twenties who was employed by the City of Las Vegas by day.

Jackson has, in fact, been linked romantically over the years with a number of women, including Brooke Shields and Tatum O'Neal, who accompanied him to various functions. He once gave an interview in which he claimed that O'Neal was his first love and that she seduced him. But in her autobiography, the actress strongly denied the story, claiming that they only kissed once, when she was twelve and he was seventeen.

> At 12 I didn't have much to say about sex—all I knew was that it went on, pretty steadily, in my father's room next to mine. But Michael was intensely curious about anything and everything sexual, though in an incredibly sweet & innocent way.

He was a huge star, but it seemed he barely even dated & knew little about life. He once came to my house & asked to come upstairs b/c he'd never been in a girl's bedroom before. He sat on the bed, & we kissed very briefly, but it was terribly awkward. For all my passionate crushes on people like Dustin Hoffman, I was just 12 & not at all ready for a real-life encounter. So I said, 'I can't.' Michael, who was sweating profusely, seemed as intimidated as I was. He jumped up nervously & said, 'Uh, gotta go.' That's the closest I ever got to Michael, which is why I'm amazed by his recent claim on national TV that I'd seduced him but he was too shy to carry it through. I absolutely adored Michael—as a friend—& I admire him to this day. I believe that he fell in love w/me. I'm told that he wrote the song "She's Out of My Life" on his album *Off the Wall* for me. What an honor. At the time of the supposed seduction, I was barely pubescent, & what I'd seen of sex so far was unappealing & gross. It may have been Michael's fantasy that I'd seduce him—and it's a little sad that he cast himself as failing, even in his dream—but it just didn't happen.

In 1988, Tatiana Thumbtzen, a Juillard-trained dancer who appeared in his 1988 *Moonwalker* video, became the first person to ever kiss Jackson in public. Afterward, he told the media, "I love her because she's warm, caring, and exciting." She was also photographed several times accompanying him as his date to various functions, and in 1994, during the height of the Jordan Chandler allegations, Thumbtzen told a reporter that she had once been romantically involved with the singer. But years later, in her book *The Way He Made Me Feel*, she admitted that she lied to the media about their romance.

Whether or not he is gay, straight, or asexual, to most people it was obvious why Jackson had married Lisa Marie Presley. He needed to give the appearance of heterosexual normalcy following the Jordan Chandler scandal. The real question is why she would agree to marry him and subject herself to the ridicule that followed. She certainly didn't need the money.

When the couple divorced just nineteen short months after they married, Lisa Marie was again interviewed by Sawyer, this time alone. The veteran broadcaster began her questioning by expressing undisguised bewilderment at the short-lived marriage, introducing the segment by sarcastically announcing, "Lisa Presley marries Michael Jackson? How weird can it get!"

Sawyer continues the barrage. "Okay. Michael Jackson? Michael Jackson? Why did you marry Michael Jackson? What were you doing?"

Presley immediately goes on the defensive. "It's unfortunate that not a lot of people know who he really is," she responds. "He doesn't let anybody see it. He was very quick to sit me down the first time I met him and say, 'Listen, I'm not gay. I know you think this and I know you think that. He started cursing, he started being a normal person and I was like, Wow! . . . Wow, you're so misunderstood. Oh my god."

Repeatedly expressing disbelief that Lisa Marie

could have ever been sexually attracted to Jackson, Sawyer clearly shows she doesn't buy the story.

Most of the speculation centered on the fact that Lisa Marie was an aspiring singer and that she believed Jackson could help her recording career. Did Elvis's daughter really need that kind of help?

As Lisa Marie told Diane Sawyer, "I'm not gonna marry someone for a recording career, just to clear that up as well."

I may have stumbled upon another explanation. The Church of Scientology.

There was one group in particular that had more than a passing interest in gay celebrities.

In 2005, I happened to be working on a book and documentary project about the Church of Scientology, the secretive religion that had swept Hollywood, attracting a number of A-list actors such as Tom Cruise, Will Smith, and John Travolta to its fold. They also had more than their fair share of lesser known celebrities, including one woman who most people had barely heard of before she married Michael Jackson.

There had long been rumors of a special church program that promises to "convert" homosexuals and turn them straight. Scientology frequently lauded its ability to help struggling actors find the spiritual grounding they needed to achieve success, offering a number of acting workshops and programs.

So for my project, I decided to pose as an aspiring actor who believed my homosexuality might be an impediment to stardom.

The Church of Scientology had been founded in the 1950s by an obscure writer of science fiction novels named L. Ron Hubbard, who devised a series of spiritual self-help systems he called Dianetics based on his writings, which involve a dictator of the "Galactic Confederacy" who, 75 million years ago, brought billions of his people to Earth in a DC-8-like spacecraft, stacked them around volcanoes, and killed them using hydrogen bombs.

A few years earlier, Hubbard had told a friend that the "easiest way to make a million dollars would be to start my own religion."

In the years since, his church had established a multibillion-dollar business empire, gained tens of thousands of followers worldwide, and generated considerable controversy, including myriad accusations that the religion was in fact a sinister cult.

As early as 1965, the Australian state of Victoria issued a report of a Board of Enquiry into Scientology, concluding that Hubbard falsely claimed scientific and other credentials and that his sanity was "to be gravely doubted."

In the mid-seventies, the FBI raided Scientology offices throughout the United States looking for documentation of Hubbard's Operation Snow White, an espionage network run by the church, which involved illegal wiretaps and the theft of documents from government offices. A number of top-level church officials, including Hubbard's wife and second-in-command, Mary Sue, were indicted and convicted on federal charges of conspiracy against the United States government.

Hubbard himself was named as an "unindicted co-conspirator."

Early on, Hubbard had identified celebrities as a key to the expansion of Scientology, establishing a series of Celebrity Centers where prominent Hollywood actors could be catered to and pampered while attending to their training. He also exhibited considerable hostility toward homosexuality, describing it in church literature as sexual perversion and a "mental aberration."

Such people, he wrote, engaged in "irregular practices which do anything but tend toward the creation of children" and "efforts which tend not toward enjoyment but toward the pollution and derangement of sex itself so as to make it as repulsive as possible to others and so to inhibit procreation."

When I first visited the church's L.A. headquarters and told them my story, the woman who greeted me immediately attempted to banish my cameraman from the premises, which would have been a major blow to my documentary. I quickly explained that my uncle in Canada—who had become exceedingly rich after inventing the hotel key card—is very interested in joining the church and has asked me to document my experiences on video. At the mention of my millionaire relative, her eyes light up and she authorizes the camera to stay. She then insists on processing my membership personally.

As a result, I became, according to the London *Daily Mail*, "the only journalist to successfully infiltrate the Church of Scientology," and I captured it all on film.

After we walked through what can only be described

as a shrine to L. Ron Hubbard, which reminds me of a trip I once took to Soviet Russia where Lenin's photo and writings were everywhere, she asks me to take a written test.

She tells me it will give me a bird's-eye view of what's going well and what can be improved. The questions are relatively innocuous such as "Do you have any regrets about past misfortunes?" and "Do you have the stomach to kill an animal to put it out of its pain?" I decided to answer each question the opposite of how I really feel just to see what will happen.

While I'm waiting for the results, I ask my Scientology handler whether the church can really help my acting career take off. "Obviously I'm not at the level of a Travolta or Cruise, but are there any classes for me to take to help me become a star?"

"Absolutely," she replies. "I mean, that's what we do. We have courses that people can take where they learn how to, on the one hand, handle certain things in life that are causing trouble. It could be marriage, money, or any other problem you might be having."

"And you'll be able to tell with this test?" I ask.

"Yeah, it's actually very accurate," she responds.

I proceed to tell her that I'm actually having a big problem. I'm gay.

"That's why I'm here, because I think my homosexuality is ruining my career. Is there any way to get over that?"

"Possibly," she replies matter-of-factly.

I ask her how.

"Through auditing," she replies.

"What's auditing?" I ask.

"Auditing is spiritual counseling."

She suggests I am now ready for the e-meter test.

Soon enough, she is hooking me up to the church's bizarre science-fiction-inspired Hubbard Electrometer, otherwise known as the e-meter. The device, according to the church's literature, measures electronic response in the skin and is supposed to "reflect or indicate whether or not the confessing person has been relieved from spiritual impediment of his sins." In other words, it's a primitive lie-detector test. The e-meter became the subject of a U.S. government crackdown over deceptive practices in the early sixties when more than one hundred E-meters were seized by U.S. marshals during the founding of the Church of Scientology building in Washington, D.C. The church had been accused of making false claims that the devices effectively treated some 70 percent of all physical and mental illness. In 1971, U.S. District Judge Gerhard Gesell, called Scientology "a pseudo-science that has been adopted for religious purposes" and referred to Hubbard's ideas as "quackery."

He ruled that the church could no longer advertise its services as a scientific cure and forced the church to label the devices as ineffective in treating illness.

More controversially, the e-meter is often used in something Scientology refers to as the "sexual and criminal security check," where members are forced during various phases of their career to hold on to the e-meter while they are asked about past criminal acts, crimes against Scientology, and "sexual deeds or misdeeds."

The information, often embarrassing and incriminating, is then allegedly put in dossiers that can be used against a member if they try to leave the church.

After I am hooked up, my handler explains that if the needle moves, it indicates stress points, and if it moves far enough to the right, it's a "fail," which would indicate how much I need Scientology.

Other than the prospect of being discovered as an undercover journalist and sent for "re-education" or being forced to watch the John Travolta Scientology epic *Battlefield Earth* for hours with my eyes propped open, I don't have a care in the world. I am then asked a series of questions such as "Are you nervous about something coming up in your life?" The needle fails to move at all, making my handler somewhat nervous. Finally, in response to a question, the needle moves a little teenie bit. "You see," she shouts with glee, "that demonstrates a problem."

After a while, she tells me to concentrate on "something, anything in your life and focus on it." My mother had just died a few weeks earlier so that's what I decide to focus on. And this time the needle jumps to the right, about an inch. I think she may have had a tiny orgasm as she watched the needle jump. She can barely contain her excitement.

I tell her I was focusing on my homosexuality and how it is sabotaging my career.

"We can definitely help you with that," she says. "You need auditing."

When my written test comes back, it shows that I am "stressed, depressed, insecure, emotionally fragile, and slightly unstable."

"As I expected," she declares, "you are under severe emotional turmoil, but you do have potential. I think Scientology can definitely help you with that. We have courses that you will benefit from greatly. It will turn your life around."

Later, I manage to get an interview with the Celebrity Center's vice president Greg Laclaire, this time as a journalist, but only after I tell him about my uncle who is thinking of joining. Laclaire assures me that the principles of Scientology are undoubtedly the factor behind the success of its celebrity members. What strikes me about the interview is not his predictable defense of Scientology. It is the point in the middle of the interview when I notice a guy had jumped out from behind some bushes and is filming me filming Laclaire.

"Greg," I ask, "is he filming us?" pointing to the cameraman.

"Oh, he's just my guy," Laclaire responds, embarrassed. "He's just filming this because we might use it someday."

For several months, I investigated the Church of Scientology, sometimes as a journalist, sometimes undercover. Along the way, I cultivated a number of current and former members as sources, discovering an astonishing amount of information about church practices. During this period, I was particularly interested in the church's focus on celebrities. It was during this phase of my research that two separate Scientologists told me the same thing—the Church of Scientology had plotted and arranged the unlikely marriage of Michael Jackson and Lisa Marie Presley.

"The church needed to reel in a big fish and they set their sights firmly on Jackson," said one former high-ranking church official. "They did what they had to do to get him, and they used one of their most loyal followers to do what had to be done."

The church had always devoted considerable efforts to recruiting celebrities and had opened up its first Celebrity Center in Los Angeles in 1969, dedicated to artists and celebrities, because, it said, "those are the people who are sculpting the present into the future." A large-scale effort was then undertaken to bring in prominent show business recruits. By the 1990s, the policy had already met with considerable success, with a rapidly increasing stable of Hollywood celebrities joining the ranks. Among the most prominent was an actor who had actually joined Scientology long before he achieved stardom, John Travolta. The church, in fact, often pointed to Travolta as a shining example of how Scientology can help achieve success. He may have also been a poster child for another notorious church practice.

In 1991, *Time*, one of the world's most respected news publications, published a devastating exposé headlined "Scientology: the Thriving Cult of Greed and Power," detailing many of the church's more unsavory practices. Among the revelations contained in the cover story was the suggestion that Travolta was practically being held hostage by the church because of his alleged homosexuality:

> High-level defectors claim that Travolta has long feared that if he defected, details of his sexual life

would be made public. "He felt pretty intimidated about this getting out and told me so," recalls William Franks, the church's former chairman of the board. "There were no outright threats made, but it was implicit. If you leave, they immediately start digging up everything." Franks was driven out in 1981 after attempting to reform the church. The church's former head of security, Richard Aznaran, recalls Scientology ringleader Miscavige repeatedly joking to staffers about Travolta's allegedly promiscuous homosexual behavior. At this point any threat to expose Travolta seems superfluous: last May a male porn star collected $100,000 from a tabloid for an account of his alleged two-year liaison with the celebrity. Travolta refuses to comment, and in December his lawyer dismissed questions about the subject as "bizarre." Two weeks later, Travolta announced that he was getting married to actress Kelly Preston, a fellow Scientologist.

It was the quickie marriage to Preston just as *Time* was preparing to run its piece speculating on Travolta's sexuality that particularly intrigued me about the story. Especially after I heard the rumors about Jackson and Lisa Marie. So I decided to track down a man named Michael Pattinson.

Michael Pattinson is a prominent gay Beverly Hills artist who in 1998 filed a lawsuit against the Church of Scientology in U.S. District Court claiming that, over the course of almost twenty-five years, the church had promised to turn him straight and that he had paid more than $500,000 in fees for "auditing" courses but that he was still gay. He also claimed that they had frequently used Travolta as an example of a success story for their homosexuality cure.

Pattinson told me he traveled in the same Scientology circles as Travolta. "I joined pretty well the same time he did, knew all the same people. In fact, I was considered a celebrity, I think, even before he was, and was even featured on the cover of the church's magazine, *Celebrity*. Everybody knew about him early on. It was pretty obvious. Travolta was the role model for the cure, especially after he got married. I thought, well, if he could get married, then he must be cured, and I took even more courses and spent even more money, just waiting for the day when I would also be cured of what they called 'my ruin.'"

By the time he left the church, Pattinson said, he had achieved a very high rank.

"I was treated by the same handlers, or Terminals as they're called, as any other celebrity, such as Travolta, such as Tom Cruise, such as Kirstie Alley. I know that it is very important for public relations that within the industry some of these people are seen to be straight while actually being gay and trying to handle it within Scientology . . . All this, of course, would be in their 'pre-clear' folders under an assumed name, a code name because all their innermost secrets are there. But it's very important to have that paradox going on. Maybe they have something in the industry which would seem to be terrible and yet they have to be shown to be straight. They would probably be very inclined to go into an arranged marriage."

In the years following her father's death, Lisa Marie Presley descended into a spiral of depression, bad behavior, and drugs. It didn't help that she had to fight off her mother's live-in boyfriend, who she claimed regularly made advances toward her while Priscilla was on the set filming her hit TV show, *Dallas*.

By the time she was eighteen, she had come off a four-year drug and alcohol binge that had people worried she was headed for the same fate as Elvis.

"I was on a 72-hour bender," she later recalled. "Cocaine, sedatives, pot, and drinking—all at the same time . . . I don't know how I lived through it. I woke up one day with a bunch of people on the floor, and the coke dealer was in the room, and I said, 'Everybody get the fuck out! That's it. I'm done.'"

She claims that's the day she drove to the Church of Scientology and said, "Somebody fucking help me right now."

It was the same year that she started to receive annuities from her father's hundred-million-dollar estate, which she was entitled to as Elvis' sole heir and which she inherited outright at the age of twenty-five, according to the terms of the will.

For the past nine years, that fortune had been managed very competently by her mother, Priscilla, who had taken the debt-ridden shambles that Elvis had left when he died in 1977—thanks in large part to the questionable practices of his manager, Colonel Tom Parker—

and turned it into a model of business efficiency and a money-making machine that saw her frequently described as one of America's savviest businesswomen. She had help.

Priscilla Presley has been an ardent Scientologist since at least the early eighties, devoting herself to a wide array of church causes and donating vast sums of money to church coffers. She even purchased a multimillion-dollar mansion in Clearwater, Florida, near the church's spiritual headquarters. Priscilla has also closely relied on Scientology advisers to help manage the Elvis estate while taking great pains to distance Elvis Presley Enterprises from Scientology in the public eye for fear of tarnishing the lucrative Elvis image. The only time she summoned her ex-husband's name, in fact, was in connection to the church's crusade against prescription drugs.

"I wish that [Elvis] knew what Scientology was before he died," Priscilla told reporters at the opening of a church-run drug rehab center in 2002, adding that the church's staunch antidrug policies could have "helped Elvis a lot" in fighting his own addiction to prescription drugs.

But it appears that Elvis did know about Scientology and that he had firmly rejected it in no uncertain terms. According to Lamar Fike, a longtime member of Elvis's entourage, known as the Memphis Mafia, Elvis once had a revealing encounter with the church.

"One day, in L.A., we got in the limousine and went down to the Scientology center on Sunset [Boulevard], and Elvis went in and talked to them," recalls Fike. "We waited in the car, but apparently they started doing all

these charts and crap for him. Elvis came out and said,
'Fuck those people! There's no way I'll ever get involved
with that son-of-a-bitchin' group. All they want is my
money.' He stayed away from Scientology like it was a
cobra. He'd shit a brick to see how far Lisa Marie's gotten into it."

Although Lisa Marie did not formally join the
church until she was eighteen, she was no stranger to
the world of Scientology, having attended the church-
run Westside Apple School for years, where she was exposed to Hubbard's teachings and philosophy, though
she says she was usually too stoned to pay much attention.

Once she joined in 1986, however, she threw herself into it full throttle, becoming one of its most ardent
devotees.

"Were it not for Scientology, I would either be
completely insane or dead by now," she wrote in a book
published by the church called *What Is Scientology?* "I
am forever grateful for the technology of Scientology
and to Mr. Hubbard, who dedicated his life to helping
man and this planet, as well as to the people who have
dedicated their lives to helping others through Scientology." Her devotion to the church extended to her
personal life, and in 1988 she married a fellow Scientologist named Danny Keough, whom she had met at
the Church of Scientology Celebrity Center International in Los Angeles and had been dating since she
joined the church.

The couple had two children and were, by most
accounts, happily married when all of a sudden it was

announced that they were getting a divorce. "Danny and I will always love each other," Lisa Marie said at the time. "However, friendship was more suitable for us than marriage. We have two wonderful children and we plan to have joint custody of them." Twenty days later, Lisa Marie flew to the Dominican Republic to marry Michael Jackson.

Perhaps the most unusual thing about the Jackson-Presley wedding, besides the unlikely nature of the couple itself, was that it was attended by Danny Keough's younger brother, Thomas, a Scientologist, who served as a witness.

Was the divorce and wedding a scheme concocted by Scientology to lure Jackson into the fold?

In 1955, L. Ron Hubbard had created a Scientology program called Project Celebrity, offering rewards to Scientologists who recruited targeted celebrities. A 1976 church policy letter states that "rehabilitation of celebrities who are just beyond or just approaching their prime" enables the "rapid dissemination" of Scientology.

Hubbard decreed that Scientologists should target prominent individuals as their "quarry" and bring them back like trophies for the church. Among those he listed as suitable prey at the time were: Edward R. Murrow, Marlene Dietrich, Ernest Hemingway, Howard Hughes, Greta Garbo, Walt Disney, Groucho Marx, and other big names of the era.

"If you bring one of them home you will get a small plaque as a reward," Hubbard wrote in a Scientology magazine.

According to one of my Scientology sources, the church had long considered Jackson a potential recruit because of his history with another controversial religion, the Jehovah's Witnesses. Jackson grew up a devout follower of the sect and even went door to door evangelizing for the Witnesses long after he became famous.

"The church did their homework and discovered that Jackson donated huge amounts of money to the Jehovah's Witnesses before he left the faith and he even helped finance the construction of their headquarters. To Scientology, that's the Holy Grail."

According to Michael Pattinson, a former Scientologist who knew Lisa Marie well, "That's exactly the kind of modus operandi they employ. Jackson would have been a big catch." Pattinson said he also heard rumors but nothing concrete.

Before he defected in the mid-nineties, Jesse Prince was one of Scientology's highest officials, reaching the rank of Deputy Inspector General, External. In this position, he had close contacts with the church leadership, including the head of Scientology, David Miscavige. Prince claims that he witnessed what may have been the early stages of the plan to recruit Jackson.

"David Miscavige just had an insane fascination for Michael Jackson," Prince recalls. "The whole crew had to listen to his music. We would have special showings [to] make sure you watch the *Thriller* video."

While he was not privy to any direct recruiting efforts, Prince does recall one conversation with Miscavige that suggested Jackson's recruitment was a high priority.

"While [all] of this was going on, David would proudly announce how we just almost got Michael Jackson, we're doing everything that we can, and Lisa Marie, and I guess it didn't work out."

However, he says that at one point the relationship between Jackson and Scientology was so good that Jackson arranged for the executive producer of *Thriller*, Bruce Swedien, to work on the *Battlefield Earth* album that the church of Scientology was producing, based on Hubbard's novel. That arrangement fell apart, he says, because Swedien's wife arrived in the studio one day wearing cologne, which is a big no-no in Scientology circles. When she was rudely chastised for the "stink," Swedien ended his involvement in the project.

Prince, who maintains that he witnessed Scientology frequently arrange both marriages and divorces, also claims the divorce between Lisa Marie and Danny Keough was closely monitored by the highest levels of the church and "got done very quickly" to ensure the Jackson marriage would be expedited.

Indeed, my sources tell me that during the short-lived marriage, there were high-level efforts to persuade Jackson to go through an auditing program, the euphemism the church used for spiritual counseling, but that he continually resisted.

"At one point, Michael complained that he thought they might be trying to brainwash him," says an associate who worked with Jackson at the time. "He said he found those people very *creepy*."

In the Diane Sawyer interview, when she asks him at one point whether he's a Scientologist, Jackson replies, "I believe in spirituality and I believe in a higher source, such as God. But I'm not a Scientologist. I read everything. I like to read. I love to study."

After the divorce, Lisa Marie claimed that the couple had been "sexually active" during the marriage, but others say they rarely spent time together and that Lisa Marie spent considerably more time with her ex-husband, Danny Keough, than with Michael during this period.

"We always wondered whether Lisa Marie had ever really stopped being married to Keough," says the Jackson associate. "It didn't seem like it."

Shortly after she divorced Jackson, in fact, Keough moved into the guesthouse on Lisa Marie's property, where he still lives today.

TEN

The crowds below were screaming with adoration. "Michael! Michael! Michael!" came the frenzied roar from the thousands of fans who had gathered in Berlin's central square, across from the landmark Brandenburg Gate, on November 19, 2002.

Above, on the balcony of his $10,000-per-night Adlon Hotel suite, stood the object of their affection, Michael Jackson, who had just arrived in the German capital to receive an award as "Artist of the Century."

Suddenly the screams intensified as Jackson walked onto the balcony holding what appeared at first to be a doll with a towel over its head. As Jackson briefly dangled it over the fourth-floor balcony railing by one arm, and its legs started to wriggle, it became obvious that the doll was in fact his nine-month-old baby son, Prince Michael II, better known as Blanket. Jackson then retreated back inside.

Nobody in the crowd appeared particularly troubled by what they had witnessed. Instead, they started to chant, "Fuck the press, Michael, you're the best!"

A few moments later, he came back to the balcony and threw down a pillow on which he had written, "I love you with all my heart—Michael Jackson."

That evening, oblivious to the coming uproar, Jackson headed to a local video store where he bought a copy of *E.T.*—which he claims to have seen at least five hundred times—and watched it with his family.

The following morning, Americans woke to the video footage of the baby dangling incident and immediately expressed shock and revulsion. "MAD BAD DAD!" screamed one tabloid headline.

Child protection experts were quick to respond to the incident. Katharina Abelmann-Vollmer of the German Child Protection Association called for an immediate investigation after German police announced that they would not press charges. "When it is someone else other than Michael Jackson dangling their child sixty feet above the street, then there would definitely have been a prosecution. There is one rule for the rich and famous and one for ordinary people," she said.

Britain's National Society for the Prevention of Child Cruelty was more circumspect with its spokesperson issuing a polite statement: "We advise anyone not to put babies or children at risk by dangling them over a balcony," said a spokesperson.

"Considering Mr. Jackson started a charity to protect children, this was alarmingly irresponsible behavior with a child," said Kevin Kirkpatrick of Prevent Child Abuse America. "Holding a child like that with what appeared to be one arm while leaning over a fourth-floor balcony window is pretty careless, to say the least."

"That kid could have been killed. Something needs to be done. He should be charged with child endangerment," echoed Dr. Patricia Farrell, a New Jersey psychologist.

Even his friends and fans were shocked. "I have always loved Michael's music, but he should be arrested for that sick stunt. It's a bloody disgrace the authorities haven't made a move to at least questioning him about it. What was he playing at?" a thirty-three-year-old American housewife told a reporter.

"I can't believe what I saw. Obviously, Michael is somehow out of control," said Donald Trump, who had frequently hosted Jackson as his guest at New York's Trump Towers and at his sprawling estate, Mar-a-Lago, in Palm Beach.

As usual when he was under fire, Jackson's family circled the wagons. Michael was "caught up in the excitement" when he dangled the baby, his brother Jermaine told CNN. "You judge a person by their intentions. He is a wonderful father. He's a great dad. He's great to our kids, my kids."

Never passing up an opportunity for publicity, Jordan Chandler's onetime lawyer Gloria Allred wrote to the California Department of Social Services asking for an investigation into whether Jackson had endangered his infant son.

"Given the height of the balcony and the fact that Mr. Jackson was only holding the child with one arm as he held the child over the side, the child was at risk of falling and being injured or killed," Allred wrote.

Responding to the outcry, Jackson issued a written statement of apology.

"I offer no excuses for what happened," he said. "I made a terrible mistake," he wrote. "I got caught up in the excitement of the moment. I would never intentionally endanger the lives of my kids."

But the psychologist Joyce Brothers was not satisfied with the tone of the statement, telling reporters, "It helps him to try to apologize, but that's not an apology. I really don't think he's capable of putting himself in someone else's shoes, to have empathy to feel how others feel."

One newspaper did attempt to put the incident into perspective and dial back the invective, noting, "The moment where he dangled his baby over a hotel balcony in Berlin was foolish, but greater cruelty to children can be observed in any supermarket car park." But defenders of his actions were few and far between.

As reaction poured in from around the world, Jackson seemed to only make matters worse when he tried to portray himself as a normal father by taking his two older children, Paris and Prince Michael, to the Berlin Zoo the day after the incident.

The outing, however, quickly turned into a surreal spectacle, as the beleaguered singer hid his kids' faces from the public under purple hoods and burka-like veils while paparazzi swarmed around them.

According to one account, "Jacko's three-year-old daughter, Paris Michael Katherine Jackson, had the look of a mourner at a funeral as she strained to view an exhibit of monkeys through her thick gauze."

Throughout the controversy, both supporters and detractors expressed bemusement about what could possess Jackson to be so reckless. Even Rabbi Shmuley

Boteach, Jackson's close friend and spiritual adviser, was perplexed: "Why he would do this? I don't know," he told a reporter. "It's so out of character for him."

A few years later, during the course of my investigation, I may have stumbled upon an explanation. According to one of his associates who was present in Berlin during the incident, "Michael was as high as a kite."

Although he managed to hold on to his son as he dangled him over the balcony, Michael Jackson was clearly losing his grip. The years following the Jordan Chandler settlement had clearly taken their toll.

Not long after the divorce with Lisa Marie was made final, Jackson again shocked the world in November 1996 with news out of Australia that he had just married a thirty-seven-year-old nurse, Debbie Rowe, who was six months pregnant at the time.

Rowe had been working for Jackson's dermatologist, Arnold Klein, and had gotten to know Jackson when he came in for his regular visits. She had just been recovering from a breakup with her first serious boyfriend and was enamored of Jackson, on whom she had always had a schoolgirl crush. When he spoke of his longing to be a father, she offered herself for the task.

The wedding itself was bizarre in keeping with Jackson's reputation. The best man was an eight-year-old boy—one of his "special friends."

The tone of Jackson's marriage to Rowe was set on his wedding night. Following their nuptials, Jackson gave his new wife a peck on the cheek. That night they slept in separate suites at the Sheraton Hotel.

She was quickly nicknamed the "Queen of Pop" by the tabloid press. Three months later, Rowe gave birth to a son who they named Prince Michael, and fourteen months after that, Rowe gave birth to a girl, Paris Katherine Jackson.

It was clear to most observers that if Jackson's marriage to Lisa Marie Presley had been designed to imply heterosexual normalcy, the plan had failed miserably. Nobody, it seemed, believed that the Presley marriage was real or that the couple had ever had sex, no matter how many times they protested. Now speculation centerd on whether fathering children with a wife was meant to quell the public's long-held doubts. By marrying and then fathering two children, he could at least leave the impression that he had sex. But if that was the intention, the new plan was also doomed. Almost immediately there was speculation that the children had been born through artificial insemination, as indeed they were. One tabloid report even suggested that Rowe had been paid as much as $1.7 million to give birth to her first child. The actual figure was $6 million.

"Before signing a contract with her he made her undergo hundreds of medical tests at a private medical clinic in Beverly Hills. He wanted to make sure she had a clean bill of health and had a stellar medical past," revealed a Jackson friend. "He asked the doctors that everything be divulged about Rowe's condition. Even if it was as minute as a pimple, nothing was to be kept secret. He was extremely paranoid and needed to know everything. Each time the doctors sent him a medical report he'd spend days and weeks studying it to make sure there were no red flags."

It soon became clear to observers that the so-called marriage was a sham when Rowe continued to live in her housing complex in the Los Angeles suburb of Van Nuys.

According to a Neverland chef's account in the London *Times*:

> Debbie was not a significant presence, like you would expect of a new mother. We only saw her a few times. The baby was cared for by a team of six nannies and six nurses. They all worked eight hours each, in shifts. So the baby would always have two nurses and two nannies by his side. They were kept under constant video surveillance which was monitored by members of Jackson's security team. The nannies all have special training. The day team do all these exercise drills with the baby to build up his strength. The night team began reading and singing to Prince when he was only three weeks old. When Prince cries, he seems to be calling for his mama. That's only natural. In Mr. Jackson's home, there is really little sign of Ms. Rowe. It's eerie, it's almost as if the baby doesn't have a mother at all. There are no pictures of Debbie I ever saw. Mr. Jackson just has one photo by his bed and that's of Lisa Marie as a child, in the year when the two of them met.

Rowe fueled the rumors by admitting that she rarely saw her children, stating that she is perfectly happy to have Jackson care for them by himself.

"Neverland is heaven," she told a Los Angeles TV crew. "It's where Michael can get away and be Dad and be a kid with his kid. Whenever the baby is awake, he is with Prince the whole time, unless he's on tour. When the baby is napping, he will lie with him for a while, then steal away to work, to write music, to dance."

"I don't need to be there with the baby," she added. "Michael pays so much attention to the baby, I would have nothing to do. It's not my duty and Michael understands that. I need my independence. My friendship with Michael is the most important thing to me. And if this marriage gets in the way of that friendship, then we'll put the marriage aside, but I want to go on as friends. I have always felt for Michael and now I feel for him even more."

Uncomplaining, she told a British newspaper, "I may be Mrs. Michael Jackson. But if he's the king, then I'm the queen in exile."

A friend of Rowe recounted her reaction to a bizarre story about the birth of their second child.

"After the baby came out from the womb, Michael wrapped Paris in a towel and fled with the newborn. Debbie was devastated. I don't think she really ever got over that," the friend said. "Maybe he was trying to make it easier for her later on, make sure she didn't have a chance to bond with the baby." After being cleaned up and examined, the baby was taken to Neverland, where a team of nannies were standing by to care for her.

Later, Rowe confirmed that her second child was not conceived through natural means.

"Of course it was artificial insemination," she told the London *Daily Mail*. "Paris was conceived in Paris, that's how she got her name. Michael wanted to call her Princess, but I thought that was stupid." And despite her revelation, she never discussed whose sperm was used to inseminate her.

At the time, the media was never allowed to see or photograph the children's faces because their heads were covered whenever they went out. If there had been media coverage, the rumors would only have intensified. When the public got their first look at Prince Michael and Paris years later, they were struck by an obvious thought: the children were white. When Michael was young, he was a relatively dark-skinned African-American child who gradually transformed into a virtual white man through means unknown. And although it is possible for the children of mixed race couples to take on the racial characteristics of only one parent, experts say it is rare to have it happen twice in a row without acquiring any of the father's features. It was obvious to many that the children were not Michael's biological offspring, though he had repeatedly denied it.

The children's "lack of any negroid features has the tittle-tattle going full tilt in Hollywood," wrote one British newspaper, typical of the gossipy tone of the coverage.

When problems with Rowe's second pregnancy— she almost died of a hemorrhage during the birth— meant that she could no longer have children, her usefulness had come to an end.

"I had so many problems when I was pregnant with

Paris," she later recalled. "After that I couldn't have any more children. Michael was upset about that, he couldn't understand it. He wanted more babies."

As one account put it, Rowe was then "put out to pasture" with a generous settlement and the couple divorced in 1999, citing irreconcilable differences. Three years later, in August 2002, Jackson showed up at a Siegfried and Roy show in Las Vegas, where he brought a six-month-old infant backstage and introduced him to the illusionists and gathered media, saying: "This is my third child, Prince Michael II." He gave no explanation about where the child had come from or who his mother was. His identity has been a closely guarded secret ever since.

Despite the skepticism and curiosity about their lineage, the children appeared to be the one bright spot in Jackson's life. The rest of his life was not going as smoothly.

In 1995, Jackson released a new album, *HIStory*, a double album comprising old hits and a selection of new material. From the moment it was released, it was clear that Jackson was obsessed with using the album to exact revenge on those who had done him wrong.

One song in particular, entitled "D.S.," is a clear attack on Tom Sneddon, with Jackson appearing to call out his name at one point, even though the lyric sheet says "Dom Sheldon," probably to avoid a lawsuit. In the song, Jackson repeatedly calls Dom Sheldon a "cold man," singing he wants to "get my ass dead or alive" and asking whether he is a "brother with the KKK." He uses another song on the album, "Tabloid Junkie," to attack the media, whom he blames for the ongoing persecution against him. But the track that inspired the most controversy is entitled "They Don't Care About Us." It contains a line that was immediately labeled as anti-Semitic by *The New York Times* and a number of Jewish groups: "Jew me, sue me, everybody do me / Kick me, kike me, don't you black or white me." Most critics suspected he was buying into the widespread notion that Jews control the media, which he regards as the source of all his troubles. The resulting outcry prompted Jackson to issue a new version without the offending lyrics. He also issued a statement denying that the song targeted Jews.

"It's not anti-Semitic because I'm not a racist person . . . I could never be a racist. I love all races," said Jackson, adding that many of his closest friends and employees are Jewish.

The album itself sold about two million copies in the United States, respectable sales figures for almost any other singer, but a far cry from his previous colossal hits, including *Thriller*, which sold more than 13 million copies in the U.S. alone.

Still, Jackson had vowed to put the Jordan Chandler controversy behind him and to get on with his career and he was making some progress. But he couldn't quite escape his legal problems.

In December 1994, a group of five former Neverland employees joined together to sue Jackson for wrongful termination. The former employees alleged that they were fired because they had cooperated with investigators looking into the Jordan Chandler allegations. One of the fired guards, Ralph Chacon, claimed that he had once seen Jackson giving oral sex to Chandler in a Neverland shower room. Another, Kasim Abdool, recalled being asked by Jackson to deliver a jar of Vaseline late one night. When he arrived with the jar, he noticed that Jackson was "sweaty" and that his pajama bottoms were undone. In the room with him were two young boys, including Jordan. Another guard, named Melanie Bagnall, also had a disturbing story to tell. She claims she saw Jackson riding in a golf cart with a young boy, sitting close together. When she got near, she noticed Jackson's hand cupping the boy's crotch.

In their lawsuit, the guards claimed that they were intimidated, harassed, and eavesdropped on by Jackson's handlers, who were using illegal surveillance devices to spy on them.

Their charges confirmed similar accusations leveled against Jackson with his most vocal media critic, Maureen Orth, who has written a series of devastating critiques of the singer since 1993. Orth, too, has painted a picture of constant intimidation, threats, and harassment against critics, potential witnesses, and recalcitrant employees, dating back to Jackson's association with Anthony Pellicano and continuing through subsequent security teams. It is unclear, however, whether Jackson himself has orchestrated the Kafkaesque conditions that Orth has portrayed in her coverage.

This time Jackson, still bitter over the Chandler settlement, vowed to fight the charges in court. He even filed a countersuit, which went to court in 1997. A Superior Court judge eventually ruled in his favor, finding that the employees had not been wrongfully terminated. He ordered two of them to pay Jackson $60,000 to satisfy his countersuit, along with punitive damages because the two had acted "with malice." It emerged during the trial that the five had sold their stories to a supermarket tabloid and that two of the employees had been caught stealing items from Neverland.

The story of the Neverland Five, however, paled in comparison to a scurrilous little book called *Michael Jackson Was My Lover*. By the terms of the 1994 settlement, Jordan Chandler was barred from talking about his case or from discussing the allegations against Jackson outside a court of law. Suddenly, in the mid-nineties, a Chilean tabloid journalist named Victor Gutierrez started shopping around a book based on the "secret diaries of Jordie Chandler," which he purportedly obtained from Jordan's uncle, Raymond Chandler. The book is a salacious account of Jordan's relationship with Jackson, complete with supposed interviews with witnesses as well as detailed descriptions of Jackson's alleged unsavory sexual practices, including the use of tampons and enemas. It also contained enough documentation, such as Jordan's report card, to suggest that he did have some legitimate inside information.

When Gutierrez was unable to find a publisher, he began to shop its sordid revelations around to various tabloids known to pay for such stories, including the *National Enquirer* and *Hard Copy*. As we know from various "witnesses" who have come forward to accuse Jackson of wrongdoing over the years, the juicier the anecdote, the bigger the payday. Gutierrez was not making any money on his book. He needed something to spark the interest of those who wrote the cheques. He had just the story and Diane Dimond was all too willing to give him the forum to tell it.

Appearing on *Hard Copy*, Gutierrez claimed that he had seen a twenty-seven-minute video of Michael Jackson having sex with a boy. Not just any boy, but Jackson's own nephew Jeremy—the son of his brother Jermaine with his former common-law wife, Margaret Maldonado. He also told Dimond that the Los Angeles Police Department was reopening the child molestation investigation against Jackson. The next day a police spokesperson told the *Los Angeles Times* that the department had seen no such videotape, they were not looking for it, and there was no renewed investigation into molestation allegations as Gutierrez had claimed.

Margaret Maldonado, who is estranged from the family, paints an unflattering picture of the Jackson clan in her book, *Jackson Family Values*. Nevertheless, she is eager to set the record straight about what she calls an outrageous lie:

> I received a telephone call from a writer named Ruth Robinson. I had known Ruth for quite a while and respected her integrity. It made what she had to tell me all the more difficult to hear. "I wanted to warn you, Margaret," she said. "There's a story going around that there is a videotape of Michael molesting one of your sons, and that you have the tape. If anyone else had said those words, I would have hung up the phone. Given the long relationship I had with

Ruth, however, I gave her the courtesy of a response. I told her that it wasn't true, of course, and that I wanted the story stopped in its tracks. She had been in contact with someone who worked at the *National Enquirer* who had alerted her that a story was being written for that paper. Ruth cross-connected me with the woman, and I vehemently denied the story. Moreover, I told her that if the story ran, I would own the *National Enquirer* before the lawsuits I brought were finished. To its credit, the *National Enquirer* never ran the piece. *Hard Copy*, however, decided it would. *Hard Copy* correspondent Diane Dimond had reported that authorities were reopening the child molestation case against Michael. She had also made the allegations on L.A. radio station KABC-AM on a morning talk show hosted by Roger Barkley and Ken Minyard. Dimond's claims were based on the word of a freelance writer named Victor Gutierrez. The story was an outrageous lie. Not one part of it was true. I'd never met the man. There was no tape. Michael never paid me for my silence. He had never molested Jeremy. Period.

The episode left an indelible stain on Dimond's reputation and left the Jackson camp determined to fight back before the fictitious story could gain circulation. They filed a multimillion-dollar slander suit against Gutierrez, *Hard Copy*, Diane Dimond, KABC-AM—a radio station where Dimond had repeated the story on air—and Paramount Pictures. The latter four defendants were later dismissed from the suit on First Amendment grounds, but on April 9, 1998, a Los Angeles jury ordered Victor Gutierrez to pay Michael Jackson $2.7 million for slander. At the trial, Gutierrez failed to produce the alleged tape or name his source, citing his journalistic ethics.

Jackson's attorney, Zia Modabber, laughed at that assertion. "Gutierrez told a district attorney investigator and two witnesses who testified at the trial that the boy's mother was his source," Modabber said. "He told anyone who would listen. The only people he would not tell were the ladies and gentlemen of his jury—that's when he became ethical. Now he's getting on his high horse saying he's protecting his source."

Evan Chandler himself was back in the headlines in 1996 when he sued Jackson and Lisa Marie for $60 million in damages because of the interview they gave Diane Sawyer two years earlier. What irked him was Jackson's assertion that "the whole thing was a lie." Eventually, a three-person public arbitration panel dismissed his claims, but one unpublished court document from the case was particularly revealing.

In a deposition, Chandler claimed that the marriage between Jackson and Lisa Marie was a "sham" and that Jackson had promised her a percentage of the profits from his *HIStory* album if she married him. Chandler claimed the marriage was an elaborate conspiracy to make it appear that his son had been lying and to create public sympathy for Jackson. Bizarrely, he claimed that the marriage to Elvis's daughter had turned him and his family into targets for angry Michael Jackson fans who felt sure the nuptials were a confirmation of his innocence.

Despite the victories, the continuous legal battles and negative headlines were taking their toll.

According to a former Jackson musician, "He was a changed man. He used to be so innocent and carefree. Now he was always suspicious, paranoid. Most of the time he was a complete basket case. That's why it cost so much money to record his albums. He was out of control."

Again, drugs may have been the explanation. Jackson's longtime business partner Myoung-ho Lee told Maureen Orth that he employed Dr. Neil Ratner to detox Jackson in Seoul in 1999 after he collapsed on a private jet during a flight to Frankfurt, Germany. "We were getting Michael off what he was addicted to, Demerol and morphine. His problem is a sleep disorder. He's up forty-eight hours at a time and then crashes."

In 1993, just after the Chandler allegations became public, Elizabeth Taylor had reportedly spirited Jackson off to a private rehab in Switzerland when she realized that his addiction was out of control. At the time, many in the media speculated that the rehab story was a ploy designed to distract attention from the Chandler case and avoid giving a deposition. But Lee says it was all too real, recalling that a doctor from the clinic called up one of Jackson's advisers one day, saying that Jackson thought he was Peter Pan.

"Either the drugs are going to kill him or he's going

to die by flying out of a window, because he thinks he can fly," the doctor said. "You better get someone here he'll listen to."

"I had always been told he was just so medicated," a former Sony employee told *Vanity Fair*. "Half the time you don't know where what he says is coming from."

Although Lee claims that Jackson was detoxed in 1999, there is evidence to back up the associate's claim. To me, at the time of the 2002 baby dangling incident, Jackson was still addicted to drugs.

I discovered a deposition that Jackson gave in a 2007 lawsuit involving unpaid bills that speaks of his addiction until at least several months after the November 2002 Berlin incident:

Attorney: As of March 31, 2003, were you still impaired because of the taking of prescription medication?

Jackson: I could have been.

Attorney: During the period of time you were impaired by the taking of prescription medication, was this an impairment that lasted, like, all your waking hours, or did it come and go?

Jackson: It comes and goes, not all of the waking hours, of course not.

The associate told me that shortly before Michael dangled the baby in Berlin, his "vitamin doctor" had given him a heavy dose of meds designed to treat the symptoms of his deteriorating physical and mental health. "He could have easily dropped his son that day and killed him because he really had no control over his actions as he was all doped up," I was told.

Indeed, British journalist Martin Bashir arrived in Jackson's suite just moments after the incident. He later described the scene: "I was worried. There was a manic quality that I had never seen before and he was loving the attention of the screaming fans outside the hotel."

According to the associate, painkillers aren't the only drugs that Jackson takes: "He pops Demerol and morphine, sure, apparently going back to the time when he burned himself during the Pepsi commercial, but there's also some kind of psychiatric medication, anti-anxiety or something like that. One of his brothers once told me that he was diagnosed with schizophrenia or something when he was younger, so it may be to treat that."

From the reliable information provided by both his supporters and his detractors, there was reason to believe Michael Jackson was a liar. Given his propensity for stretching or demolishing the truth, should anybody believe him when he claims that his obsession with young children is completely innocent? That's what I still had to figure out.

The most notorious of his lies was his unequivocal assertion that he only ever had plastic surgery twice in his career. In his autobiography, and many times since, he claimed that he has only had two nose jobs, attributing the change in the structure of his face to puberty, weight loss, a strict vegetarian diet, a change in hairstyle, and stage lighting. Nobody was buying it.

Early in his career, as Jackson's appearance began to gradually transform and there were unconfirmed reports that he was trying to look like his Motown mentor and onetime idol, Diana Ross. Indeed, the resemblance was uncanny for a while. Later, as his original black features began to disappear and the singer gradually became whiter and whiter, people joked that he was trying to look like his new idol, Princess Diana.

But in 1999, Dr. Stephen Hoefflin, a Los Angeles plastic surgeon who operated a number of times on Jackson's nose, said he did not believe the singer was trying to appear less African American. "I think he wanted a feature that bothered him to be made smaller, more sculptured. And certainly not to erase the ethnicity," Hoefflin said, adding that Jackson had had more surgery than he recommended.

The prominent German cosmetic surgeon Werner Mang says he was summoned by Jackson's medical team for a radical reconstruction of the star's nose in the late nineties.

Mang says that the work Jackson had done on his face early in his career—a subtle slimming of his nose—had turned out fine, but had since gone too far.

"The doctor should have stopped after the [1982] album *Thriller*," he said. "Because after *Thriller*, Michael Jackson was very good looking, all was okay."

But by Wang's estimate, in the following years, Jackson underwent at least another half-dozen operations in Hoefflin's Santa Monica clinic.

"I think Michael Jackson wants to change from a black man to a white woman. He always came to Stephen Hoefflin and told him, 'Could I have a tattoo? Could I have the nose thinner?'" said Wang.

"Stephen Hoefflin told me that after each album [Jackson] has an aesthetic plastic surgery," he added.

"I think he is obsessed with aesthetic surgery, and every serious plastic surgeon has to stop . . . because it's dangerous for his health and for his skin."

After Jackson was photographed several years ago with a bandage over his scarred nose, ABC News asked a prominent U.S. plastic surgeon, Dr. Pamela Lipkin, to study the way Jackson's face had changed over the years.

"Probably he's trying to look Caucasian," Lipkin concluded. "His skin is whiter. His nose is getting thinner every six months. His lips are getting thinner. His eyebrows are getting higher. His eyes are getting wider every time. His cheekbones are getting bigger."

Lipkin said she believed something had gone wrong with his latest surgery, though she admitted she hadn't examined him personally.

"What I think happened recently is that something in his nose—a graft, an implant, something—has now come out through the skin,' said Lipkin, a nasal specialist. "He's really got a hole in his skin."

"Michael Jackson has what we call an end stage nose, a crippled nose, a crucified nose—one that's beyond the point of no return,' she said. "People who have had so many surgeries on their nose that it becomes hard to breathe through are called nasal cripples," Lipkin said.

Indeed, Maureen Orth claims that Jackson is reduced to wearing a prosthetic nose because he has lost so much cartilage. "One person who has seen him without the device says he resembles a mummy with two nostril holes," she writes.

His rapidly changing appearance was troubling to many observers.

"If Michael Jackson had ever come to me, I wouldn't have treated him," Washington-based dermatologist Dr. Tina Alster told *Vanity Fair*. "He doesn't have a realistic view of how he looks. I get a number of these people, and I send them to someone for psychological evaluation. Michael Jackson is an extreme and very public example."

My own sources in Jackson's camp tell me that he had between twenty and thirty cosmetic surgery procedures in the span of his career. "When you're Peter Pan, you're never supposed to grow old," says one of his associates. "That's Michael's ultimate goal and he'll do anything to achieve it." And it seems that it isn't simply plastic surgery that accounted for Jackson's changing features.

According to an affidavit given by former Santa Barbara sheriff's deputy Deborah Linden during her investigation of the Jordan Chandler case and obtained by Maureen Orth, Jackson's maid Blanca Francia told her that Jackson said he bleached his skin because he did not like being black and he felt that blacks "are not liked as much as people of other races." To whiten his skin, he supposedly used a powerful bleaching agent called Benoquin. According to the affidavit, Jackson once told his dermatologist, Dr. Arnold Klein, Debbie Rowe's former employer, that one day he had got Benoquin on his genitals and that it burned. When investigators seized Michael Jackson's personal memorabilia from a New Jersey warehouse in 2004, they found two tubes of a skin-bleaching agent called Eldopaque.

During my own investigation, I interviewed a prominent TV broadcaster who is very close to Jackson and who doesn't believe that he is a child molester. However, he did confirm that Jackson is bleaching.

"Michael definitely whitens his skin," he said. "I saw him doing it a few years back when I accidentally arrived an hour early for a TV interview with him. He was taken aback and claimed he was putting cream on his body because he had an infectious rash. I know he lied because I was able to read the cover on the ointment he was taking when he turned his back."

In May 2009, *The Sun* reported that Jackson was suffering from the early stages of skin cancer. Observers found this to be remarkable because he is virtually never exposed to the sun, carrying an umbrella whenever he ventures outdoors.

Perhaps a clue can be found in a 2006 report by the U.S. Food and Drug Administration that proposed banning over-the-counter skin bleaching creams because of the risk of skin cancer.

"What's the harm?" a veteran Hollywood reporter asked me one day when I mentioned these issues. "Do you really think that makes Michael Jackson different than any other celebrity? Everybody in this town lies about plastic surgery, except maybe Joan Rivers. As for the whitening, the guy's an eccentric. He's obviously got serious psychological issues, but, again, who doesn't around here? I've been covering him since he was thirteen and he's also done a lot of good. A lot!"

At the time, I asked if she would appear on camera to say that.

Her reply: "I don't think so. It's not a great career move to be seen defending Michael Jackson these days, though God knows he could use somebody to stick up for him."

Her reaction underscored an attitude that had been building for some time, at least in the United States, where polls showed that a significant number of people no longer held Jackson in high esteem.

In 2001, when he released a new album, *Invincible*, the reaction was less than overwhelming. Despite generally good reviews, the public was no longer buying his material the way they used to, though he could always count on the diehard fans to ensure it wasn't a complete flop.

Invincible was said to have been the most expensive album ever made, due to the enormous amount of time Jackson spent in the studio, doing constant revisions, hiring and firing personnel, and spending vast amounts of time "disoriented," according to a musician who worked with him on the album.

To finance the album, which Jackson committed to paying for himself, Sony Music Entertainment advanced him as much as $50 million. In the old days, this kind of money would have been a drop in the bucket for an entertainer who, according to *Forbes*, was making as much as $45 million a year at one point. But Jackson's finances were in disarray, in part because of his never-ending legal woes and in part because of his lavish lifestyle. To ensure their investment, Sony asked Jackson to put up as collateral a portion of his most lucrative asset, the Northern Songs catalogue he had acquired—at the urging of Yoko Ono—a decade earlier. He had bought it for the bargain basement price of $47.5 million when his friend Paul McCartney failed to bid, despite the fact that the catalogue included publishing rights to the entire Beatles repertoire, along with the song catalogues of many other musical greats. In 1985, Jackson merged Northern Songs with his record company Sony, to form a joint venture, Sony/ATV Music Publishing, of which Jackson retained half ownership. In 2002, *Forbes* estimated Jackson's 50 percent stake in the company to be worth $450 million.

Jackson was livid when Sony chief Tommy Mottola forced him to put up his most prized asset, but he was convinced that the album would more than pay for itself even if it generated the kind of worldwide music sales that his less successful albums had enjoyed. Sony had for years expressed interest in acquiring Jackson's half of the ATV catalogue, but the singer—always a shrewd businessman—had held firm. When *Invincible* was released, sales were respectable, but much lower than Jackson's previous efforts. The revenues didn't begin to approach the levels needed to repay the advance. "He's a drain, a money pit," a Sony official told *Vanity Fair*, expressing their frustration.

Jackson and his advisers became convinced that Sony had deliberately failed to promote the album in the hopes of forcing him to sell his share. Paranoid or not, the potential conflict of interest was glaring, even though Jackson certainly did his part to contribute to flagging sales by refusing to tour to promote the album.

With his finances a shambles and no hope of repaying Sony's advance any time in the near future, Jackson decided to go on the offensive, leading to a remarkable press conference on July 6, 2002.

Jackson trekked to a place where he had rarely been seen, Harlem, to join the controversial black activist the Reverend Al Sharpton and his former lawyer Johnnie Cochran, who had formed a group called the National Action Network to investigate whether artists were being financially exploited by record labels.

At a press conference called by Sharpton, Jackson took to the microphone and unleashed what can only be described as a tirade against Mottola, saying, "He's mean, he's a racist, and he's very, very, very devilish." He also claimed that Mottola had been heard using the word nigger to describe an unidentified black artist. (Michael's brother Jermaine later went on a talk show to claim Mottola had been heard referring to the rapper Irv Gotti as a "fat black nigger.")

"The recording companies really, really do conspire against the artists," Jackson said. "They steal, they cheat, they do everything they can, especially [against] the black artists . . . People from James Brown to Sammy Davis Jr., some of the real pioneers that inspired me to be an entertainer, these artists are always on tour, because if they stop touring, they would go hungry. If you fight for me, you're fighting for all black people, dead and alive."

The backlash was immediate, with many Sony artists rushing to Mottola's defense and pointing out that he had married Maria Carey, who is half black. Sony called the remarks "ludicrous, spiteful, and hurtful." Even Sharpton rushed to distance himself from the accusations and Jackson was widely mocked in the media for suddenly embracing his black roots after practically turning himself white for years.

And though Jackson's charges were clearly ridiculous and were probably just an excuse for his poor record sales, there was something quite significant about his outburst.

If, as his critics constantly charged, Jackson was ashamed of being black and had lightened his skin to discard his heritage, why would he suddenly portray himself as a black militant?

The world may have forgotten that Jackson was a black man, but he never forgot what it was like to grow up in Indiana, a stronghold of the Ku Klux Klan. Racism was still rampant during his childhood. For example, going door-to-door selling the magazine of the Jehovah's Witnesses, *The Watchtower*, he and his siblings were greeted more than once with the words: "Get lost, nigger." Real or imagined, Jackson was convinced that his skin color was a major factor in his troubles.

According to his friend Rabbi Shmuley Boteach, "In a conversation I had with Michael in the winter of 2000 he told me that he thought that some of the attacks against him were motivated by race."

"Michael was never embarrassed about his blackness," one of his former African American confidants, Luther Crawford, told me. "He always said his hero was Nelson Mandela and he brought in literally thousands of poor black kids from the L.A. ghettos to play in Neverland. I think he was quite conscious of his black roots. That's a media creation, that charge. The white skin and face isn't meant to diss the Negroes, it's meant to be this persona that he created to get attention. Everything Michael does is very carefully crafted and always meant to get attention. Nothing is left to chance."

The controversy over Mottola and the racism charges merely served as an excuse for the media to dissect Jackson's flagging career and predict his demise as a recording artist.

His close friend the psychic Uri Geller was worried about the toll the continuous criticism and financial woes were having on Jackson. The star had retreated further into his own world, isolating himself at Neverland with his three children.

"They do not have a normal family life as you or I would know it," Geller revealed to an inquiring reporter. "Michael is very lonely, you know. Things are so difficult for him."

Jackson's friends and advisers saw only one solution. If he were ever to revive his career and reputation, Jackson needed to take concrete steps to rehabilitate his image in the eyes of the world.

Martin Bashir seemed like just the person to help him do it.

ELEVEN

Michael Jackson was obsessed with Princess Diana, and that's where his troubles began.

In 1995, a rising BBC journalist named Martin Bashir landed the interview of a lifetime when the Princess of Wales agreed to sit down for a candid one-on-one interview about her recent troubles.

The princess spoke from the heart about her battles with bulimia, her affair with James Hewitt, and the breakdown of her marriage to Prince Charles, which led to their divorce a year later.

It was during this interview, in fact, that she uttered the memorable line: "There were three of us in this marriage, so it was a bit crowded." Of course, she was referring to the prince's relationship with his mistress, Camilla Parker Bowles.

The interview was watched by millions around the world and made Bashir a star overnight, but few watched it as intensely, or as often, as Michael Jackson, who believed he and the princess shared a special bond.

After her death in 1997, Jackson claimed that the late

princess used to regularly telephone and confide in him. "The press were hard on her in the same way they were hard on me, and she needed to talk to someone who knew exactly what she was going through," he said. "She felt hunted in the way I've felt hunted. Trapped, if you like."

He said he offered her the advice that helped get him through his own troubles: "Be strong, and be determined, and nobody can hurt you. Only you can hurt yourself, so be defiant."

He made another unusual claim. "Diana desperately wanted me to meet her children, and we talked about it many times."

They met only once, when Jackson performed at London's Wembley Stadium in 1988, after which he and the princess had a lengthy chat. It was during this conversation that she told him that his song, "Dirty Diana," was one of her favorites. He was enamored of her ever since.

So when the man who had earned the trust of the princess called, Michael Jackson was all ears.

Displaying the charm that had become his trademark, Bashir gushed about his admiration for the singer: "The world needs to see a man of your legend, your greatness, how much you mean to people. Let me do for you what I did for Diana. You're just as loved as she was."

Jackson fell for the bait. The beleaguered singer didn't know who he could trust anymore. He had been betrayed repeatedly by those around him, even members of his family. But so was Diana. Bashir had portrayed her sympathetically, while allowing her to paint Charles as the villain. This was just the man to help Michael Jackson regain his pedestal.

For eight straight months, from mid-2002 to early 2003, nothing was off limits. For the first time, Jackson allowed a camera crew into his inner sanctum, Neverland; behind the scenes at the Berlin Hotel, where he dangled his baby; and to his secretive Las Vegas retreat. Remarkably, he gave an interview with one of his special friends.

With much hype, the documentary *Living with Michael Jackson* premiered on Britain's ITV Network in February 2003. The program began innocuously enough with an introduction by Bashir explaining how it came to be: "Eight months ago," Bashir began, "I put a proposal to Michael Jackson: show me the real man, but show me everything, make nothing off limits. He thought about it and then he said yes, come to Neverland."

The documentary is a candid look into Jackson's inner child, as he takes Bashir on a tour of Neverland, showing him the "paradise" that he had created for the thousands of sick and inner-city children he brings to the ranch every year to cavort on its grounds. After he engages Bashir in a lighthearted go-kart race, there is a revealing exchange when the reporter asks him why Peter Pan seems to be a recurring theme in his life:

M.J.:   Because Peter Pan, to me, represents something that's very special in my heart. You know, he represents youth, childhood, never growing up, magic, flying, everything I think that children and wonderment and magic, what it's all about. And to me, I just

have never, ever grown out of loving that
or thinking that it's very special.

Bashir: You identify with him?

M.J.:   Totally.

Bashir: You don't want to grow up?

M.J.:   No, I am Peter Pan.

Bashir: No you're not, you're Michael Jackson.

M.J.:   I'm Peter Pan in my heart.

Further on in the documentary, Jackson offers his
most candid ever admission about his upbringing, revealing the brutal methods his father Joseph used to
prepare his sons for a life in show business.

M.J.:   You know, he practiced us with a belt in his
hand. And if you missed a step, expect to
be, whoop, whoop, whoop.

Bashir: Just let me go back. You just said that you
would practice the dance steps and your father would be holding a belt in his hand, is
that what you just said?

M.J.:   Yes. Yeah, he would tear you up if you
missed. And so we, not only were we practicing, we were nervous rehearsing because
he sat in the chair and he had this belt in
his hand. And if you didn't do it the right
way, he would tear you up, really get you.
And I got it a lot of times, but I think my
brother Marlon got it the most because he
had a hard time at first. And he tried so
hard. And it was always, do it like Michael,

do it like Michael. You know, but the others were very nervous and I was nervous, too, you know, because he was tough.

Bashir: How often would he beat you?

M.J.:   Too much.

Bashir: Would he only use a belt?

M.J.:   Why do you do this to me? No, more than a belt.

Bashir: What else would he use to hit you with?

M.J.:   Ironing cords, whatever's around. Throw you up against the wall, hard as he could. See, it's one thing to . . .

Bashir: But you were only a child.

M.J.:   I know.

Bashir: You were a baby.

M.J.:   I know. It's one thing to discipline . . .

Bashir: And you were producing successful records.

M.J.:   I know. He would lose his temper. I just remember hearing my mother scream, "Joe, you're gonna kill them, you're gonna kill him. Stop it, you're gonna kill them." You know, and I was so fast, you know, he couldn't catch me half the time. But when he would catch me, oh, my God, it was bad. It was really bad.

So far things were going according to plan. Anybody watching the first half of Bashir's documentary couldn't help but sympathize with the singer, admire his childlike innocence, even understand his "freakish" nature and odd behavior, which seemed understandable after the abuse he had suffered as a child.

Midway through, however, the program starts to take a gradual shift, as Bashir accompanies Jackson on a shopping spree at a Las Vegas mall, where he engages in an almost obscene orgy of spending, parting with more than a million dollars in less than an hour on a kitschy assortment of antiques, rugs, and artworks.

After this unseemly display of ostentatious wealth, Jackson reveals that he is worth more than a billion dollars, which Bashir correctly points out to the viewers is untrue, interviewing industry analysts who peg his actual fortune at less than $300 million, especially after his latest album failed to recoup its costs.

After delving into the baby-dangling incident, Bashir accompanies Jackson and his children to the Zoo Berlin, after which he reveals to his viewers for the first time that Jackson's behavior "was beginning to alarm me."

He returns to Neverland, where he is present when the singer hosts a busload of disadvantaged children, brought in to frolic at the ranch for a day. This, Bashir implies, is yet another example of Jackson's ostensible generosity toward children. That's when he brings out his heavy artillery—the first time the world meets a boy named Gavin Arvizo:

Bashir: The problem was, I, like everyone, knew that ten years ago children were being invited to sleep over at Neverland. One of them, a thirteen-year-old boy, accused Jackson of sexual abuse, a claim that cost him millions of dollars. I'd assumed that now he'd be more cautious, but to my utter astonishment, I discovered that children were still sleeping over, sometimes in his house, sometimes in his bedroom. And then I met twelve-year-old Gavin and his brother and sister. Gavin met Jackson two years ago after he'd been told he was dying of cancer.

Bashir: What is it, Gavin, about Michael that makes him connect so well with children? What is it?

Gavin: Because he's really a child at heart. He acts just like a child. He knows how a child is. He knows what a child thinks. See, 'cause I think that you don't necessarily have to be a child just because society says, eighteen and up, you're an adult. That doesn't really matter. You're an adult when you want to be one.

M.J.: Isn't that great? Not sick at all. No more cancer. All gone. All gone. When they told him he was going to die. Isn't that great? They told your parents to plan for his funeral.

Gavin: I had a growth spurt. I went from four ten to five four.

M.J.: See? Medicine don't [sic] know it all, do they?"

Bashir: According to Gavin, it was Michael's friendship and support that helped him beat the cancer. They've remained close friends ever since. When you stay here, do

	you stay in the house? Does Michael let you enjoy the whole premises?

Gavin: There was one night I asked him if I could stay in the bedroom. And he let me stay in the bedroom. And I was like, Michael, you can sleep on the bed. And he was like, no, no you sleep in the bed. No, no, you sleep on the bed. And then he finally said, okay, if you love me, you'll sleep on the bed. I was like, oh, man. And so I finally slept on the bed. But it was fun that night.

M.J.: I slept on the floor. Was it a sleeping bag?

Gavin: No, you packed a whole bunch of blankets on the floor.

Bashir: But Michael, you know, you're a forty-four-year-old man now.

M.J.: Yes.

Bashir: What do you get out of this? What do you get out of this?

Gavin: He's four.

M.J.: Yeah, I'm four. I love, I feel, see, I think what they get from me, I get from them. I've said it many times, my greatest inspiration comes from kids. Every song I write, every dance I do, all the poetry I write, is all inspired from that level of innocence, that consciousness of purity. And children have that. I see God in the face of children. And, man, I just love being around that all the time. Are you guys still staying up late? Sometimes I call your house, it's so late.

	But you tell me to call. You tell me to call late.
Bashir:	When people hear that children from other families have come and they've stayed in your house, they've stayed in your bedroom.
M.J.:	Well, very few.
Bashir:	But, you know, some have. And they say, is that really appropriate for a man, a grown man to be doing that? How do you respond to that?
M.J.:	I feel sorry for them because that's judging someone who just wants to really help people. Why can't you share your bed? The most loving thing to do is to share your bed with someone, you know.
Bashir:	You really think that?
M.J.:	Yeah. Of course.
Gavin:	You're taking a position that you use every single night that you go into. You sleep and you're sharing it with another.
M.J.:	I said, you can have my bed if you want. Sleep in it. I'll sleep on the floor. It's yours. Always give the best to the company. Like, to him, I said, 'cause he was gonna sleep on the floor. I said, no, you sleep on the bed, I'll sleep on the floor.
Bashir:	But haven't you got a spare room or a spare house here where he could have stayed?
M.J.:	Yes. We have guest units. But whenever kids come here, they always want to stay with me. They never want to stay in the

guest, and I have never invited them in my
room. They always just want to, they say,
can I stay with you tonight? I go, if it's okay
with your parents, yes, you can.

Bashir: Were your parents happy that you were
here with Michael?

Gavin: Yeah, my mom is very, very, very happy.
And I know they're happy because I was
happy.

Bashir: Do they come with you?

Gavin: Yeah, most of the time. But I wasn't
really with my parents, I was mainly with
Michael.

Bashir: But they were happy that you were here?

Gavin: Yeah.

Bashir ends the segment with a voiceover, expressing his reaction to the exchange: "I felt very uneasy after
this conversation. I knew I had to confront Jackson
about what I thought was an obsession with children. It
just couldn't be avoided."

Before he presents this confrontation, however,
he decides to broadcast an exchange that is clearly designed to demonstrate for his viewers an example of the
singer's credibility, or lack thereof.

The segment begins with Jackson revealing that
when he was a child, his father used to tease him about
his appearance, taunting him with insults such as "God,
your nose is big. You didn't get it from me." The British
journalist uses this as a segue to bring up long-standing
rumors about plastic surgery:

Bashir:	If I look at some of the photographs of you in your adolescence . . .
M.J.:	Yeah, I change. People change.
Bashir:	But even after, when you did the *Thriller* album, your lips are very different now to what they were then.
M.J.:	No, no, no.
Bashir:	But they do look different.
M.J.:	No, sorry. Same lips.
Bashir:	You don't think so?
M.J.:	Nope.
Bashir:	But, you know, on a serious point, in some ways I can understand it because . . .
M.J.:	I'm happy with my lips.
Bashir:	No, forget the lips, specifically. But . . .
M.J.:	And everybody in Hollywood gets plastic surgery. Plastic surgery wasn't invented for Michael Jackson.
Bashir:	(wondering if these adolescent experiences in the spotlight had led Michael Jackson to remake his face, to create his own mask) What do you say to people who say, "Well, when Michael Jackson was a boy, he was a black kid but now as an adult, he looks like a white man"?
M.J.:	Well, you gotta ask God that. That has nothing to do with me, okay? And that's ignorant.
Bashir:	Are you trying to be other than what you are?
M.J.:	No.

Bashir: So when they say things like you've had implants in your cheeks.

M.J.:   Oh, God.

Bashir: You've had a dimple made in your chin?

M.J.:   Oh, please, please. That's, please.

Bashir: You've had your lips enlarged.

M.J.:   Oh, please. That's stupid.

Bashir: You had your eyelids reconstructed.

M.J.:   It's stupid.

Bashir: None of it's true?

M.J.:   Come on, none of it's true. None of it's true. It's BS. They made it up. They lie. They don't want to give me credit for anything. One paper said I had each little hair transplanted into my face with a laser, lasered in, 'cause I was growing a little beard. How ignorant is that? I can't even grow a beard now? Ignorant fool who wrote such a thing. So don't believe that stupidity. Don't waste your money on it. Because when you're buying it, you're not buying something based on what's true. It's not the truth. It's garbage.

At this point in the program, Bashir returns to the confrontation he had promised earlier.

Bashir: When you're talking about children, we met Gavin. And it was a great privilege to meet Gavin because he's had a lot of suffering in his life.

M.J.:   Yeah.

Bashir: When Gavin was there, he talked about the fact that he shares your bedroom.

M.J.:   Yes.

Bashir: Can you understand why people would worry about that?

M.J.:   Because they're ignorant.

Bashir: But is it really appropriate for a forty-four-year-old man to share a bedroom with a child who is not related to him at all?

M.J.:   That's a beautiful thing.

Bashir: That's not a worrying thing?

M.J.:   Why should it be worrying? Who's the criminal? Who's Jack the Ripper in the room? This is a guy trying to help heal a child. I'm sleeping in a sleeping bag on the floor. I gave him the bed because he has a brother named Star. So him and Star took the bed. And I'm on the floor in the sleeping bag.

Bashir: Did you ever sleep in the bed with them?

M.J.:   No. But I have slept in a bed with many children. I slept in the bed with all of them. When Macaulay Culkin was little, Kieran Culkin would sleep on this side, Macaulay Culkin on this side, his sisters in there. We all would just jam in the bed. And we'd wake up like dawn and go in the hot air balloon. You know, we have the footage. I have all that footage.

Bashir: But is that right, Michael?

M.J.: It's very right. It's very loving. That's what the world needs now, more love, more . . .

Bashir: The world needs . . .

M.J.: . . . more heart.

Bashir: The world needs a man who's forty-four, sleeping in a bed with children?

M.J.: No, no, you're making it all wrong. That's wrong.

Bashir: Well, tell me. Help me.

M.J.: Because what's wrong with sharing a love? You don't sleep with your kids or some other kid who needs love who didn't have a good childhood?

Bashir: No. No, I don't. I would never dream of sleeping . . .

M.J.: I would. I would. Because you've never been where I've been mentally.

Bashir: What do you think people would say if I said, well, I've invited some of my daughter's friends around, or my son's friends around, and they're going to sleep in a bed with me tonight?

M.J.: That's fine.

Bashir: What do you think their parent would say?

M.J.: If they're wacky, they would say, you can't. But if you're a close family, like your family, you know them well and . . .

Bashir: But, Michael, I wouldn't like my children to sleep in anybody else's bed.

M.J.: Well, I wouldn't mind. If I knew the person well, and, like, I'm very close to Barry

	Gibb. Paris and Prince can stay with him anytime. My children sleep with other people all time.
Bashir:	And you're happy with that?
M.J.:	I'm fine with it. They're honest. They're sweet people. They're not Jack the Ripper.
Bashir:	I suppose the problem for many people is what happened in 1993 or what didn't happen.
M.J.:	What didn't happen?
Bashir:	Just cast your mind back. What was that like when you first heard the allegations that were being made against you?
M.J.:	It was shocking, and I'm not allowed to talk about this by way of law, so . . .
Bashir:	But how did you feel about what was being said? I'm not asking you to talk about what was said.
M.J.:	I was shocked because God knows in my heart how much I adore children.
Bashir:	But isn't that precisely the problem? That when you actually invite children into your bed, you never know what's going to happen.
M.J.:	But when you say "bed" you're thinking sexual. They make that sexual. It's not sexual. We're going to sleep. I tuck them in. I put little, like, music on. Story time. I read a book. Very sweet, put the fireplace on. Give them hot milk. You know, we have little cookies. It's very charming, very sweet.

At one point, Bashir asks Jackson what he has to say to people who think this is all a bit strange:

"People can always have a judgment about anything you do, so it doesn't bother me," Jackson responded. "Everything can be strange to someone. This interview is strange to some people out there. So who cares, right?"

Indeed, when Bashir's documentary was broadcast in the UK in February 2003 to a massive audience of 15 million viewers, nobody seemed to care. The bulk of the coverage the next day focused more on Jackson's lavish shopping spree and less than candid admissions about plastic surgery than his sleepovers with children, though more than one newspaper did call this revelation "disturbing."

The media agreed that Jackson had done himself no favors by allowing Bashir into his life, but the fallout was minimal. Nevertheless, Jackson issued a written statement expressing his shock and devastation over how he had been portrayed:

> I trusted Martin Bashir to come into my life and that of my family because I wanted the truth to be told. Bashir persuaded me to trust him that his would be an honest and fair portrayal of my life and told me that he was "the man that turned Diana's life around." I am surprised that a professional journalist would compromise his integrity by deceiving me in this way. Today I feel more betrayed than perhaps ever before; that someone who had got to know my children, my staff and me, whom I let into my heart and told the truth,

could then sacrifice this trust and produce this terrible and unfair program. Everyone who knows me will know the truth, which is that my children come first in my life and that I would never harm any child. I also want to thank my fans around the world for the overwhelming number of messages of support that I have received, particularly from Great Britain, where people have emailed me and said how appalled they were by the Bashir film.

Indeed, Jackson's fans immediately went on an offensive against Bashir, pointing out to anybody who would listen that the latter had been publicly rebuked by Britain's media watchdog for an ethical lapse a year earlier. The father of a sixteen-year-old runaway had complained that Bashir had "blackmailed" him into giving an interview by promising to help find the girl. In its report, the Broadcasting Standards Commission said Mr. Bashir had misled Farooq Yusof into believing he was investigating the role of the authorities in the disappearance of his daughter Sufiah. In addition, Princess Diana's biographer Andrew Morton claimed in a book that Bashir and the BBC had tricked Princess Diana to sit down for her *Panorama* interview by using "forged documents" and bank records to convince her that she was being spied on by Britain's intelligence services. Both Bashir and the BBC have always denied the charge.

Despite the attacks on Bashir's integrity, however, there was enough interest in the documentary to spark a bidding war in the United States, which ABC won.

When the program was aired a few days later by the news program *20/20*, it promised "unprecedented" revelations, though a number of American newspapers had already reported the highlights after it aired in the UK.

The fallout was almost instantaneous.

The first to react was Jackson's nemesis and Jordan Chandler's former attorney, Gloria Allred, who took the opportunity to call for an immediate inquiry:

> I am hopeful the Child Welfare Services will initiate a much-needed investigation into Mr. Jackson's activities with children at Neverland. I think it's highly inappropriate for a young child to sleep in the same bedroom with Mr. Jackson, an adult male, especially in light of prior accusations against him.

Allred wasn't the only one who was calling for a probe. The day after the program aired in the United States, the howls of outrage began to be heard in all quarters from Americans. And before the credits had even rolled on Bashir's program, Tom Sneddon's phone started ringing off the hook.

Shortly after Sneddon began investigating Jackson for the second time in 2003, a journalist asked him whether he was on a vendetta against the singer. With a straight face, the Santa Barbara district attorney replied that he had barely thought about Michael Jackson during the previous decade. A sampling of interviews he gave and articles about his activities during that interval, however, demonstrates that this assertion may have been less than entirely accurate.

On August 19, 1995, for example, during Jackson's marriage to Lisa Marie Presley, the *Chattanooga Times Free Press* reported that Sneddon "had twice contacted Presley's mother, Priscilla, for information about Jackson's relationships with young boys."

On August 23, 1995, following the Diane Sawyer interview with the couple, Sneddon told the *New York Beacon* newspaper that Jackson had not been "cleared" of sexual involvement with two boys, as Sawyer had reported. "The state of the investigation is in suspension until somebody comes forward," the district attorney said.

On January 27, 1996, in an interview about Jackson with a California newspaper called *The Advertiser*, Sneddon said, "But the reality is, no matter what he does, he can't escape the fact that he paid out millions of dollars to prevent a thirteen-year-old boy from testifying against him in court." Contrary to popular belief, Sneddon added, it would be "inaccurate" to say Jackson was cleared of all charges. "The state of the investigation is in suspension until somebody comes forward and testifies," he reiterated.

On February 14, 2001—on the eve of a scheduled Jackson speech on behalf of his Heal the World Foundation—Sneddon told the *New York Daily News* that Jackson is "not out of the woods" on the 1993 charges of child molestation. "The case against Michael Jackson was never closed, and he was never exonerated," Sneddon said. "It's in suspended animation and can be reopened at any time."

In a February 2003 Court TV interview with Diane Dimond, Sneddon told her that he needed only "one more victim" to reopen his case against Jackson.

So it is safe to say that the district attorney had in fact thought about Jackson a lot since he closed the case because of a lack of evidence ten years earlier.

Some have compared Tom Sneddon and his obsession with nailing Jackson to Inspector Javert's crusade to track down Jean Valjean in *Les Misérables*. But while the character Valjean in Victor Hugo's novel had done nothing more than steal a loaf of bread, Sneddon remained convinced that the singer was guilty of the heinous crime of sexual abuse of a child. But he still had nothing to go on and he knew it. After Allred called him personally and lodged a formal complaint against Jackson, Sneddon called together his team to brainstorm how their office should respond.

The result was an unusual press release in which Sneddon summoned the original Chandler allegations:

> A number of years ago at a press conference in Los Angeles with the then L.A. County district attorney, Gil Garcetti, we described the investigation as "open, but inactive." It was stated that the case could be reactivated upon the discovery of new, credible evidence or victims willing to cooperate. Nothing has changed. The investigation remains "open, but inactive."

Judging from the media inquiries the department has received, the release continues: "It appears that the major focus centers on Jackson's statements revealing he slept in the same bed with children."

Sneddon proceeds to cite the relevant section of the California penal code about misconduct of an adult with a child to explain why he can't press charges:

> A review of these sections reveals that the act of an adult sleeping with a child without more is insufficient to warrant a filing or support a conviction. I direct your attention to these sections. If you read them you will notice that in each instance they require affirmative, offensive conduct on the part of the perpetrator and a mental state that accompanies any touching that may occur. The mere act of sleeping in the same bed with a child alone without either a touching and the required mental state would not satisfy the statutory requirements. Furthermore, while Section 803(g) allows prosecution of offenses which occurred beyond the statute of limitations, it requires as a prerequisite that the victim initiate the request to investigate by reporting the allegations to law enforcement.

Without a complainant, therefore, Sneddon makes clear he is powerless to act. However, that could change if a child comes forward and reports a crime. To facilitate such a complaint, he includes the numbers of the department's hotline. And then, just as he had done fruitlessly for more than ten years, he waited for a call to come.

This time it didn't take long.

• • • •

In the early morning hours of November 18, 2003, while
Michael Jackson was in Las Vegas recording a TV special, more than 60 police officers and investigators from
the Santa Barbara D.A.'s office descended on Neverland, armed with a search warrant. It represented more
than twice as many officers as the police had typically
used to raid the premises of some of America's most
notorious serial killers. While the officers scoured the
ranch looking for evidence, a forensic team carefully cut
a swatch from the mattresses of each bed on the premises, including the master bedroom.

As the raid continued into the afternoon, a senior deputy for the Santa Barbara Sheriff's Department
issued a terse statement. "This is based on a warrant out
of superior court and is part of an ongoing criminal investigation," he said, refusing to provide any additional
information.

As speculation reached a frenzied pitch, Tom Sneddon announced that he would hold a press conference
the following day to elaborate on the purpose of the raid.

At the conference, Santa Barbara Sheriff Jim An-
derson told the packed room that an arrest warrant had
been issued for Jackson on a charge that he had molested a juvenile and that he had been asked to turn
himself in and surrender his passport.

Announcing that he finally had a "cooperative
victim," Sneddon added, "I can assure you in a very
short period of time there will be charges filed against
Mr. Jackson—multiple counts." He refused to elaborate
on the age or even the sex of the alleged victim. To a

reporter's question, Sneddon gave an answer that would later be described as flippant. "I can tell you it's BS, but that isn't going to change people's observations," he said. "Like the sheriff and I are really into that kind of music," he added sarcastically. Earlier, he had greeted the roomful of reporters with another attempt at humor: "I hope that you all stay long and spend lots of money because we need your sales tax to support our offices."

These exchanges prompted Loyola University law professor Laurie Levenson to express dismay at Sneddon's approach. "It was baffling, perplexing, and it didn't have a particularly serious tone," she said. "A good defense lawyer is going to say he was too personally invested and you can't trust the investigation."

Meanwhile, Diane Dimond, who was the first reporter to break the news of the Neverland raid, was offering her own take on the latest twist to the Jackson saga: "The district attorney and the sheriff here are charging that Michael Jackson not only molested a child, but he molested a sick child. I don't know, it, it almost defies credibility."

Still, most legal analysts agreed that Tom Sneddon would not have pressed charges after all these years unless he had an airtight case.

It did not look good for Michael Jackson.

TWELVE

Considering that it was a TV interview that got Jackson into his current predicament—facing as many as forty-five years in prison—it was all the more remarkable to see Michael Jackson sitting down across from Ed Bradley for a Christmas Day 2003 interview with the hard-hitting U.S. television newsmagazine *60 Minutes*.

The surprises didn't stop there. In the middle of the wide-ranging interview, which touched on Jackson's reaction to the Neverland raid a month earlier, as well as his arrest, Bradley asks the singer whether he still considers it acceptable to share his bed with children.

"Of course. Of course. Why not?" Jackson replies. "If you're gonna be a pedophile, if you're gonna be Jack the Ripper, if you're gonna be a murderer, it's not a good idea. That I'm not. That's how we were raised. And I met . . . I didn't sleep in the bed with the child. Even if I did, it's okay. I slept on the floor. I give the bed to the child."

He tells Bradley that he would slit his wrists before he would hurt a child. Jackson then provides his first public account of his relationship with Gavin Arvizo. He had met the twelve-year-old boy a year earlier for the first time and was determined to help him in his battle against cancer:

> When I first saw him, he was total bald-headed, white as snow from the chemotherapy, very bony, looked anorexic, no eyebrows, no eyelashes. And he was so weak, I would have to carry him from the house to the game room, or push him in a wheelchair, to try to give him a childhood, a life. 'Cause I felt bad. Because I never had that chance, too, as a child. You know? That the—and so, I know what it—it felt like in that way. Not being sick, but not having had a childhood. So, my heart go out to those children. I feel their pain. He had never really climbed a tree . . . And—I helped him up. And once he went up—up the tree, we looked down on the branches. And it was so beautiful. It was magical. And he loved it. To give him a chance to have a life, you know? Because he was told he was going to die. They told him. They told his—his parents to prepare for his funeral, that's how bad it was. And I put him on a program. I've helped many children doing this. I put him on a mental program.

During the same interview, Jackson claimed that he had been manhandled by police during his arrest. "They manhandled me very roughly," he tells Bradley. "My shoulder is dislocated, literally. It's hurting me very badly. I'm in pain all the time. This is, see this arm? This is as far as I can reach it. Same with this side over here."

Santa Barbara police authorities would later provide tapes of the arrest disproving Jackson's account by pointing to video footage of the singer waving to cheering crowds as he left the police station to show that he was probably lying. Most legal analysts assumed the story was part of a defense strategy designed to portray Jackson sympathetically in advance of his trial. Yet it was one more assault on his credibility, which was already badly strained.

Meanwhile, The Smoking Gun website had obtained a report from the Los Angeles Department of Children and Family Services (DCFS) revealing that the department had investigated claims that Gavin Arvizo had been molested by Jackson and concluded that the claims were "unfounded."

Shortly after the Bashir documentary had aired on ABC, an official from Gavin's school called in a Child Abuse Referral on the DCFS hotline, alarmed at the child's admission that both he and his younger brother, Star, had slept in Jackson's bed.

According to the subsequent investigation, the department interviewed the boys' mother, Janet Arvizo, who stated that she believed the media had taken everything "out of context." Jackson, she said, was "like a father" to her children and was like part of her family. She told the investigators that her son had shared a room with Jackson, but had not slept in the same bed.

Gavin was interviewed separately and he too denied that any sexual abuse had occurred. Instead, he claimed

238 IAN HALPERIN

the boys enjoyed visiting Neverland. His sixteen-year-old sister Davellin, who frequently accompanied her brothers for sleepovers, was also interviewed and she too denied seeing anything sexually inappropriate.

The family's comments to the investigators appeared to contradict the claims they had made to the D.A.'s office, which prompted the molestation charges against Jackson. It was not the only time their statements appeared to be at odds with their later claims. Shortly after the Bashir documentary aired, the Jackson camp revealed that they had their cameras rolling at the same time as Bashir, shooting all the same footage he did to ensure he did not present a distorted record. Their footage, they claimed, painted a very different picture than the one Bashir had showed his audience.

Jackson negotiated a $5 million fee for the rights to a special using his footage, which aired on Fox—hosted and narrated by the tabloid talk show host Maury Povich—as *The Michael Jackson Interview: The Footage You Were Never Meant to See*.

In this version, Bashir is seen flattering Jackson endlessly, especially in describing his "so natural, so loving, so caring" relationship toward his children. "Your relationship with your children is spectacular," he said. "In fact, it almost makes me weep when I see you with them."

In his documentary, Bashir described "the disturbing reality" of Neverland, where Jackson admitted to sleeping with children. In the unaired footage, he describes it as "nothing short of spiritual."

In his documentary, Bashir implies that it was Jackson who made his children wear masks. That's because he failed to include the interview he conducted with ex-wife Debbie Rowe in which she reveals that it is she, not Michael, who insisted on the masks.

For the rebuttal special, Jackson's cameraman also interviewed Gavin Arvizo and his family, who had not yet come forward with their allegations. In this interview, Janet Arvizo said, "The relationship that Michael has with my children is [a] beautiful, loving, father-son and daughter one. To my children and me Michael is part of the family." She claimed that Bashir had taken her son's relationship out of context and said she was contemplating legal action against the British journalist.

Although the rebuttal special dealt a blow to Bashir's journalistic credibility, the fact remained that Jackson had admitted to sharing his bed with a twelve-year-old boy. In the eyes of most Americans, that was not normal or acceptable behavior.

By the time Tom Sneddon finished presenting his case against Jackson to the grand jury, he had secured an indictment on ten separate felony counts allegedly committed against Gavin Arvizo, identified as "John Doe" in the legal documents because he was still a minor.

The most significant element of the indictment, however, was not the many allegations against Jackson. It was the fact that the lewd acts he was charged with were alleged to have taken place between February 20 and March 12, 2003—*after* the airing of the Bashir documentary. Bizarrely, Jackson was being accused of molesting Gavin Arvizo only after the worldwide controversy erupted over sharing his bed with the boy.

During this period, Jackson was said to have "willfully, unlawfully, and lewdly commit[ed] a lewd and lascivious act upon and with the body and certain parts and members thereof of John Doe, a child under the age of fourteen years, with the intent of arousing, appealing to, and gratifying the lust, passions, and sexual desires of the said defendant and the said child."

Of the ten counts he was charged with, four involved administering a "toxic agent," namely alcohol, to a minor with the intent of sexually molesting him. Later, three additional counts were added—conspiracy involving child abduction, false imprisonment, and extortion. According to these counts, Jackson was said to have imprisoned the Arvizo family in Neverland at one point when they wanted to leave.

Anthony Pellicano was no longer associated with the Jackson legal team, but that didn't mean they had stopped using private detectives to dig up dirt on the singer's enemies. They didn't have to search far to find incriminating evidence to discredit the Arvizo family.

In November 2003, shortly after his arrest, and before the accuser had been officially identified by most media outlets, the media suddenly "learned" that the Jackson case wasn't the first time that the Arvizo family had made abuse allegations.

In November 2001, the JCPenney department store chain paid the Arvizos a settlement of $137,500 to end a lawsuit alleging that three security guards at a Southern

California store beat Gavin Arvizo, his mother, Janet, and his brother, Star, in a parking lot in 1998 after Gavin left the store carrying clothes that hadn't been paid for. To up the ante, Janet even added an allegation two years after the incident, claiming that the guards had sexually fondled her breasts and pelvic area for "up to seven minutes" while they were trying to detain her.

A month before the settlement, Janet filed for divorce from her husband, David, in a case which would see her allege abuse and false imprisonment, both of which mirror the charges she made in the subsequent Jackson case.

Later, David's attorney, Russell Halpern, said Janet had lied about the abuse and had a "Svengali-like" ability to make her children repeat her lies.

When social workers from the Department of Children and Family Services were summoned to the Arvizo home in October 2001 to investigate an altercation, they questioned the children, who told them there had been no abuse by their father.

"There was no hitting, just yelling, and not a lot of yelling," the children stated. But when Janet Arvizo returned home and discovered that the DCFS had interviewed her children without her presence, she immediately got in contact with the agency and demanded they return. This time the children's stories changed drastically and they claimed abuse had taken place.

More significantly, Halpern claimed, David Arvizo had once showed him a script that his wife had allegedly written for their children to use when they were questioned in a civil deposition. "She wrote out all their

242   IAN HALPERIN

testimony. I actually saw the script," he recalled. "I remember my client showing me, bringing the paperwork to me."

Whether coincidentally or not, the psychiatrist hired by JCPenney to evaluate Janet Arvizo found her to have "rehearsed" her children into supporting her story and to be both "delusional" and "depressed."

At the height of the Jackson trial, David Arvizo later told reporters that "my children are routinely rehearsed by their mother Janet to do or say whatever she wishes."

Even Janet's attorney in the divorce, Michael Manning, appeared to question her accusations against Jackson when reporters asked him about the JCPenney case.

Manning told the Associated Press that Janet had never indicated to him that Jackson had sexually abused Gavin. He remembered her saying positive things about Jackson as recently as April or May 1993. "'He was really good to us'—that's what she said at the time," Manning recalled.

In the years since the Arvizo abuse trial, Jackson supporters have routinely claimed that Janet Arvizo retained as her attorney Larry Feldman, the same lawyer who had previously represented Jordan Chandler and won a $15 million civil settlement against the singer. Therefore, they argue, her intention was always to extort money from Jackson. Although there is significant evidence to question Janet's motives, this story isn't quite accurate.

Initially, Arvizo retained a lawyer named Bill Dickerman, not to sue Jackson, but to try to stop additional airings of the Martin Bashir interview. It was

Dickerman who had referred her to Larry Feldman, who in turn referred Gavin to a therapist when he discovered that the boy had been acting out in school.

The therapist was a Los Angeles psychologist named Stanley Katz. He interviewed Gavin and his younger brother, Star, twice in his Beverly Hills office, once in May 2003, once a month later. It was during one of these sessions that Gavin revealed for the first time that he had been molested by Michael Jackson, which triggered an automatic report to the police just as it had in the Jordan Chandler case ten years earlier.

When a detective from the Santa Barbara County Sheriff's Department phoned Katz a month later to get his opinion of Gavin's allegations, the psychologist offered a rather surprising assessment.

In a tape-recorded conversation, Katz told Detective Paul Zelis that Jackson "is a guy that's like a ten-year-old child. And, you know, he's doing what a ten-year-old would do with his little buddies. You know, they're gonna jack off, watch movies, drink wine, you know. And, you know, he doesn't even really qualify as a pedophile. He's really just this regressed ten-year-old." The detective concurred, replying, "Yeah, yeah, I agree."

Katz also revealed that it took considerable time for Gavin to trust him, noting that he was aided by Janet Arvizo, who "had to really spell out" that the psychologist was "helping us, working for us."

Katz then told Gavin: "You know, you don't want Jackson to do these things to kids again, do you?" At this point in the conversation, Katz reveals that Gavin summoned the name of Jordan Chandler. "Well, Jordy Chandler did not stop him," Gavin had said.

The media were having a field day. If the O. J. Simpson murder case had been the trial of the last century, the charge against Michael Jackson certainly was being treated as the trial of the new one. And Diane Dimond loved every second of it. As the acknowledged authority on Jackson's travails, she seemed to be everywhere. Other reporters were falling all over themselves to pick Dimond's brains about the case and to perhaps glean a morsel or two of gossip. Court TV had hired her to be their analyst during the trial and she was even a staple on CNN, a far cry from her tabloid TV roots.

Not the least of her appeal was the widespread assumption that Tom Sneddon was using her to leak information and therefore she often knew what was going on before any of her colleagues. The relationship with Sneddon went way back when he detected that her sympathies lay with the prosecution. But that was also true of many crime reporters, who could often parlay their sympathies into valuable leaks from the district attorney's office. Few, however, were willing to return the favor.

In March 2004, Dimond learned about a New Jersey businessman named Henry Vaccaro who had come into possession of Michael Jackson's vast memorabilia collection after the singer failed to pay the $60,000 rental fee for the storage of the items at Vaccaro's warehouse in Asbury Park, New Jersey. She quickly hopped on a plane to New Jersey and filed a report for Court TV on the extensive collection. Among the items she featured in her report was a pair of soiled white briefs, which she is seen lifting on camera and speculating that they "might contain DNA evidence." When the cameras were turned off, Dimond did not merely pack up her equipment and leave. Instead, according to Vaccaro, she said she was going to call the prosecutor about this potential evidence.

If she did this, it would be a potentially serious breach of journalistic ethics, according to her critics. Dimond herself denies the allegation. But a letter Vaccaro sent Sneddon in 2005 requesting the return of the items seems to confirm the businessman's account: "I was contacted by your office after Diane Dimond of Court TV informed you that there were various items of potential interest to you among the contents of a warehouse in Asbury Park, N.J."

My personal belief is that if Diane Dimond found evidence that could shed light on a serious allegation of child abuse, she had an obligation to report it, ethics notwithstanding. I know I would have done so.

Jackson's supporters have long painted her as one of the villains in this case, obsessed with sending Jackson to prison, and this is the kind of story that merely reinforces those beliefs. Indeed, throughout the trial, she gleefully speculated about how somebody like Jackson would fare in prison, given the attitudes of most prisoners toward child abusers. And Dimond undoubtedly provided a forum for a number of extortionists and crackpots with axes to grind against Jackson.

But it's important to remember that she also provided some superb investigative reporting over the years, often doing a better job of tracking down facts than the district attorney's office, with its vastly superior resources. She also regularly cautioned her viewers against the danger of false accusations. And in one piece, aired not long after the Jordan Chandler case was settled, Dimond did a particularly memorable job of illustrating just how easily such accusations could get by if the media and the district attorney weren't vigilant. And, although the piece aired years before the Arvizo case surfaced, it provides a particularly compelling, and relevant, cautionary tale.

In the segment, produced for *Hard Copy* not long after the Chandler case was settled, Dimond reveals that yet another boy had come forward with allegations that he was molested by Jackson.

As the boy, his face blurred because he was only fifteen, looked into the camera, he told his story about how he and another teenage boy were abused by the singer:

> He started just, touching like our stomach and things. Like, he'd rub our stomach and then he'd get lower and then that's when I started saying like, "What are you doing?" He said, "It's okay. Don't worry, your bodies are meant to be touched."

Over the next few days, Dimond explains, she spoke with the boy for hours and he never wavered. His story stayed consistent. The boy said he met Michael Jackson at a Canadian video arcade. He said he was supposed to spend the weekend with a friend, but changed his mind after Jackson invited him to visit Neverland. He was flown there in a private jet.

The boy proceeded to describe in detail the people in Jackson's entourage, the layout of the ranch, and even Jackson's family home at Encino.

"Later, he would draw us incredibly detailed maps of both Jackson homes," Dimond reveals. "It was clear either the boy was telling the truth, or he had been well coached."

The boy's story, she reveals, had originally been sent to her as a videotaped statement by a Toronto man named John Templeton. He called *Hard Copy* several times to ensure that it had arrived. Dimond flew to Toronto to meet with the boy and Templeton in order to learn more. She explains what happened next:

> The plan was to meet the pair in the lobby of [an] airport hotel. But when I arrived, the only one to greet me was the young boy. He came with me into town and told me that he lived on the streets of Toronto—in a section called Boy's Town, where the street kids gather. He explained that his mother had kicked him out of the house, and that John Templeton was just a man he'd met on the streets.

Over the following days, a *Hard Copy* team conducted hours of extensive interviews, quizzing the boy and trying to trip him up. Standing by were police officials in both California and Toronto. They were waiting to conduct their own investigation of the boy's charges. On camera, Dimond confronts him about his motives:

Dimond: People are going to think that you're out for his money.

Boy: I don't care about his money.

Dimond: They're going to think you're making it up.

Boy: I know. You know, I know. But I don't care about his money. He can keep it.

Dimond: You're telling the absolute truth?

Boy: Yeah.

Finally, they decided to give him a test. They showed the boy a number of photographs, including several Neverland employees. He identified all of them perfectly.

Then Dimond took him downtown to the Toronto police headquarters, where he was questioned for six straight hours. He stuck to his story without wavering that Michael Jackson had molested him.

"I found him fairly believable," a detective named Campbell tells Dimond.

The only reason the story fell apart is because *Hard Copy* had been receiving similar reports for some time from the same Toronto suburb where the boy lived. It was all uncovered when a man named Rodney Allen called claiming a Jackson family member had molested him years ago. Rodney Allen and John Templeton were the same person. The whole story was in fact a scam. Having established this, Dimond interviews him:

Dimond:	I care about this one kid, who gave me all sorts of information about Neverland, about Havenhurst, about Disneyland, about Michael Jackson's body. Where did he get all of that information?
Allen:	He got it from me.
Dimond:	You planted all this stuff in that kid's head?
Allen:	I didn't plant it in his head. He was asking questions. I answered them the best I can. I told him what I could tell him about the place because I want Michael to face it.
Dimond:	So this kid is an A1 number one liar?
Allen:	Professional.

Toronto police arrested Rodney Allen and charged him with public mischief for concocting the story about Jackson. Four years later, he was arrested again for allegedly molesting a number of boys.

If Diane Dimond was convinced that Jackson was guilty of molestation and deserved to go to prison for his crimes, her onetime coanchor Geraldo Rivera had a very different take on the case. Before embarking on a career as a successful syndicated talk show host, specializing in pop culture topics, Rivera was one of the most respected investigative journalists in the United States, winning an Emmy Award for his investigation into the neglect of mentally retarded patients at a state institution. Rivera, whose trademark mustache was instantly recognizable to most Americans, was also the first journalist to report that Elvis Presley had died of a prescription drug overdose rather than a heart attack—an investigation that caused the state of Tennessee to revoke the medical license of Elvis's doctor for overprescribing medication.

As a former investigator for the New York Police Department, Rivera was particularly suited to crime-related stories. When the news broke of Michael Jackson's arrest, Rivera decided to conduct his own investigation, which lasted for months. On the final eve of the trial, Rivera prepared to announce the results to his audience. If Michael Jackson was convicted, he had vowed to shave off his mustache.

THIRTEEN

On February 28, 2005, *The People of the State of California v. Michael Joseph Jackson* trial got under way in a Santa Barbara courtroom more than a year after Jackson was first arrested on charges of child molestation.

In America, a citizen on trial is entitled to a "jury of his peers," but when Michael Jackson looked across the room at the twelve jurors who would be deciding his fate, he didn't see a single black face.

Tom Sneddon was determined to avoid a replay of the O. J. Simpson fiasco where a group of mostly black jurors acquitted the former football player after his attorneys skillfully played the race card. During jury selection, Sneddon had taken great pains to weed out anybody who might be considered sympathetic to the singer—above all, Michael Jackson fans and black people. After Sneddon summarily rejected two black women from the jury pool, Jackson's lead attorney Tom Mesereau objected on constitutional grounds, arguing they were being removed because of their race. The judge overruled his objection.

The result was a mostly white jury. The deck appeared to be stacked against Jackson.

Heading for opening day of the trial, Tom Sneddon appeared to believe his case was a sure success, though most legal analysts were puzzled about his boundless confidence. Given the credibility of the Arvizo family, which had already been dissected and found wanting by the media, did Sneddon have something else up his sleeve? DNA evidence? A surprise witness?

Shortly after the arrest, Diane Dimond had teased her viewers with a revelation that seemed to spell doom for Jackson's chances when she revealed that Jackson had written a series of "sensational" and "salacious" love letters to Gavin Arvizo. When she later appeared on CNN's *Larry King Live*, she said that the letters had gone missing before police raided Neverland. After she said, "I absolutely know of their existence," King confronted her about their existence. Dimond was then forced to admit that she had never actually seen or read the letters. Understandably, Jackson's supporters pointed to the story of the letters as yet another example of her bias against the singer.

The first chance the world had to examine Sneddon's actual case was during opening arguments when he laid it out piece by piece for his captive audience.

For three hours, the district attorney told the jury that Michael Jackson had held a thirteen-year-old cancer patient and his family captive at Neverland, supplied the boy with alcohol, showed him pornographic magazines, and improperly touched him. He then engaged in an elaborate conspiracy with his associates to prevent the Arvizo family from leaving the ranch.

"You see," said Sneddon in a plodding tone, "the private world of Michael Jackson reveals that instead of reading them *Peter Pan*, Jackson is showing them sexually explicit magazines. Instead of cookies and milk, you can substitute wine, vodka, and bourbon."

The gist of the case, he elaborated, was that the boy met Jackson through an organization that put stars in touch with sick children. During August 2000, after Gavin came home from the hospital, his brother, Star, who was nine, and his parents and sister were picked up in a limousine and taken to stay at Neverland for a few days.

On the night before their last day at the ranch Jackson took Gavin aside and said, "Gavin, why do you not ask your parents if you can spend the night in my bedroom at the dinner table tonight?"

The parents agreed. The singer and his personal assistant Frank Tyson then allegedly showed the Arvizo boys porn on a computer in a bedroom in an effort to "groom" him for a later seduction. He said the boys spent the night in the bed, but Jackson and Tyson slept on the floor.

The abuse was said to have started only *after* the Bashir documentary aired and when the singer allegedly tried to imprison the family to keep them from cooperating with authorities. It was claimed that Jackson forced them to make a tape praising the singer for the rebuttal video used to discredit the Bashir film.

Perhaps the most effective element of Sneddon's presentation was when he played sections of the documentary for the jury. When Jackson says, "That's a beautiful thing. It's very loving . . . It's very sweet" after Bashir asks him if sleeping in a bed with young boys was a good idea, several jurors were seen to cringe.

When it was the defense's turn to address the jury, Tom Mesereau leaped up in a dramatic flourish and went on the attack. "I'm here to tell you these accusations are false, they are bogus, and they never happened," he said, his trademark white hair flowing past his shoulders. "These charges are fake, silly."

Mesereau promised to prove that Janet Arvizo, whom he referred to as Jane Doe, was a con artist who coached her children on how to lie for profit. He told jurors about the settlement with JCPenney and more recently how she attempted to use her son's cancer in both successful and unsuccessful efforts to gain sympathy and cash from celebrities like Jay Leno, Chris Tucker, and George Lopez.

He said another actress would testify that she gave the family $20,000 to prepare a room for Gavin on his return from the hospital. She was shocked to find it had been spent on a big-screen TV.

"We will prove that the mother, with her children as tools, wanted to find a celebrity to latch on to, to give them the advantages and opportunities they did not have."

He pointed out that Janet had also fraudulently claimed to many people that she was destitute and that her son needed money for chemotherapy. In truth, he said, the boy's father was a member of a union that covered his medical bills.

"The most known celebrity, the most vulnerable celebrity, became the mark—Michael Jackson," Mesereau said.

Addressing the actual molestation charges for the first time, he said that despite two massive police swoops on Jackson's Neverland Ranch, no DNA evidence was found indicating that the boy or his younger brother had engaged in sexual acts.

"The . . . children's DNA was never found in Michael Jackson's bedroom after searching and testing," he said.

"There is one witness," Mesereau promised the jury, addressing the alcohol charges, "that will tell you that Mr. Jackson ordered some alcohol for himself and his guests, and the children stole it. They [the Arvizo kids] were caught intoxicated. They were caught with bottles. Mr. Jackson was nowhere around. We will prove to you that they are now trying to say that he was behind all this. And it's false."

Most legal analysts agreed that Mesereau had presented the more compelling opening arguments.

"If style mattered over substance, and sometimes it does in court, then the defense has the advantage after the first day of the trial," said the analyst for CBS News. "Sneddon's opening statement was plodding and included way too many dates, names, and petty details. Moreover, it meandered back and forth along the timeline that jurors will need to grasp if they are to convict Jackson. By the end, the monologue seemed like a book about Russian history, where all the names are so jumbled together and unfamiliar that they lose most of their meaning. That's not a recipe for a good start to a long criminal trial."

As Jackson left the courthouse at the end of the day, he was greeted by a deluge of fans and protesters. "Michael, we love you," one supporter shouted. Another responded, "Michael, how does it feel to put your hands down a boy's pants?"

If all went according to plan, Tom Sneddon's star witnesses would be the Arvizo family themselves—not just Gavin, but his younger brother, Star, and his older sister, Davellin, as well as the mother, Janet. All were prepared to present devastating testimony about what they had seen and heard at Neverland between February and March 2003. Their testimony would be especially crucial to secure a conviction against Jackson on the serious count of abduction and false imprisonment.

After testimony from Martin Bashir and others about the documentary that set the stage for the current case, it was time for the jury to hear from Gavin's older sister, Davellin. Sneddon walked her through the timeline and she talked about how she and her brothers had been introduced to Jackson through Jamie Masada, the owner of an L.A. comedy club, the Laugh Factory. After Gavin was diagnosed with cancer at the age of ten, he presented a dying wish list to meet Chris Tucker, Adam Sandler, and Michael Jackson.

Soon after, at Masada's behest, Jackson called her brother in the hospital, telling him to "eat up all the cancer cells like Pacman." Jackson, she said, was attempting to teach Gavin a visualization technique whereby he could picture the healthy cells eating unhealthy ones. When Gavin eventually recovered, Jackson invited him and the whole family to visit him at Neverland. Eventually, Davellin testified, after the Bashir documentary had aired, that there was a "conspiracy" to fly her and the family to see Jackson in Miami aboard Chris Tucker's private jet.

Once they returned to Neverland, she continued, she and her family were given a "list of nice things to say" about Jackson for the rebuttal video. That's when she felt they were being held captive.

"We were scared by the whole situation," she said. "The whole situation, the secrecy. The—just real aggressive. I was just scared." Davellin also said she had never consumed alcohol until she was given a drink by Jackson at Neverland.

When it was Mesereau's turn to cross-examine her, he showed her the video she had made with her family praising Jackson. "He's a very caring, humble man. He took us under his wing when no one else would," says Davellin on the video about Jackson as tears stream down her face.

Earlier, she had told Sneddon that Jackson allowed no one in the family to watch the Bashir video. Yet on the rebuttal video, Janet Arvizo suggests she and her son mimic a specific scene from the Bashir interview. It showed the boy holding hands with Jackson and leaning his head on the singer's shoulder.

Despite this obvious contradiction, Davellin still insisted that none of her family members had seen the Bashir video.

Mesereau also focused on an interview that she

had given to the California Department of Children and Family Services where she denied that Jackson had acted inappropriately with her brother.

She admitted that she lied in this interview.

"So you'd lie about certain things and tell the truth about certain things, depending on what you are asked, right?" Mesereau said.

"Yeah," she softly replied.

After Davellin, it was her brother Star's turn, the first witness to actually claim to see sexual activity involving his brother and Jackson. Star, who was twelve at the time of the incident, testified that he twice caught Jackson molesting his brother.

"I saw directly into the bedroom and my brother was on top of the covers. I saw Michael's left hand in my brother's underwear and his right hand in his underwear," the boy said.

He said he saw the alleged molestation as he climbed a stairwell leading to the singer's bedroom, where he and Gavin usually slept during their visits to Jackson's Neverland Ranch.

"What was [Gavin] doing?" Sneddon asked him about the first incident.

"He was asleep. He was kind of snoring," the boy recalled, adding that Jackson was "rubbing himself" while touching his brother.

A second similar incident happened again two days later, the boy said.

Another time, Jackson even pretended to have sexual intercourse with a female mannequin about the size of an eight-year-old.

"He was fully clothed and acting like he was humping it," Star said, as he laughed wildly.

Jackson also once had a "cussing contest" with Gavin on a day when he had given the boy red wine, Star testified.

"I saw my brother stumbling around with a soda can in his hand . . . I saw red, light red around the top of his 7-UP can," the boy testified. His brother was "not well" the next day.

Moreover, Jackson also showed both brothers porno magazines, which he stored in a black Samsonite briefcase, according to Star. Authorities had found more than seventy magazines during their raids on Neverland, all featuring adult *heterosexual* sex. Yet Tom Sneddon had continuously reminded the jurors of Jackson's porn stash. Legal analysts were puzzled as to why he would emphasize this fact if he was trying to paint Jackson as a gay pedophile. The media would later consistently report that two books were found during Neverland raids featuring child pornography or full frontal nudity of boys, contributing to the public perception of Jackson as a pedophile. But as the jury discovered, both books were well-respected art books by well-known fashion photographers, which featured nude children only in passing and could not be defined as child pornography by any legal definition. One was sent to him by a fan. Most experts in pedophilia were, in fact, surprised that in the many searches of Jackson's residences, not a single example of child pornography was found, highly unusual in the case of a true pedophile, who usually feasts on such images.

The boys and Jackson flipped through the magazines on two occasions, once in the singer's bathroom and once in his bedroom, Star testified. Among the titles were *Barely Legal* and *Juicy, Ripe and Ready*.

On another occasion, Jackson discussed masturbation, saying "everyone does it, you should try it," the boy added.

It was riveting testimony, and extremely damaging for the defense. Until Tom Mesereau finally strode up to the witness box for his cross-examination.

Mesereau produced an interview that Star gave to the sheriff's deputies in which he said that he was lying on a couch pretending to be asleep when he witnessed the second molestation, contradicting his testimony to the jury.

"I was pretending like I was sleeping. I was in his couch, the little couch," Jackson's attorney quoted from a transcript.

"I was nervous when I did the interview," the boy said.

"So because you were nervous you didn't get the facts right," the attorney asked.

"Yes," the boy said.

Mesereau then produced another transcript of an interview the boy gave to a therapist, Stan Katz, which again contradicted his account on the stand.

Star had told Katz that he saw Jackson put his hand "on top" of Gavin's underwear, not inside, as he said on the stand.

"I don't remember," the boy said in response to Mesereau's reminder.

Referring to a second incident, Mesereau questioned him with the transcript in hand. "Didn't you tell

Stan Katz that Mr. Jackson touched your brother's butt, not his crotch?"

"I never said he touched his butt!" Star replied testily.

When Davellin was on the stand, she testified that she drank wine with Jackson and her brothers in a wine cellar. But Star told Mesereau that his sister had actually received alcohol from Jackson in the kitchen and that it was vodka, not wine.

"It wasn't in the wine cellar?" Mesereau asked.

"No," replied Star, contradicting his sister.

He then got Star to admit that it would have been almost impossible to "catch" Jackson molesting his brother because Jackson's bedroom was equipped with a high-tech security system that warns him when somebody is coming.

"So there were sensors that you tripped, an alarm that went off and the camera?" Mesereau asked.

"Yes," Star conceded.

Mesereau then played the witness a video in which he, his brother, mother, and sister sing Jackson's praises and said he was a loving and compassionate father figure to them.

"Everything you said [in the video] is a lie?" Mesereau asked.

"Basically yes," Star replied.

He proceeded to ridicule claims that the family was held prisoner at Neverland, pointing out that the family had left the ranch twice and had later returned to the estate.

"How many times do you think your family escaped

from Neverland and went back so that they could escape again?" the attorney asked sarcastically.

When Mesereau showed him a copy of a porn magazine titled *Barely Legal*, asking if this was the exact edition that Jackson had showed the boys, Star testified it was.

"Are you sure?"

"Yes."

Mesereau then pointed out that the magazine he had showed Star was dated August 2003, months after the boys visited Neverland for the last time.

Finally, Mesereau got the boy to admit that he had lied under oath in a deposition for another case when he swore that his mother and father never fought and that his father never hit him during the civil suit against the department store years earlier.

"Did someone tell you to lie in the JCPenney case?" the lawyer asked.

By the time Star left the stand, it was clear that his and his sister's credibility had been reduced in the eyes of the jury, who began to look over at Jackson regularly for the first time.

The next day, a Santa Barbara newspaper, *The Independent*, published an editorial questioning whether the public and the media had perhaps unfairly prejudged Jackson:

> What if Michael Jackson is innocent? That should be an obvious consideration, given our country's "innocent until proven guilty" legal mantra, yet it's a question worth special attention in the ongoing child molestation case against the King

of Pop. Ever since the Neverland raid in 2003, most people across the globe—save a devoted but waning fan base—automatically assumed that Jackson must be guilty in some regard.

It was finally time for Jackson to face his accuser. On March 15, 2005, Tom Sneddon called Gavin Arvizo to the stand, where he told much the same story as his brother and sister. He also added a shocking new allegation. He said that before Jackson masturbated him, the singer told him that if men don't masturbate, they end up raping women. The comment made a number of jurors gasp.

But when Mesereau stood up for the cross-examination, he held in his hand Gavin's police statement from 2003. At that time, he told investigators that it was his grandmother who told him that men have to masturbate to avoid raping women.

Confronted with his inconsistency, the boy was understandably flustered. But he had a ready explanation. Jackson had told him the same thing as his grandmother did "around the same time."

"Michael tried to explain to me first," he added. "He was more pushing it on me . . . I guess my grandmother saw I was very confused about sexuality. She didn't make the identical quote."

It was a bizarre day at the trial, which started when Mesereau told the judge that Jackson was in the hospital with a health problem after he allegedly tripped and injured his back while getting dressed. The judge was unsympathetic and ordered the attorney to produce his client, resulting in the odd spectacle of Jackson arriving in court wearing only his pajamas.

Mesereau also produced the statement of a surprise witness, an administrator from Gavin's school who says he questioned the boy about the abuse in the wake of the Bashir documentary, but that Gavin had twice denied anything improper had occurred.

Mesereau quoted the school official as saying to the boy: "Look at me, look at me . . . I can't help you unless you tell me the truth—did any of this happen?"

Gavin acknowledged the conversation with Alpert, who was dean at John Burroughs Middle School in Los Angeles.

"I told Dean Alpert he didn't do anything to me," the boy said, adding that he lied because he didn't want to be teased by his classmates.

Throughout Gavin's testimony, he claimed that he had been molested by Jackson twice. But when Sergeant Steve Robel, lead investigator for the Santa Barbara Sheriff's Department, took the stand, he testified that Gavin had actually twice claimed to investigators the singer had molested him five to seven times, "but he could not articulate exactly" what happened every time.

The defense was intent on portraying the entire Arvizo clan as "rapacious financial predators" who used celebrities to make money, and Mesereau pursued this line.

When he asked Gavin during his testimony whether he had ever called talk show host Jay Leno, for example, the boy admitted it, but said he never spoke directly to the comedian, claiming he reached an answering machine. He also denied his mother was present when he made the call, saying there was a woman present, but that she was a family friend.

However, ABC News obtained the police transcript of a conversation where Leno told investigators a very different story.

"A while back the mother called, 'Oh, my son, he's twelve years old, oh, he loves you,'" Leno said, contradicting Gavin's sworn testimony. "I'm not that much of an egomaniac, I don't know why a twelve-year-old would be infatuated with a fifty-five-year-old guy who does political jokes . . . and I said 'Well, what can I do for you?'" Leno said.

"It all sounded very rehearsed to me," he added.

The investigator then asked Leno whether the mother and son were "looking for money."

"I think so. It just sounded a little suspicious . . . I don't know if he's reading from a script, but it just sounded coached," he replied. Leno would eventually take the stand to testify on behalf of Jackson's defence even though he also told police he thought Jackson was guilty of the charges against him.

Leno wasn't the only celebrity that had been hit up for money, apparently.

The comedian Chris Tucker, who introduced Gavin to Jackson, would testify that he had met Gavin at a benefit in 2000 while the boy was fighting cancer and the two became friends.

"He was really smart and cunning at times, and his brother . . . was definitely cunning," he recalled. He told the jury that Gavin was constantly asking for gifts and that he had one day taken Jackson aside and warned him to "watch out" for Janet Arvizo because he had grown suspicious of her.

Another celebrity, CNN talk show host Larry King, had a similar story to tell about Janet Arvizo, but the judge wouldn't allow him to tell a jury, ruling it irrelevant. Nevertheless, King told the court that he had spoken to the Arvizos' former civil lawyer, Larry Feldman, trying to get him to come on his popular show to discuss the case. Feldman declined, he said, but not before telling King that he didn't want to take Janet's case because he didn't find her credible.

"He just said she is a wacko," King recalled in testimony that would have been devastating to the prosecution if the jury had been allowed to hear it. "He said she is in it for the money," King stated.

When the jurors finally heard from Janet Arvizo herself, she gave them a rambling, often contradictory account of the family's time at Neverland and painted a sinister picture of Jackson.

"He never cared about us or my son," she charged.

Turning to the jury, she regularly made speeches during her testimony.

"He managed to fool the world," she announced. "Now, because of this criminal case, people know who he really is."

For five days, Arvizo stayed on the stand, allowing Tom Mesereau the opportunity to destroy her credibility time and again. He returned repeatedly to the JC-Penney lawsuit, presenting photos from the incident that seemed to contradict her version of events.

Nevertheless, perhaps the most damaging part of her testimony concerned a story that she had arranged about her son in a local newspaper saying that the family was poverty-stricken and required to pay $12,000 for each chemotherapy treatment Gavin received. The story included an address to send contributions.

Under cross-examination, Arvizo first claimed that the figure was a typographical error and that it should have read $1,200, but she finally acknowledged that the family was actually paying nothing for the treatments because her husband's insurance covered the chemotherapy.

After the trial, Arvizo was charged with perjury and welfare fraud for illegally collecting more than $18,000 in welfare benefits by falsely claiming she was indigent. She pleaded no contest to the charges and was sentenced to community service.

If the Arvizo family had come across as scheming gold diggers while Mesereau tore apart their credibility on the stand, Tom Sneddon still had some powerful artillery to strengthen his rapidly deteriorating case, especially after the judge ruled that the prosecution could introduce previous accusations against the singer to demonstrate a pattern of abuse.

On April 5, 2005, Sneddon called twenty-four-year-old Jason Francia to the stand. This was the son of maid Blanca Francia, who had sold her story to *Hard Copy* for $20,000 years earlier. Blanca claimed she had seen Jackson showering naked with young boys. In a sworn deposition taken by Jackson's legal team years earlier, Blanca admitted to embellishing parts of her story to *Hard Copy*. Under oath, she admitted that she had never actually seen Jackson shower with anyone nor had she seen him naked with boys in his Jacuzzi. They always had their swimming trunks on, contrary to the story she had told Diane Dimond.

Francia told the court that Jackson abused him three times starting in 1990 during a tickling session while watching cartoons at Jackson's Century City condo. He testified that the first two times, Jackson fondled his testicles for a few minutes outside his pants and then stuck a $100 bill down the boy's pants after it was over.

The third time, Jackson reached inside his underwear, Jason Francia said emotionally. Even more startling, Jackson had quietly settled an abuse claim with his mother for $2.4 million years earlier to head off a civil suit. It was the most powerful and damaging testimony against Jackson to date.

In his cross-examination, Mesereau reminded Francia that he had originally denied the molestation when police questioned him in 1993. He suggested that detectives had bullied him into his accusations, pulling out the transcript of a statement Francia had made about his interrogation in which he claimed, "They made me come up with a lot more stuff. They kept pushing. I wanted to hit them in the head."

After the trial jurors said they didn't find Jason's account credible because there were too many loopholes. Nevertheless, Francia's testimony certainly appeared more believable than another prosecution witness,

Ralph Chacon. He was a security guard and part of the Neverland Five that sued Jackson for wrongful termination years earlier. The group subsequently sold their story to *Hard Copy* for a large payout.

Chacon told the jury he was doing his rounds one day when he saw Jackson and a boy in a Jacuzzi near Neverland's amusement arcade.

"I saw Mr. Jackson caressing the boy's hair, he was kissing him . . . sucking his nipples," he testified.

But under cross-examination, Mesereau was quick to hit back, accusing Chacon of having tried to "extort" $16 million from Jackson in a lawsuit and lengthy trial that the guard lost, forcing him into bankruptcy. He also pointed out that Chacon had been fired for stealing from Neverland.

"After a six-month trial, this is a good way to get even with him, isn't it?" asked Mesereau, drawing an objection from the prosecution. "Do you have any motive to get even with Mr. Jackson?" asked Mesereau.

"No, sir," Chacon replied.

The prosecution witness garnering the most headlines, however, was Adrian McManus. She had worked as a Neverland maid between 1990 and 1994. McManus drew gasps after testifying she had seen Jackson molest Macaulay Culkin as well as two other boys.

When Mesereau cross-examined her, he asked her why she never mentioned Culkin during her deposition in the 1994 wrongful termination case.

"I didn't tell the truth. I said I didn't see anything," she said, explaining that she was afraid of Jackson because he had threatened to report her to her superiors if she ever did anything he didn't like. She added that she needed the job because her husband had been laid off and a house payment was due.

Mesereau pointed out that in the original lawsuit she was found to have stolen an Elvis Presley sketch drawn by Jackson that she then sold to a tabloid. She originally claimed that she had found it in the trash. More damaging to her credibility, however, was a lawsuit involving her and her husband in which they were discovered to have defrauded three children of more than $30,000. Finally, McManus acknowledged that she had been completely untruthful throughout a deposition she gave during the Jordan Chandler case in 1994.

"Do you know how many times you lied under oath in the . . . deposition?" asked Mesereau.

"The whole time," she replied. "I believe I didn't tell the truth."

The case dragged on for another two months with jurors forced to sort through mounds of contradictory evidence and scores of witnesses on both sides, including Culkin himself, who was called by Jackson's side because of McManus's startling claim.

The actor vehemently denied that anything improper had ever occurred between him and Jackson, as did two other former Jackson "special friends," Australians Brett Barnes and Wade Robson. The trio's testimony in defense of Jackson was a particularly bitter pill for Tom Sneddon to swallow because he had long hoped he could persuade the three to back up his case. He was so confident, in fact, that he had listed all three as potential prosecution witnesses at the outset of the trial.

On June 3, the jurors retired to deliberate, but not before they heard a powerful closing argument from Tom Mesereau attacking the Arvizos one last time. "It's the biggest con of their careers," he boomed. "They're trying to profit from Michael Jackson. They think they have pulled it off. They're just waiting for one thing, your verdict."

Tom Sneddon had made a number of serious missteps during the three-month trial, and so he left his closing argument to his deputy Ron Zonen. He painted Neverland as an elaborate palace of temptations and Jackson's bedroom as a "world of the forbidden" where prepubescent boys "learned about human sexuality with someone who was only too willing to be their teacher."

For ten days, the jurors met behind closed doors as they tried to sort through a complex maze of legal arguments and testimony. Many legal analysts were predicting that Jackson would be found guilty on at least some of the counts against him, perhaps of serving alcohol to a minor.

By the time the judge had finished reading the last count of not guilty, Michael Jackson appeared close to collapse.

He was so overtaken by emotion as he filed out of the courthouse for the last time minutes later that he hardly noticed the large sign that had been hoisted by one of his supporters:

MICHAEL, ON BEHALF OF MANKIND,
WE'RE SORRY.

FOURTEEN

I'm sitting in the back room of a dance rehearsal studio smoking a joint with a legend, but things aren't exactly going as planned.

For months, with mixed success, I have been attempting to track down those who know Michael Jackson best. My potential sources range from current and former household staff to associates, to Sony employees, musicians, and "special close friends." But the Holy Grail is an interview with Jackson's best friend, Elizabeth Taylor. My usual modus operandi is to pose undercover, but Taylor is in poor health and doesn't go out much, leaving my options limited. Short of infiltrating her household staff, it seems like a lost cause.

A number of media commentators had noted Taylor's low profile during the Arvizo trial, in marked contrast to her seemingly constant media presence a decade earlier when she was repeatedly called on to defend her friend's reputation. Had she finally seen the light and decided to distance herself from Jackson's troubles?

But in May 2006, the seventy-four-year-old Taylor

appeared on *Larry King Live* and was as vigorous as ever in her defense of her old friend, telling King, "I've never been so angry in my life," at the child abuse charges. When King asks her whether it doesn't look strange for a man in his forties to spend the night with children, Taylor is quick to respond.

"All right," she says. "I'll answer that, because I've been there, when his nephews were there, and we all were in the bed, watching television. There was nothing abnormal about it. There was no touchy-feely going on. We laughed like children, and we watched a lot of Walt Disney. There was nothing odd about it."

"So you think they were out after him?" King asked.

"I do," replied the grande dame of American cinema.

If I couldn't get to Taylor, I knew who my second choice had to be. One of the oddest spectacles of the last few years had to be the 2002 wedding of Liza Minnelli—the legendary Oscar- and Tony-winning daughter of gay icon Judy Garland—to impresario David Gest, the strangest-looking man I have ever met. Despite the almost universal snickering over Liza's choice of groom and nonstop jokes about Gest's sexual preferences, the wedding itself was unlike anything New York had ever seen, with a star-studded guest list right out of Who's Who.

Gest chose Michael Jackson to be his best man, citing their close friendship since childhood and the fact that it was Jackson who introduced the couple at his 2001 reunion concert. The two had more than friendship in common. The odd-looking Gest had undergone multiple face-lifts years earlier by Jackson's plastic surgeon, Steven Hoefflin, and forever regretted it, saying, "I hate my looks." For her maid of honor, Minnelli chose Elizabeth Taylor. When the moment came, however, it was Jackson who held Liza's train as she walked down the aisle. He also gave the bride away.

The marriage itself lasted less time than the singer's ill-fated union with Lisa Marie, but Jackson and Liza remained close friends, and Minnelli was said to know where the bodies were buried. Like Taylor, however, she was conspicuously silent during the Arvizo trial, and I wondered why.

For several months, I had posed undercover as a paparazzo for another forthcoming book project, so I was well acquainted with the various nooks, crannies, and watering holes where New York–based celebrities liked to hang out. In Liza's case, that was a dance studio called Luigi's, where she always rehearsed. But I still needed a hook.

Taking a chance, I decided to trade on my onetime friendship with the legendary Hollywood actress Ava Gardner, whom I knew years before in London. I met Ava one day after busking near London's Hyde Park when she sat beside me on a park bench while exercising her corgis. When she saw my sax, she asked me what kind of music I play. When I told her jazz, she said casually, "Oh, I was married to a couple of jazz musicians." When I asked her who she meant, she replied, "Artie Shaw and Frank Sinatra." From her response, I probably should have known who she was, but at the time I wasn't very familiar with pop culture. That may have been why we struck up a friendship. She invited me up for tea in her apartment at Hyde Park Towers, where she had a photo prominently displayed of herself with the queen—explaining that the two had bonded over their mutual love of corgis—and we had many enjoyable get-togethers until her death in 1990.

During our friendship, Ava shared many stories about her Hollywood days, especially her tempestuous marriage to Frank Sinatra. One day she wiped off some makeup and showed me a scar above her lip, where she said Sinatra had struck her with something in a fit of rage.

She told me she was living in England because "Frank's boys" had made it clear to her that he wanted her on the other side of the Atlantic as far away from him as possible. "He couldn't handle the thought of bumping into me with another man," she said, hinting at the obsessive jealousy that I had always heard about from the man who apparently never got over losing Ava.

"When he wasn't drinking or womanizing, he could be very sweet," she emphasized, adding that he was "hung like a mule."

I knew that Liza Minnelli was close to Sinatra, who was good friends with her mother. Growing up, she always called him "Uncle Frank," but I gambled that she had fonder memories of Ava Gardner than he did.

So one day after rehearsal, I cornered Liza and told her that I was Ava Gardner's hair and makeup artist during her later years. I knew that would impress her on two counts. First, I was obviously gay—a definite plus for one of the world's best known fag hags—and second,

I was a friend of a friend. Sure enough, at the sound of Ava's name, Liza got sentimental.

"You knew Ava? She was so beautiful. When I was younger, I always wanted to have her looks," she gushed. "Come back with me and tell me about her."

The next thing I knew we were sitting in the back room with a couple of other dancers and a joint was being passed around as we experienced Liza being Liza. I told her a little about Ava, whom she knew when she was a child, but I was careful to leave out the stories Ava had told me about Sinatra's violent tendencies. I figured Liza probably wouldn't have responded well to unflattering tales about Uncle Frank.

I needed a segue to bring up Jackson, so I told her that Ava was a huge fan of Jackson and used to practice some of his dance moves. At that, she let out a trademark Liza Minnelli laugh. It proved to be infectious, prompting everybody present to collapse into hysterics, especially after Liza stood up and did an impression of Ava Gardner attempting to moonwalk.

Sensing an opportunity, and hoping the pot would loosen her tongue, I broached the subject. "You know Jackson, don't you?" I asked innocently. "I love Michael," she replied, "but I haven't talked to him for months. It's terrible what they did to him, just awful."

But didn't he bring it on himself a little bit? I asked, reminding her that he shared his bed with children even after the Jordan Chandler settlement.

"It's ridiculous. If you saw him with those kids, you'd see how innocent it all is. I've been to Neverland. It's so terrific what he does for kids there. Believe me, I've seen just about everything in Hollywood, and I mean *everything*. There are more sickos than you can shake a stick at. Michael Jackson is not one of them."

The encounter was fun, but not terribly enlightening. But the very next day my luck would change when I ran into another longtime acquaintance of both Minnelli and Jackson, the legendary *New York Post* gossip columnist Liz Smith, coming out of the Eighth Avenue office of American radio and TV personality Joe Franklin. It was Franklin who mentioned to her that I was working on a documentary about Michael Jackson, saying, "You could tell him a thing or two about that guy, Liz." The mention of Jackson's name seemed to infuriate Smith. "Jackson still has lots of demons that have not been disclosed," she warned. "Beware."

I told her I'd be happy to disclose them in my film if she had been privy to anything in particular that the world needs to know. However, like everyone else who issued similar warnings, she was less than forthcoming about the details, saying only, "I hear things."

During my time undercover in Michael's camp, I had more than a glimpse of the real Michael. I spent more than five years inside his "camp," on and off, sometimes posing as a fan, other times as a driver, once as a florist— always in disguise, I saw him face-to-face extensively.

My own attempts to meet Jackson had been consistently thwarted since I began my investigation. Once again I needed to summon my best investigative skills. So in 1997, when I heard that Jackson was going to be in New York to do a photo shoot for Italian *Vogue*, I knew that this was the opportunity I had been searching for. One of my earliest undercover ventures was an investigation into the fashion industry, where I posed undercover as a male model to expose its underbelly. In the process, I actually landed a modeling assignment for the Fubu fashion line. From that experience, I knew a considerable amount about the chaos surrounding a fashion shoot. With that in mind, I contacted one of my sources, who told me that the shoot would take place in Jackson's luxury suite at Manhattan's Four Seasons Hotel.

After I managed to get past hotel security, I discovered where the shoot was taking place by telling a concierge that I was a lighting technician for *Vogue*. I then got past the security team on Jackson's floor by claiming the same thing. When I got to the massive suite, however, I needed a different story. I told an assistant that I was part of the stylist team. She told me that the shoot wouldn't be starting for hours but that I could help myself to the food that had been set up in one of the rooms.

Jackson was nowhere in sight.

While I drank a mineral water, I started to chat with another assistant and asked her what was involved. It was during the course of this conversation that she informed me Jackson's "hairpiece" would have to be styled and fitted.

"Is it elaborate?" I asked.

"It depends which one he uses," she explained, revealing that he travels with four wigs depending on the occasion. "It takes forever to get them right."

Twenty minutes later, there was a commotion. Jackson was on his way. At this point, a member of the singer's security team asked to see the credentials of everybody present. When he came to me, I told him that I had accidently left my credentials in the cab on the way there. Minutes later, I was being escorted out of the hotel lobby in a polite but menacing manner, close to my goal, although ultimately thwarted.

A few months later my luck would change. Through a mutual friend I had with Jackson I finally got to meet the King of Pop. Jackson was in L.A. on an outing with two of his three children at a Hollywood pizza parlor. All of them were in disguise. My friend alerted me that he'd be there. I got in my hairdresser's disguise and sped to the pizza joint in my rented car. When I got there, they were all sitting at a corner table, munching on slices of pizza and drinking pop. I was nervous I'd be found out the second I entered. But when my friend introduced me to Michael, it was the most amazing experience I ever had. We talked about old Hollywood movies and hairstyles, which I had researched for months before I took on this undercover persona. Michael went on and on about the Hollywood hairstyles of the silver screen during the forties and fifties. "It was Hollywood's most glamorous time," Michael said in a frail but lucid voice. "No one has come along with such class and style since Deborah Kerr, Dorothy Lamour, and Susan Hayward," he said. When Jackson talked about how beautiful Ava Gardner was, I told him about my close friendship with her. After hearing that, Michael treated me like part of his family. He was infatuated with my stories about Ava and asked me for all the juicy ones I had about Ava's relationship with Frank Sinatra.

At one point during our conversation at the pizza joint, Jackson put his hand over mine. I then wondered if the singer was hitting on me. After staring at me for over a minute in complete silence, he told me my blue eyes reminded him of Frank Sinatra, ironically Ava Gardner's ex-husband. He made me extremely nervous. I had visions in my mind of Michael leaning over and kissing me on the lips. Thank God he didn't. It was one of the most intense moments I have ever experienced looking into another man's eyes. I felt Michael's sexual energy from the get-go. I left feeling most uncomfortable and spent the next few weeks trying to figure out whether he was actually hitting on me. To this day, I believe he was.

In North America, I've been known as an authority on Michael Jackson. I have established beyond doubt, for example, that Jackson relied on an extensive collection of wigs to hide his salt-and-pepper hair. Short of their luxuriance, the Peter Pan of Neverland cut a skeletal figure. In my final meeting with Michael, I had been trying to persuade him to change his look to a platinum blond wig with a streak of ocean-blue down the middle. He had told me he wanted a fresh start. Some liked to snigger at his public image, and it is true that flamboyant clothes and bizarre makeup made for a comic grotesque; yet without them, his appearance was distressing.

Following the Arvizo verdict, Jackson had vowed never to live in the United States again. When Larry

King asked Elizabeth Taylor about this a year later, she snapped, "Well, really, why should he? He's been treated like dirt here." Indeed, a Gallup poll taken immediately following his acquittal showed that 48 percent of Americans disagreed with the verdict. Only 38 percent thought the jury got it right.

For a while, he took up residence in Bahrain, where a prince who fancied himself an amateur songwriter offered him refuge at one of his stately palaces. He even built Jackson a $300,000 recording studio. But Jackson found life in the Muslim state stifling and he was reduced to dressing as an Arab woman in order to move about freely.

He needed a permanent home and he had narrowed the possibilities to three locations. He had always had an affinity for Britain, where the fans had always treated him with kindness and affection. Polls there showed that the majority of Britons believed him innocent of the child molestation charges. The only drawback was the tabloids. They had originally coined the nickname Wacko Jacko and seemed determined to make his life a living hell whenever he visited. Still, Jackson brought his three children to the British countryside in March 2006 and the family had a great time staying at Cliveden, a mansion located in Berkshire that served as the backdrop for the infamous Profumo sex scandal in the early sixties involving call girls, Russian spies, and state secrets. In fact, the Jackson clan was holed up in the estate's Spring Cottage, where a number of notable orgies took place, setting off the original scandal. "It would surprise no one if Michael ended up staying in Britain," Jackson's spokesman announced at the time. "Michael has been in the UK for several weeks now. It is very unlikely he will return to the United States. Europe, and Britain in particular, feel like a safe haven to him at this time." Cliveden provided just the seclusion Jackson was looking for, but when he attempted to buy it, he was informed by the owners that it was not for sale at any price.

His second choice was Berlin, the scene of the notorious baby-dangling incident years earlier. Jackson had never forgotten the reaction of Berliners who rallied around him when the rest of the world howled with outrage over the episode.

"Michael is a fan of Germany, and has fallen in love with the city of Berlin. The Jackson family also really likes the city of Potsdam," said his adviser Shawn Andrews. Michael's father, Joe Jackson, told reporters the same thing.

"Michael wants to move to Europe," Andrews said. "He is positive about that. He feels at home in Berlin. No one in Germany ever let him down during the trial," he said. "Michael himself can't explain why he's fallen so deeply in love with Berlin."

In fact, I've learned that Jackson had been seriously contemplating building a replica of Neverland in preparation for the day when he sells the original and moves out of the United States. After he was cleared of the molestation charges, he vowed he would never again live in the original Neverland, saying it had been "violated" by the police officers who raided it in 2003.

Although Berlin had long been his first choice for his new home, he found it difficult to find the right location in the outskirts of that city and had been looking at alternative locations farther east, where the land is cheaper and more readily available. The only thing standing in the way, I had been told, was his ongoing financial woes.

"After the next tour, he should be flush with cash," an associate told me. "I think that's when he'll finally make his move once and for all. Germany is probably at the top of his list, though I suspect he will choose more than one home."

I discovered Jackson's third preferred location by chance because it just happened to be my hometown of Montreal, even though I was living in New York at the time. For some reason, Jackson had always had a special affection for Quebec, and it happened to be the only jurisdiction in North America where polls showed that the majority of residents firmly rejected the child abuse allegations against him, perhaps because Quebeckers know what it's like to be persecuted.

"I was backstage with Michael at one of his concerts in Montreal in the mid-1980s and I overheard him talking to a French journalist," the late Montreal broadcaster Ted Blackman told me years ago.

They were discussing whether or not Quebec would be better off being separate from Canada. Jackson replied "oui, oui." I was amazed. Jackson said he thought Quebec could be another Paris and that Canada was too culturally lame to sustain Quebec. It seemed to me that Jackson was a separatist, which bothered me at the time because I don't support separatism and I was afraid that he would influence young Quebeckers if he spoke out publicly. I remember he ignored the English journalists and spoke in broken French to the French media. He also accepted a key chain with a fleur-de-lys from a journalist from *La Presse*. The entire scene was surreal.

There was another Quebec connection as well. In 2002, Jackson's Neverland Entertainment Group had been in negotiations with a Montreal film company to open a new film production division called Neverland Pictures. MDP Worldwide Entertainment Inc., with offices in both Los Angeles and Montreal, announced that a deal had been done. Mark Damon, chief executive officer of MDP, said Jackson committed to invest $20 million of his own money to become a partner and major shareholder in MDP, which had taken over the Montreal firm Behavior Communications in 2000. Damon, a veteran film producer, said Jackson would be a producer, actor, and director for Neverland Pictures. Jackson was introduced to Damon through his old film producer friend Raju Sharad Patel. He had produced a number of major films, including the 1994 film adaptation of Rudyard Kipling's *Jungle Book*—cofinanced by Damon—and Tom Hanks's breakthrough film, *Bachelor Party*, in 1984.

"Michael Jackson and I have been friends for years, and every time we would meet, Michael would express his interest and desire to form an independent film company," said Damon at the press conference unveiling the new partnership. "Now we have been able together to create Neverland Pictures to make Michael's long-cherished dream come to fruition. This partnership will significantly expand MDP's production and financing capabilities as well as bring Michael's creative vision as a filmmaker—demonstrated in so many pioneering video productions such as *Thriller*—to film audiences around the world and we are thrilled to be working with him."

The deal eventually fell apart due to Jackson's ongoing financial troubles. "It wasn't pretty," a longtime associate of Damon told me. "Michael lied repeatedly, hoping that MDP would decide to go ahead with the project even if he didn't cough up the money he was supposed to invest. It got very messy and the deal eventually collapsed."

Yet the end of the business relationship with MDP didn't sour Jackson on Montreal. In June 2007, I attended a gathering following Montreal's Grand Prix Formula One race, where I was introduced to one of the city's leading Realtors. She announced to our small group that she was in the process of selling Michael Jackson a house and that he had already been to Montreal twice to look at potential properties. "He came incognito," she revealed. "He even attended a hockey game while he was here."

She said that she had already shown him a number of potential locations in the city's exclusive Westmount and Outremont districts, but that he still hadn't found the right place. "Privacy's the key," she said, revealing that the singer had his sights set on a swanky mansion once owned by the Bronfman family—scions of the Seagram fortune. However, it wasn't for sale.

It was this revelation that prompted me to start digging a little deeper.

FIFTEEN

More than a year later, Jackson still had not left the United States. He appeared to be spending an inordinate amount of time in Los Angeles, in a country he had vowed to leave after the verdict three years earlier. I knew for a fact that it was not an empty threat and that he been searching diligently for new quarters. So why was he still here?

I flew to Los Angeles and started to mine my various sources, none of whom had been particularly helpful in providing strong revelations. When I asked one of my sources, somebody on Jackson's payroll, why the star was spending so much time in Los Angeles, the answer surprised me. "It's because of his condition." What condition? I asked. "Alpha something, it's genetic."

A few weeks after that, a photographer named Mike Lopez snapped a photo of Jackson being pushed by an aide in a wheelchair and wearing a surgical mask. Lopez told the TV show *The Insider* that Jackson didn't look well. "He's very frail," he said.

I thought back to what my source had told me

about his "condition" and started to do some research, interviewing a number of doctors. The name "Alpha" triggered a recollection with one of the doctors I interviewed, who said, "It could be Alpha-1." Sure enough, I looked up Alpha-1 in a medical dictionary and I discovered that it was a genetic condition called alpha-1 antitrypsin deficiency, which is caused by the breakdown of a substance in the body that protects tissues from enzymes of inflammatory cells. In severe cases, it could lead to emphysema, especially in smokers. According to *Scientific American*, Alpha-1 is not all that rare.

"It is very much underrecognized," Dr. James Stoller, an expert in the disease, tells the publication. The best estimate in the United States is that there are probably about 100,000 severely affected Americans. If one looks at carriers of the disease, it probably affects 3 percent of Americans. It's quite common—one of the most prevalent genetic variants in the United States.

Could this be why Jackson had been photographed for years wearing a surgical mask in public, to protect his lungs from the ravages of the disease?

When I returned to my source inside the Jackson camp for confirmation, he said, "Yeah, that's what he's got. He's in bad shape. They're worried that he might need a lung transplant but he may be too weak. Some days he can hardly see and he's having a lot of trouble walking."

When I reported the story in December 2008, attracting worldwide headlines with my claim that he had "six months to live," the Jackson camp was quick to issue a denial, calling the report a "complete fabrication" and insisting that the singer was in perfect health. However, less than a month earlier, I discovered Jackson's own lawyers had argued that he was too ill to travel to London to testify in a $7 million civil suit brought against him by a Bahraini prince, Sheikh Abdulla Bin Hamad Al-Khalifa.

"It would be unwise for him to travel, given what's [sic] he's got now," Jackson's attorney Robert Englehart said at the time, but declined to elaborate "for the obvious reasons." Al Khalifa's lawyer, Bankim Thanki, called the medical evidence presented by Jackson's legal team "very unsatisfactory," noting "it's not the first time a sick note has been presented by Mr. Jackson."

In January 2009, I issued a public challenge for Jackson to submit to a complete medical examination at the Mayo Clinic at my expense and prove that his health was sound. It was ignored. A medical expert who once worked on Jackson's respiratory system agreed to meet me in private. I had to agree to sign an agreement guaranteeing his anonymity. I met him at a downtown Los Angeles Mexican restaurant and we talked for 45 minutes.

He told me to beware of Jackson's litigious nature. He warned me that he had to be careful of what he disclosed because he "could not risk losing my medical license." "You hit the nail on the head," he told me. "I can only reveal to you that Michael has had extreme lung problems and other ailments connected to it for years. There's a reason why he always wears a surgical mask. Of course his people will deny it. They might try to sue you and tie you up in court just to quiet you down. Be careful."

Meanwhile, Fox News columnist Roger Friedman had his own theory about Jackson's condition, dismissing the rumors completely. "Everyone can relax," he wrote. "Reports of his ailing health have been extremely exaggerated. Reports over the weekend that Jackson has some newly revealed sickness requiring a lung transplant are totally hokum, I can assure you. Yesterday I spoke to one of Jackson's regular insiders, who reported that the kooky former King of Pop is just fine, playing with his kids, and living large in a house he can't afford in Beverly Hills."

Friedman, who has always been one of the fairest and most accurate chronicler of Jackson's activities, added, "He's also a publicity hound who thinks that news of illness will make him sympathetic to the public. He learned this from Elizabeth Taylor, his onetime best friend."

Had I been duped into circulating a story to make Jackson look more sympathetic? I wondered. When I confronted my source, he told me that the story was accurate, though he added that "Michael is a bit of a hypochondriac so maybe he's being overdramatic about his condition." Still, he insisted that Jackson had been diagnosed with Alpha-1.

"Why do you think that he's staying in L.A.? It's to be close to his doctor. They're giving him shots to reverse the condition."

Indeed, Jackson had recently rented a luxury mansion in Beverly Hills and had been photographed weekly visiting the nearby clinic of his longtime dermatologist, Dr. Arnold Klein, whose offices had served as a base for years for his various medical treatments.

Picking up on what my source had told me about

Jackson getting "shots," I realized that he was undoubt-edly visiting the clinic to receive regular injections of alpha-1 antitrypsin, a substance that is derived from human plasma and which is often used to effectively treat the symptoms of Alpha-1. The treatment is said to be remarkably effective in reversing the effects of the condition and can enable a sufferer to live a normal life.

I had heard something was up, but the announcement was still as much a surprise to me as anybody else. A few weeks before Jackson held a London press conference announcing his fifty-concert comeback at the O₂ Arena in July, one of my sources in his camp told me that he had been offered $3 million to perform at a party for a Russian billionaire on the Black Sea in Spring 2009.

"Is he up to it?" I asked.

"He has no choice. He needs the money. He can't say no. His people are pushing him hard."

My first thought was his health. Could he even stand on a stage for an hour-long concert?

"He can stand. The treatments have been success-ful. He can even dance once he gets in better shape. He just can't sing," said the associate, explaining that Jackson would have to use lip-synching technology to get through the performance. "Nobody will care as long as he shows up and moonwalks."

He revealed one more piece of information. Jackson had been offered well in excess of one hundred million dollars to play Las Vegas for six months. "He said no, but his people are trying to force it on him. He's that close to losing everything."

Indeed, by all accounts Jackson's finances were in a shambles. The Arvizo trial itself was a relative bargain, costing a little more than $30 million in legal bills. But the damage to his career, already reeling before the charges, was incalculable.

Years of lavish spending had taken their toll, with one British newspaper calling Jackson the "King of Debts." After the Arvizo trial, a Bahraini sheikh hosted Jackson in his palace, underwriting his lavish lifestyle, but a few years later, the prince sued his former guest, demanding repayment for his hospitality. Jackson claimed he thought it had been a gift, and so it appeared to the rest of the world. But Roger Friedman has his own theory: "For one year, the prince underwrote Jackson's life in Bahrain—everything including living accommodations, guests, security and transportation. And what did Jackson do? He left for Japan and then Ireland. He took the money and moonwalked right out the door. This is the real Michael Jackson. He has never returned a phone call from the prince since he left Bahrain."

Although Jackson settled with the sheikh on the eve of the trial that would have aired his financial dirty laundry for the world to see, the settlement only put him that much deeper into the hole. It was a hole that kept getting bigger, but it was guaranteed by Jackson's half ownership in the Beatles' catalogue.

"Jackson is into Sony for hundreds of millions," a source familiar with his financial troubles told me in Spring 2009. "No bank will give him any money so Sony has been paying his bills. The trouble is that he hasn't been meeting his obligations. Sony has been in a

position for more than a year where they can repossess
Michael's share of the [Beatles] catalogue. That's always
been their dream scenario, getting full ownership. But
they don't want to do it because they're afraid of a backlash from his fans. Their nightmare is an organized Boycott Sony movement worldwide, which is the only thing
standing between Michael and bankruptcy at the moment." She said at the time that the scheduled London
concerts wouldn't completely clear Jackson's debts—
estimated at almost $400 million—but they would allow
him to get them under control and, more important, get
him out of default with Sony.

According to two separate sources in Jackson's camp,
the singer put in place a well-thought-out contingency
plan to ensure his children would be well taken care of
in the event of bankruptcy.

"He has as many as 200 unpublished songs that he
is planning to leave behind for his children when he
dies. They can't be touched by the creditors, but they
could be worth as much as $100 million or more that
will ensure his kids a comfortable existence no matter
what happens," one of his collaborators revealed.

Another producer that Jackson collaborated with
said some of the songs Jackson penned and produced
were in considerably different styles than his fans were
used to hearing. "When he dies, his unpublished catalogue will consist of many surprises," the producer said.
"There's [sic] lots of ballads, children's lullabies, African
beats, and even some country. Michael liked to experi-
ment a lot when he fooled around in the studio. He'll
leave behind more unpublished songs than any rock star

ever left behind. It's the only way to ensure that his kids will be properly taken care of forever."

The producer added that Jackson's unpublished catalogue would also consist of numerous homemade films and artwork. "Michael has a whole library of films he made, many of them shot on a home video camera. He was always creating new things. He also drew a lot, but was always reluctant to release his drawings in fear that they would be criticized. He was the most sensitive artist I ever met. And the most eccentric. With Michael you never knew what to expect when it came time to create. He once told me if he could start all over he'd focus more on visual art than music. He really had an eye for film and art. He often compared himself to great artists like Van Gogh and Rembrandt. You never heard Michael comparing himself to musicians." The producer remembered a seven-hour conversation he once had with Michael about Renaissance art. "Michael was a real renaissance man," he said. "One night we were supposed to record in the studio. Michael said he had some new beats he wanted to lay down. Instead we spent all night talking about art history. He knew everything. I never met anyone more educated on art and its origins. We ended up not recording a note that night. We didn't even take a break for a glass of water. That's how intense it was."

It appears that for the circle of handlers who surrounded Jackson during his final years, their golden cow could not be allowed to run dry. Bankruptcy was not an option.

Whatever the final autopsy results reveal, it was greed that killed Michael Jackson.

Friends and associates paint a tragic picture of the last weeks and months of his life as Jackson was goaded into a concert tour that he could never have logically completed.

"The vultures who were pulling his strings somehow managed to put this [London] concert extravaganza together behind his back and then they presented it to him as a fait accompli," said one aide. "The money was just unbelievable and literally all his financial people were telling him he was facing bankruptcy. But Michael still resisted at first. He didn't think he could pull it off. They were talking about a lot of shows."

Eventually they wore him down, the aide explained, but not with the money argument. "They told him that this would be the greatest comeback the world had ever known. They were armed with all these studies conducted by a London agency showing that Michael could still sell out a stadium for weeks at a time on the other side of the Atlantic. That's what convinced him. He thought if he could emerge triumphantly from the success of these concerts, he could be the King again."

According to Jackson's associates, the financial details of the London O_2 concerts are still murky, though various sources have revealed that Jackson was paid as much as £10 million in advance, much of it went to the handlers who negotiated the lucrative deal. They would have eventually seen Jackson receive as much as £100 million, if the concerts had been completed.

The London concert promoter, Randy Phillips, Rod Stewart's former manager, had been trying to coax Jackson out of retirement for years, but each time he had been rebuffed by the singer's former handlers. "I was turned down twice by his representatives. I was told he wasn't ready to go back onstage, both physically and psychologically," Phillips revealed. However, Jackson had replaced many of his veteran staff, the same people who had seen him through the aftermath of the Arvizo trial and who had been protecting his fragile emotional health to the best of their ability.

This housecleaning had apparently been engineered by his children's nanny, Grace Rwaramba, who was gaining considerable influence over Jackson and his affairs and had been described as the "queen bee" by those around Jackson, until she quit or was fired in late December 2008. One longtime Jackson associate told *People* magazine that Rwaramba had brought the powerful black militant organization the Nation of Islam and its security guards to Jackson's camp. It is unknown whether Rwaramba was ever a member of the Nation, but she would later lament its increasing influence over Jackson's affairs.

According to Rwaramba, Jackson rented a Beverly Hills house from the Nation for the staggering sum of $100,000 a month, but she believes he was taken advantage of.

"The Nation of Islam was telling him that the house we had in Los Angeles, after Neverland was sold, cost $100,000 a month," she complained to a reporter after his death. "I checked with many real estate agencies. To rent this house should not have cost more than $20,000 to $25,000. He had no clue."

During the Arvizo trial, the Nation was supplying

Jackson's security detail and Louis Farrakhan's son-in-law, Leonard Muhammad, was appointed as Jackson's business manager, though Muhammad's role had lessened significantly in recent years.

In late 2008, a shadowy figure who called himself Dr. Tohme Tohme suddenly emerged as Jackson's "official spokesman." Tohme has been alternately described as a Saudi Arabian billionaire and an orthopedic surgeon, but he is actually a Lebanese businessman who has, by his own admission, never held a medical degree. At one point, Tohme claimed to Fox News that he was an ambassador at large to the nation of Senegal, but the Senegalese embassy claimed that they had never heard of him.

Tohme's own ties to the Nation of Islam came to light in March 2009, when the famed New York auctioneer Darren Julien was conducting the sale of Michael Jackson memorabilia.

Julien filed an affidavit in Los Angeles Superior Court that month in which he described a meeting he had with Tohme's business partner, James R. Weller. According to Julien's account of the meeting, "Weller said if we refused to postpone [the auction], we would be in danger from 'Farrakhan and the Nation of Islam'; those people are very protective of Michael. . . . He told us that Dr. Tohme and Michael Jackson wanted to give the message to us that 'our lives are at stake and there will be bloodshed.'"

A month after these alleged threats, Tohme Tohme accompanied Jackson to a meeting at a Las Vegas hotel with Randy Phillips and the AEG group to finalize plans for Jackson's return to the concert stage. Jackson's handlers had twice before said no to Phillips. This time, with Tohme Tohme acting as his confidant, Jackson left the room agreeing to perform ten concerts at London's O_2 Arena.

Before long, however, ten concerts had turned into fifty and the potential revenues had skyrocketed. But those who knew Jackson best knew he was in no shape to perform ten shows, let alone fifty. "We knew it was a disaster waiting to happen," said one aide. "I don't think anybody predicted it would actually kill him but literally nobody believed he would end up performing." Their doubts were underscored when Jackson collapsed during only his second rehearsal. "Collapse might be overstating it," said the aide. "He needed medical attention and couldn't go on. Not sure what caused it."

Meanwhile, everybody around him noticed that Jackson had lost an astonishing amount of weight in the months leading up to the London concerts. His medical team even believed he had become anorexic. "He goes days at a time hardly eating a thing and at one point his doctor was asking people around him if he had been throwing up after meals," one staff member told me in May. "He suspected bulimia, but when we said he hardly eats any meals, the doc thought it's probably anorexia nervosa. He seemed alarmed and at one point said, 'People die from that all the time. You've got to get him to eat.'" Indeed, one of the known consequences of anorexia is cardiac arrest. This is what killed another iconic pop singer, Karen Carpenter, who admitted to suffering from anorexia shortly before her death in 1983.

After spotting him leave one of his rehearsals, Fox News reported that "Michael Jackson's skeletal physique is so bad that he might not be able to moonwalk anymore."

"I never saw anybody weigh him, but he couldn't have weighed more than a hundred pounds in the last month," says one member of his L.A. staff who saw him every day. At Jackson's official height of five foot ten inches, that represents a body mass index (BMI) of 14.3, which according to the National Eating Disorders Association may indicate anorexia. The normal BMI for somebody Jackson's height is between 18.5 and 24.9, meaning Jackson is at least 25 percent under the normal weight for a healthy male. Anything under 15 percent falls within the category of a potential anorexic. Although eating disorders such as anorexia are much more prevalent in women and girls than men, according to the association, as many as one million men suffer from the disease, which, curiously, is twice as prevalent in gay men. By any definition, Jackson's rapid weight loss clearly indicated something was wrong.

For the first time, those in Jackson's inner circle began to urge him to cancel the shows, but their pleas fell on deaf ears.

"There was just too much money at stake," recalls one aide. "The people who had his ear told him he would be a laughingstock if he canceled. They had to have known he was in no shape to go on, he was so frail, he kept canceling rehearsals. We wondered if somebody was going to cash in whether or not he performed. It just didn't make any sense. I know his family was concerned, especially his brother Jermaine, but Michael was kept very isolated during those last weeks."

One of Jackson's closest friends claimed a month before Jackson died that Michael told his daughter, Paris, he had only weeks to live. "He called her into his room and told her not to get mad at him if he didn't make it to Father's Day. He had a premonition that his days were numbered. He felt extremely ill. Unfortunately, no one wanted to help him. His closest advisers tried to control him with medication, drugs, and false hopes. They wanted to make sure he didn't bail on the O_2 gigs and that they would not be paid the money Jackson owed them."

The friend said that Jackson spent the final months of his life writing extensively. He thinks it was a long farewell, and not that Jackson simply wanted to write to his fans. "He'd hole himself up in his room for hours, sometimes days, and not move," the source said. "I asked him if he was writing a novel. He replied, 'Just some thoughts on my journey on this earth. I want to leave something to my children.'" This alarmed the friend. "After he told me that, I was concerned Michael was suicidal and that he was writing a long note to say farewell. His emotions during his last few weeks were completely erratic; I had never seen him more depressed. He knew he could not come back because of his failing health and that he wouldn't be able to pay all his debts. He told me three times that he felt like dying. At first I thought he was joking. Michael always liked to play the victim and convince people he was terminally ill. This time he was serious. He seemed to be convinced that he was dying. I wish I had taken him more seriously and tried to get him help. Unfortunately, Michael was like the boy who cried wolf—any time he complained, there was always doubt about his authenticity. He had spent years and years fooling people."

Although the financial details of his arrangement with AEG won't fully emerge until the estate is settled in 2010 and beyond, most of Jackson's longtime inner circle suspect that the people who had the most to benefit from the London concert were those associated with the complex web of businesses associated with Tohme Tohme, including the giant real estate firm Colony Capital LLC. Colony Capital had saved Neverland from foreclosure more than a year earlier by purchasing a $23.5 million credit note in a deal brokered by Tohme. Somehow this action allowed Jackson to retain his prized estate.

On May 20, 2009, concert organizers suddenly announced that the first London concerts had been delayed for five days while the remainder have been pushed back until March 2010. At the time they denied that the postponements were health-related, explaining that they needed more time to mount the complex technical production, though skepticism immediately erupted among ticket holders. Their doubts were well placed.

Behind the scenes, Jackson's mental and physical health was rapidly deteriorating. According to a member of his household staff, he was "terrified" at the prospect of the London concerts:

He wasn't eating, he wasn't sleeping and when he did sleep, he had nightmares that he was going to be murdered. He was deeply worried that he was going to disappoint his fans. He even said something that made me briefly think he was suicidal. He said he was worried that he was going to end up like Elvis. He was always comparing himself to Elvis as long as I knew him, but there was something in his tone that made me think that he wanted to die, he was tired of life. He gave up. His voice and dance moves weren't there anymore. I think maybe he wanted to die rather than embarrassing himself onstage.

The most obvious comparison between the King of Pop and the King of Rock and Roll was their all-consuming prescription drug habit, which in Jackson's case had significantly intensified in his final months and is almost certain to be a factor in his death when the autopsy results come in. "He is surrounded by enablers," said one aide who labeled himself in this category two months before his death. "We should be stopping him before he kills himself, but we just sit by and watch him medicate himself into oblivion."

Like his longtime idol Elvis, Jackson could count on an array of doctors to write him prescriptions on a whim with little regard to medical necessity, though Jackson would always cite "pain" as the basis for his drug-taking, which also provided the enabling physicians an excuse not to ask too many questions. Among the many drugs for which he developed a fondness in recent years was

OxyContin, often nicknamed "Hillbilly Heroin." It had become quite fashionable among musicians and Hollywood stars for its instantaneous and powerful high. But although members of his entourage witnessed Jackson receiving injections from doctors on a regular basis, they all insisted that the singer never used heroin itself or any other illegal drugs.

"He always had a prescription or a doctor giving him what he wanted," said a member of his staff who witnessed Jackson's long-standing addiction escalate since the Arvizo trial. "As far as I know the drugs were always legal, unfortunately."

In fact, in late 2003, shortly after he appeared on 60 Minutes to discuss the Arvizo scandal, Jackson overdosed on prescription drugs and had to be revived by a doctor who had been treating his brother Randy. The doctor was summoned to Michael's rented Beverly Hills home in the middle of the night. After the doctor revived him, he advised that Jackson should enter a rehab clinic to treat his addiction, advice the singer ignored. On other occasions, the children's nanny, Grace Rwaramba, reportedly had to pump Jackson's stomach after he took an excessive amount of drugs.

According to the aide, painkillers aren't the only drugs that Jackson took on a regular basis. "He pops Demerol and morphine, sure, apparently going back to the time when he burned himself during the Pepsi commercial, but there's also some kind of psychiatric medication, anti-anxiety or something like that. One of his brothers once told me that he was diagnosed with schizophrenia when he was younger, so it may be to treat that."

His aides apparently weren't the only ones who recognized that the prospect of a fifty-concert run was foolhardy. In May, Jackson himself reportedly addressed a group of fans as he left his Burbank rehearsal studio. "Thank you for your love and support," he told them. "I want you guys to know I love you very much. I don't know how I'm going to do fifty shows. I'm not a big eater. I need to put some weight on. I'm really angry with them [the concert promoter AEG] booking me up to do fifty shows. I only wanted to do ten." One of his former employees was particularly struck by Jackson's wording that day: "The way he was talking, it's like he's not in control over his own life anymore," she told me in early June. "It sounds like somebody else is pulling his strings and telling him what to do. Someone wants him dead. They keep feeding him pills like candy. They are trying to push him over the edge. He needs serious help. The people around him will kill him."

"It's like he was being kept away from his family," said an aide. "His family used to be the only people he could trust, and I know for a fact that they were very concerned with his health, but it's like he was being kept isolated from them. I think he spoke to his mother occasionally on the phone, but his brothers were being kept at a distance. I think if they had been around and seen what Michael had been reduced to, they would have put a stop to the concerts. Maybe that's why they were being kept away." He revealed that various members of the Nation of Islam seemed to be in control of the singer's affairs and kept a very tight grip over Jackson's every move:

They were scary people, very intimidating. I'm not sure why Michael was so in thrall to the Nation. There were rumors that he had secretly converted to Islam and that he was one of them, but I never saw him praying to Mecca. His brother Jermaine was a devout Muslim, but I never saw any sign that Michael himself had converted. Yet the Nation of Islam seemed to be controlling his life. We couldn't figure it out.

The above echoes charges made by Jackson's former close friend and publicist, Stuart Backerman, who left the singer's employ in 2004 after the Nation first entered Jackson's domain. "They basically took over Michael's business and isolated everybody," Backerman complained. As the first London concerts approached, something was clearly wrong. Jackson had vowed to travel to the UK in order to obtain a house and acclimate himself for at least eight weeks before his fifty-show residency, but he kept putting it off. First, he said he was worried about swine flu. Then, when that abated, a new series of excuses followed. Few who knew him were buying it. "For some reason, he didn't want to leave for England," stated one aide. "The bigwigs were getting nervous that he was going to back out of the London concerts."

On June 21, 2009, Jackson told my top contact in his camp that he wanted to die. He said that he didn't have what it would take to perform anymore because he had lost his voice and dance moves. "It's not working out," Jackson told my longtime source. "I'm better off dead. I don't have anywhere left to turn. I'm done."

During the last week of his life, Jackson flew in a Houston-based cardiologist, who had treated him a number of times in Las Vegas, but wasn't his regular doctor. The doctor, Conrad Murray, was with Jackson at the end. It was first believed that Murray had given Jackson a painkiller injection that contributed to his death, according to media reports that surfaced soon after. However, the doctor claimed that he had found Jackson on the floor unconscious and that he did not give him any injections. Less than twenty-four hours after Jackson was pronounced dead, his family and advisers were demanding an independent autopsy and an investigation into Murray's role. Many Jackson aides believe Dr. Murray is being used as a scapegoat. "It's easy to try to pin the blame on this one doctor who only knew Michael for a week," said one furious member of Jackson's entourage. "But this stuff had been going on for years. Let's look at all the other doctors who wrote him prescriptions and fed his drug habit, not to mention the vultures who were content to keep him high while they spent his money and pressured him to make more. That's who should be the focus of the investigation. It's all a big smoke screen to hide the truth."

On June 24, Jackson's last night on earth, he was scheduled to rehearse with his backup singers at L.A.'s Staples Center at 7:00 p.m., fine-tuning some of the shakier numbers for his upcoming London concerts. When he finally arrived more than three hours late, he took to the stage, but seemed disoriented. "He was listless," reported one member of his entourage in attendance, adding that this was his normal state during the last few weeks when he bothered to show up at all. "To be honest, I never thought Michael would set foot on a concert stage ever again," said one aide, choking back tears on the evening of his death. "This was not only predictable, this was inevitable."

Less than forty-eight hours after Jackson's death, as the book was going to press, I was in contact with one of James Brown's close relatives, who had his own startling theory, based on a recent conversation he had with the singer. He said his father had been friends with Jackson for years dating back to the Motown days, and that he and his relatives had been close to Jackson since they were children.

"I got a call from [Jackson] about two weeks ago," he revealed. "I've never heard Michael so sad. He was crying on the phone to me. He sounded more confused than ever. He said good-bye to me and I got a tear in my eye because I thought that was the last time I would ever speak to him. Unfortunately I was right. The last thing he told me is that he wanted to go to a better place. He was tired of everything." When he heard about Jackson's death, Brown's close relative says he immediately knew what happened:

> My man, the media got it wrong. When I heard about this new doctor that was with Michael when he died, I knew what must have happened. Michael brought this doctor in to kill him. It was his way of committing suicide. But now they're saying the heart doctor didn't inject him after all. That makes more sense. Michael wanted to die and he did what he had to do to make that happen.

Brown's close relative acknowledged that he had no proof for this scenario, but insisted that "there is no other explanation." He went on to say that he is convinced that the singer's inner circle, especially Tohme Tohme, had driven Jackson to the state where he wanted to end it all. "I know that Michael was intimidated and scared of Tohme Tohme. That man was like a cancer," he declares.

Perhaps the last word here should go to the person closest to Jackson, his mother, Katherine. The day Michael died, Katherine told one of the people closest to Jackson that no matter how Michael died, she will always believe that he could have been saved. "She admitted that Michael was seriously ill, but was convinced that he had 'a bunch of undesirables around him,'" the Jackson source said. "She couldn't stop sobbing. She's one of the nicest and most sincere people I ever met. She promised me she'd look after Michael's three children forever and fight hard against anyone who attempted to take them away. It was the most emotional conversation I ever had." I can now reveal that Jackson's will, not as yet made public, demands that his three children remain with Jackson's seventy-nine-year-old mother, Katherine, in California. The mother of the third child has never been identified. I fully expect that it will emerge that the children had a test tube conception, a claim already made by Deborah Rowe.

CONCLUSION

When Michael Jackson died just as this book was going to press, it no longer seemed relevant whether or not he was a child molester, though the charges will almost certainly haunt his legacy forever.

I started my investigation convinced that Jackson was guilty. By the end, I no longer believed that. I could not find a single shred of evidence suggesting that Jackson has molested a child. In contrast, I found significant evidence demonstrating that most, if not all, of his accusers lacked any credibility. They were motivated primarily by financial considerations.

Like most people, almost everything I thought I knew about the case going in was wrong. I had my own prejudices, but I had also been influenced to a great extent by the irresponsible and heavily biased reporting of journalists seemingly out to get him.

Jackson himself, however, also deserved much of the blame. He may or may not have been a criminal, but his behavior throughout both cases—continuing to sleep with children even after the suspicions surfaced—

bordered on criminal stupidity, even if he called such suspicions "ignorant."

For years to come, there will be many suspicions and theories about how Michael died. Perhaps his closest confidant and a longtime source of mine told me two hours after he died that "Michael was tired of living. He was a complete wreck for years and now he can finally be in a better place. People around him fed him drugs like they did to Anna Nicole to keep him on their side. They should be held accountable," the source said, sobbing.

One person in Jackson's inner circle said that they had never seen Jackson more despondent than during the last few days of his life. "He admitted to me that he had completely given up and that the rehearsals he had at the Staples Center for the O_2 residency in London were "an act of futility." "Two days before he died he told me he didn't think he'd come back," the close friend said. "He seemed preoccupied and that music and performing were the last thing [sic] on his mind. Never in my life had I seen a person look so sad. I figured the end was not far off."

The friend added that most of Jackson's inner circle were concerned about how the autopsy report would play out. He also accused the Jackson family of trying to suppress Michael's health reports and guaranteed that they'd insist on hiring a private medical examiner to do a "doctored report." "That's how Michael operated for years," the source said. "Everyone who worked for him or was close to him was aware how much he lied about his health. That's why we all had to sign confidentiality agreements. Now in death his family will try to get their own independent autopsy report and pay big bucks to make sure that the real condition of Michael is covered up. I guarantee you we'll never find out a fraction of how sick Michael really was. That's how the Jackson family has always operated. They're spin doctor masters. They will make sure that Michael comes out of it all looking good and make it sound like it was all a freak accident. Everyone who knew Michael in his final years knows very well that Michael was sick and could die at any moment. He had so many complications with his health."

Michael Jackson was undoubtedly a deeply troubled and lonely man. Throughout my investigation, I was torn between compassion and anger, sorrow and empathy. But as a musician myself, even before his tragic demise, I also couldn't help be struck by another tragedy.

Michael Jackson may very well have been the most talented performer of his generation—joining the ranks of Dylan, Cobain, and Lennon and McCartney as a true musical genius. Sadly, for fifteen years this fact has been lost to a generation who may remember him only as a grotesque caricature who liked to share his bed with little boys.

Now that he's gone, maybe it's time to finally shelve the suspicions and appreciate the music.

Ian Halperin, June 2009

APPENDIX

On October 6, 1993, Jordan Chandler flew to New York City to be tested by Dr. Richard Gardner, a clinical professor of child psychiatry at Columbia University and one of the nation's leading authorities about false claims of child abuse. After administering a series of tests on Chandler, Dr. Gardner conducted the following taped interview.

Dr. Gardner: "Okay. At age twelve and a half, May '92, what happened then?"

Jordan Chandler: "I met him at Mr. Schwartz's (car rental agency). And then my stepfather took him [Michael] outside to choose a car for him to use. And I guess when my stepfather was outside he said, 'You don't have to pay for the car if you just take Jordie's number and give him a call.'"

"Why would your stepfather say that?"

"Because my stepfather knows I was interested in Michael Jackson and his music."

"And this was in your presence?"

"No. I was told this by my stepfather."

"So what happened then?"

"Then he [Michael] left."

"Did he agree to the deal, Jackson?"

"Yeah."

"Okay, then what happened?"

"I don't remember how many days later, but he called me."

"What did he say?"

"He said . . . I don't really remember, but I remember the conversations we had on the phone around the early days of our relationship."

"That was the beginning of the relationship, is that correct?"

"Right."

"How long did the first call last?"

"I don't remember. I don't remember the very first call."

"In this first phase, let's call it the telephone call phase. I would like to try to break it down into phases. This first phase was started around May of '92; that phase which was confined just to telephone calls. How long did that phase last?"

"I would say some time in late January of this year [1993]."

"How often were the calls during this phase?"

"Well, see, he went on tour during the summer so that was when I got off of school, so I would say June or so. But before that he called—I don't know, I don't want to guess wrong. I don't know."

"If you could guess the total number of calls during that first phase, over that seven- or eight-month period?"

"I don't know. Do you think I could tell you—get more specific in the phase—and let's see there? So, well, I remember—he called over there at my dad's house but my stepfather had gave him my mom's number."

"You were living primarily with your mother at that point."

"Yes."

"Okay."

"And so, I assume he—I can't really remember but I assume he was used to calling my mother's house. And so he called my dad's house. I don't know, I think my mother gave him the number. We spoke for, I remember, for like three hours."

"You had conversations for three hours?"

"Well, that one call."

"There was one phone call for three hours; we're talking about the telephone phase now."

"Well, I'm trying to be specific and then when I'm finished—"

"Was it all in that time frame now, I want to stick with that time frame?"

"Right, I know, well I have to remember what happened."

"Sure, but I'm going to interrupt you to clarify. Was there more than one three-hour telephone call during the telephone phase?"

"Yes."

"About how many, roughly, were there?"

"I don't know, it could be—"

"More than ten? Was it roughly five to ten such calls to the best of your ability? Would that be an accurate statement?"

(Inaudible.)

"Okay, that's all. I don't expect you to (inaudible) but if you could narrow it down to a rough guess and we're able to indicate that that's a guess, then that's fine."

"Okay, well—"

"What would you talk about in these three-hour conversations?"

"He would talk about things he likes to do."

"Like what?"

"Like video games. He'd talk about things he has at his Neverland Ranch."

"How is that spelled?"

"N-e-v-e-r-l-a-n-d. He told me he had animals."

"Did he tell you what animals he had?"

"Giraffes, elephants, a lion, horses, a petting zoo, and other animals. He had reptiles."

"What other things did he say that he liked?"

"Playing water fights. He has this custom-made water-fight place."

"What is that like?"

"It's sort of like a water-war zone."

"Was it some kind of a pool or something like that?"

"No, it was structures built with water guns attached to it; all different things. It has an obstacle course."

"What else did he talk about?"

"He talked about some of the friends he had."

"What did he say about his friends?"

"Well, he talked about who some of his more famous friends were."

"Like who?"

"Peter Davis."

"And who was he?"

"He's the kid from [deleted for privacy]."

"Was there anything special about that relationship at this time?"

"He said that Peter Davis was the kind of kid who likes to prank a lot, to prank people."

"Was he involved in pranks with him?"

"Sort of. He said Peter Davis sort of coerced him into going along."

"What other friends did he say he had?"

"Joshua Samuels, who was [deleted for privacy]."

"Joshua Samuels, who is he?"

"[Deleted for privacy], you know?"

"How old is Joshua Samuels now?"

"I don't know; he could be [deleted for privacy]."

"And what did he say about Joshua Samuels?"

"That he was his friend and that was it."

"In any of this period, was there anything sexual said?"

"No."

"Anything else that he'd talk about on the telephone during these conversations?"

"Other things that he had done at his ranch. He has a carnival sort of thing, a movie [theater], some golf carts that you drive around in."

"Would you say that that was the main topic of conversation, telling you about his Neverland?"

"Yeah."

"And what were your reactions to that?"

"Well, for just a regular kid it seemed pretty fantastical and overwhelming. And also, he would tell me that Neverland is named after the place that Peter Pan was, because he thought that he was Peter Pan."

"He thought that he was Peter Pan?"

"Yeah. And he said that Neverland was a place where kids had the right-of-way, on the roads, had the dominance, sort of. Could have what you want when you want it."

"Is there anything else you can tell me about these conversations? We're still talking about the telephone phase."

"No, that's about it. But after that, he went on tour in June and came back in early February, late January."

"Oh, so in this time frame during the telephone phase from May '92 to late January '93, he was on tour?"

"Except for (inaudible) May and I would say June."

"And the tour lasted how long?"

"From I would say June to February."

"So from June '92 to February '93, he was on tour? Is it correct to say then that these telephone calls were made from various parts of the world?

"Yeah."

"Do you remember some of the countries?"

"Paris, Rome. I think he was in Turkey or something. I could be wrong about that."

"Okay, anything else you want to tell me about phase one?"

"Well, actually the first time—when I was at my dad's and I spoke to him for three hours—he was at his apartment complex in Century City. We were trying to work out a time when I could go there and play with the video games."

"So there was an invitation extended?"

"Except it didn't work out because—"

"When was this to the best of your recollection?"

"May of '92, he invited you to Century City?"

"He has an apartment there which is called the Hideout."

"Why is it called the Hideout?"

"Because it's in a very public place but yet nobody knows he's there."

"He invited you with whom? Did he invite you with anybody else or was it you alone?"

"I don't remember, I think—I don't know."

"Okay, but why didn't it work out?"

"Because I had to study."

"Now, anything else you can tell me about that time?

"You used the words before, that it was fantastic and overwhelming. What I want to know is, that between these calls, did you find yourself thinking about him a lot?"

"Uh-huh."

"What kind of thoughts were you having?"

"Like, um, his house must be a great place, and everything."

"Did you dream about it?"

"I don't think so."

"Did it in any way interfere with schoolwork?"

"The calls?"

"Yeah, I mean when you're talking to him you can't do homework, but did it interfere with your concentrating on what you're supposed to do, school, and things like that?"

"No."

"What were your parents' reactions during all this time of that phase?"

"I don't remember them thinking anything bad about it at all."

"So now the next phase would be starting in January of '93. Now you know better than I—"

"That would be late January, early February."

"Okay, let's call that phase two. Now, you know better than I how to break down phases since this is from your life and your experiences. What would you like to set aside as phase two?"

"Maybe, we should call it the portion of seeing him. We could call it that."

"Okay, seeing him. So that phase two begins with actual contact with him—when two human beings are together as opposed to over the phone."

"Right."

"That's when phase two starts."

"Actually, I think we should call it more of the early part of it, because, um, things got bad as it got intimate."

"When you say it got bad, you mean what?"

"Sexual things happened."

"Okay. Let's do this now. Let's call phase two the phase when there was involvement with him—not through the telephone but you were with him together—but there was nothing sexual. Do you want to call that phase two?"

"Yeah."

"And then phase three would be sexual."

"Yeah."

"Since you mentioned the sexual, and that's, let's say, around early February?"

"Yeah."

"Early February '93 to when?"

"I think maybe my mom would know, because that was during the Las Vegas trip, where it switched. That was the first trip."

"Okay, so that's the best of your recollection. I'm going to speak to your mom and your dad later and they can fill me in on some of these details. That's one of the reasons I have your mom in the next room so if there's any discrepancies in details, I can get it from her. To the best of your knowledge—recollection—when was Las Vegas? Was it before the summer or after the summer?"

"I believe it was after the summer. After the summer of '92 but not—"

"We're in '93."

"Right. So it was before, like, I believe I had a break in school in February."

"Okay, well, you said that phase two started in February of '93."

"Early."

"Early February of '93."

"You said something about Las Vegas. So you're saying that something happened physically in Las Vegas? Is that what you're saying?"

"Yeah, that's when it started."

"You started to sleep in his bed? Did you start to sleep in his bed in early February '93?"

"No."

"Was there a time frame where—"

"Sort of later February."

"So phase two might have been a very short time, then?"

"Yeah."

"Okay, I just wanted to get an idea when there was contact. See, in phase one, there was nothing sexual, right?"

"That's right, in phase one."

"In phase two, we're still talking about nothing sexual but there was contact with him as human beings as opposed to the telephone. I would say, sleeping in bed, I'll call that sexual. Some people might not, but I would."

"Right, and I consider that too, and that's where it switched."

"Most people would consider it sexual to sleep in bed with a person. How long was the time frame from the time you first saw him in the flesh, and the time you slept in bed with him?"

"I don't know."

"But it was in February when you started sleeping in the bed with him."

"Right, right. I'm really not even sure if it was in February, but—"

"Okay, but phase two then was a short period."

"Right."

"Maybe about a month, or less [than] a month?"

"I don't know."

"Okay, we'll put that in as a question mark. Now what I want to know is, in that phase, what kinds of things did you do with him, before you slept in bed with him?"

"Well, we went to his Neverland."

"Who's we?"

"Me, my mother and Kelly, my sister, my half sister."

"What happened there?"

"Nothing happened. I slept in the guest area with my mother and Kelly, and Michael stayed in his room."

"How long were you at Neverland?"

"I think for a weekend."

"Do you know if it was Friday or Saturday or Sunday? Was it two days or three days?"

"I don't know."

"What did you do?"

"We went jet skiing on a small lake he has."

"What else did you do there?"

"We saw the animals and played video games."

"You did those things with him?"

"Yeah."

"So these activities were with him? What other kind of activities did you do with him?"

"We took golf cart rides."

"With Kelly and your mother?"

"Occasionally, like, half and half. They would go off sometimes."

"Who's they?"

"My mother and Kelly."

"How many visits were there to Neverland in that time frame?"

"I don't remember."

"So we're still in phase two now. Anything else besides the visits to Neverland in phase two?"

"We may have gone to the Century City apartment."

"Who was with you?"

"Michael and I. I can't remember if my mom (inaudible)."

"Then what happened? Is that the end of phase two? Were there calls during phase two?"

"Yeah."

"Calls lasting three hours?"

"Yeah. Oh yeah, I just remembered. When we were at Neverland we went to Toys 'R' Us, when it was closed. My sister and I could get anything we wanted."

"They opened the store for him, is that it?"

"Right."

"How much would you buy?"

"A lot. We got to take along shopping carts and fill them up."

"Do you have any idea what the cost of that was?"

"No."

"What kinds of things did you get, do you remember?"

"Video games (inaudible)."

"Anything else in phase two?"

"No."

"Going back to phase one. I know you don't have a record of the times he called you, but if you could guess offhand the total number of telephone calls in phase one, what would you say it was? Not only the three-hours calls, but the calls that were shorter as well, what would you say?"

"I believe ten."

"Now, let's go into phase three. Do you think phase three should be subdivided or would you just like to describe it as how things evolved?"

"I don't really know because—can we fill that question in later?"

"Sure."

"Phase three began, I would say, when we were on the trip to Las Vegas. We stayed at the Mirage Hotel."

"On a trip, and to the best of your recollection that was when?"

"I can't really remember. I think late February or so."

"Okay, that was after the trip to Neverland, after the Toys 'R' Us. In Century City, did anything special happen?"

"No, not that I can remember. We just played video games."

"He had the video games there?"

"When you say *we*, who was we?"

"My mother, Kelly, and I."

"What happened in Las Vegas?"

"My mom and Kelly shared a room. Michael had his own room. It was a big suite."

"Was Kelly in the same room with you?"

"No, with my mom, and I had my own room."

"You had your room, Kelly and your mom had a room, and Michael had a room."

"That's right."

"Was it connected or in separate places? Was it one big suite?"

"It was a big suite, yeah."

"Go ahead."

"Let's see, one night—"

"How long were you there?"

"I don't know, maybe a week."

"What happened that night?"

"After my mom and Kelly went to sleep, we went to watch the movie *The Exorcist*. We were in his room, in his bed. And when it was over I was scared, and he said, why don't you just stay in here. And I did and nothing happened."

"When you say you stayed in the room—"

"Stayed in the same bed."

"Slept in the same bed?"

"That's right."

"When you slept in the same bed was there any physical contact?"

"No."

"Was it a big bed?"

"Yeah, I think so."

"So there was no physical contact. What were your thoughts when he said let's sleep in the same bed?"

"Well, I was scared, and I didn't think anything was going to happen."

"You were scared of him or scared of the movie?"

"The movie. So I said, 'Okay, that's fine.' It was like a regular slumber party."

"Okay, is there anything else to say about that event?"

"Just simply that we talked about how they got the idea for *The Exorcist*. So the next morning, I was with my mom alone and—"

"Did your mother know that you had slept in bed with him?"

"Well, I'm getting to that. I said, 'I slept with Michael in the same bed last night,' and she said, 'Well, just don't do it again.'"

"Did she speak to Michael at all?"

"Well, I'll get to that. So when I told Michael the news of the fact that she said don't do that again—don't sleep in the same bed—we were alone, Michael and I, and he burst out in tears and said, 'She can't set up barricades like that,' and 'Nothing could happen, it's just a simple slumber party type thing,' and 'There's nothing wrong with it.'"

"He said, nothing will happen, there's nothing wrong with it, and it's like a slumber party?"

"Right. And so he came—I don't remember if I was crying or not but he decided that he had to confront my mom with his feelings about what she said. What he told me he said, 'There's nothing wrong with it, you should allow it because it's simple and fun and you shouldn't set up barricades.' And he got my mom feeling so guilty that she just broke down in tears and decided that, okay, I believe you. And Michael somehow got her to agree that there would be no further questions asked. And so from that point on I was in his bed till the end of our relationship."

"So, are you saying from then on you were in his bed—are you talking about the Las Vegas trip, or from then on all the time?"

"All the time."

"You said to the best of your recollection the Las Vegas trip was one week. How many times did you sleep in his bed?"

"I'd say maybe two or three."

"Okay, was there any physical contact?"

"No."

"Was there any undressing in front of you?"

"No."

"Did you undress in front of him?"

"No."

"Okay, all right, that's Las Vegas. Are we finished with Las Vegas? Is there anything else to say about Las Vegas?"

"No, that's it."

"Okay, bring me to the next step, then."

"Well, when we got back to L.A. our friendship was a lot more close than when we had left, and so we saw each other more. And we quite frequently went up to his ranch."

"And each time you were there you would sleep in bed with him?"

"Yeah. And my mom and Kelly would stay in that same guest place."

"And how far was that guest place from the room you slept in?"

"It was far, it was quite a lot. Know where the bathrooms are? From here to the bathrooms."

[Jordie is describing the distance from the interview room to the bathrooms in the building in which Dr. Gardner's office is located.]

"That's like a block away. It's the equivalent of a city block."

"No, it's smaller than that."

"Half a block away?"

"I can't really remember, but that's about right."

"Okay, I would say that's a few hundred feet."

"Well, I don't know, you should ask my mom."

"It was in the same house?"

"No."

"It was in a different house?"

"Yeah. It was like a guest complex and they stayed in that room."

"So it was a different building?"

"But Michael and I stayed in his room, which was in the main house."

"So here we are in Neverland, and then what's the next step?"

"Well, I slept in his bed there, and then each week we would go back up and it would kind of progress [to] sleeping in bed, and I think one night we were sleeping in the bed, I think it was at Neverland, and he just leaned over and hugged me or something."

"Okay, let's call that the end of phase two. Let's call phase three sleeping in the same bed and nothing else. All right?"

"Yeah."

"We'll call phase four: it was more physical contact."

"This is where it starts."

"Where the physical contact started? When would you say that started to the best of your recollection?"

"When like what time?"

"What month? I mean Las Vegas, you said, was in early February sometime."

"Las Vegas was more like later February."

"Okay, late February. When was the first hug?"

"I don't know."

"Do you have any idea?"

"No."

"Was it before the summer of '93?"

"I would think early May, middle May [1993]."

"Somewhere in May '93; that was the first hug? And that was while you were in bed?"

"Yes."

"Where were you at the time? Where was the bed—physical location?"

"Do you want me to describe what his room looked like?

"No, I'm wondering where the bed was. Were you at Neverland or were you in some city?"

"Oh, this was in Neverland. I think it may have been somewhere else, but I'm almost positive it was Neverland."

"Okay, and what happened then?"

"He hugged me and I thought nothing of it. I said, okay, whatever. And that was it and he continued that for a small amount of time."

"How long would the hug last?"

"A quick hug and that was it."

"And this was while in bed?"

"Yeah, and fully clothed."

"And did you say anything?"

"I don't remember, I think he said, 'I love you, good night,' or something. I don't know."

"Did you push him away?"

"No. I just—I don't think I hugged him back. I just said, 'I love you, good night.'"

"He said, 'I love you'?"

"I think so, I don't know."

"When you say 'I love you,' it can be said in many different ways. You understand, someone can say 'I love you' and they're really saying I'm in love, and sometimes you can say 'I love you' as a friendly gesture without romantic feelings. What kind of a way did you say that? Were you saying it with romantic feelings or—?"

"Just friends."

"Just friendly. It wasn't a romantic love?"

"No."

"Okay, go ahead."

"So after that hugging thing—"

"Are you describing now a beginning of a pattern of hugging?"

"Yes, like every time he would graduate to a new sexual act, we'd continue that and graduate some more."

"Okay, what was the next step? So are you saying there was a lot of hugging, a lot of attempts to hug?"

"Yeah."

"Did this happen in bed or under other circumstances?"

"You know, I mean it was just a regular hug that if anybody saw it they wouldn't think anything of it."

"He did it in public situations?"

"Yeah, like a good-bye kind of hug."

"Did you ever feel in those hugs that he was sexually aroused? You didn't ever feel he had an erection or anything like that?"

"No."

"Okay, the next step."

"I think he kissed me on the cheek, or something."

"When did that occur?"

"I don't know, around the same time."

"Around the same time, so you're talking about May— we're still in May of '93. He kissed you on the cheek under what circumstances? Were you in bed? Were you standing up? What were the circumstances?"

"I think we were in bed."

"What kind of kiss was it?"

"Just a peck on the cheek. I think it was a good-night peck on the cheek."

"And then what happened?"

"And so he continued that as well as the hugging and then graduated to kissing me on the lips."

"When did that occur as far as you know?"

"I don't know."

"Was it before the summer?"

"Yeah."

"Is it correct to say it was June? Would that be reasonable?"

"I don't know. I really don't know."

"But it was before the summer?"

"Yeah."

"There are different kinds of kissing on the lips. What kind of a kiss was it?"

"Just a peck."

"Was his mouth open or closed?"

"Closed."

"And how long did it last?"

"I don't know, a second, I think."

"Was this in bed?"

"Yeah."

"And then the next step?"

"Next step, I think he graduated to like kissing me for a longer amount of time, you know."

"On the lips?"

"Yes."

"Where was this? Where were most of these things happening? Was it Neverland? Was it mostly Neverland?"

"Neverland."

"Were there other places other than Neverland where this was happening?"

"Yeah. At Century City, at the Hideout."

"So primarily at Neverland and Century City Hideout? This Century City Hideout, I don't think I have a clear picture of what it's like. You said it's in an area where people wouldn't know there was a hideout there."

"Well, there are many apartments around there—"

"Is Century City [the] name of a city around there?"

"Yeah."

"You see, I'm from the East Coast, is all. Century City is part of Los Angeles?"

"Yes."

"Okay, so it's really an apartment. Right? I get the picture. So it happened there and it happened in Neverland and Century City and in your mother's house?"

"Yes."

"He was sleeping over at your mother's house?"

"Yes."

"And when he'd sleep over at your mother's house, he was in the room together with you?"

"I had my room."

"And he would sleep in your room?"

"Yeah."

"About how many occasions did he sleep in your room at your mother's house?"

"I don't know. My mom would know. I don't."

"Roughly."

"I don't know."

"More than five times?"

"Yeah."

"More than ten times, would you say?"

"Uh-huh."

"More than fifteen times?"

"I don't know."

"Twelve to fifteen would be a reasonable number?"

"It could be a whole lot more, but that's something my mom would have to say."

"Okay, what we're talking about now, is this is all before the summer?"

"I think so."

"Okay, so then, we're talking about kissing on your lips a long time."

"And then one time he was kissing me on the lips for a longer amount of time—a peck on the lips—and he put his tongue in my mouth."

"And what was your reaction to that?"

"I said, 'Hey, I didn't like that. Don't do that again.'"

"And what did he say?"

"He started crying, much like when he tried to convince my mother to allow us to sleep in the same bed."

"And what did he say?"

"He said there's nothing wrong with it. He would get me to do things and convince me that the things he was doing weren't wrong, because he would talk about people who levitate, you know, it was weird."

"He would talk about people who what?"

"Levitate."

"What does levitate mean to you?"

"Rise up from the ground by means of meditating."

"And what did he say about levitation?"

"That the people who levitate are unconditioned. It's confusing; it took me a long time to understand it."

"When you talk about unconditioned, what does that mean?"

"That they were not conditioned to believe that gravity existed, and I suppose that that meant that those who are unconditioned would find what Michael was doing was not wrong. Do you understand that?"

"Uh-huh. What else did he say to you?"

"He said, also, during phase one, the telephone phase, his cousin would go along with him on the tour. And I spoke to his cousin one time. We just said hello."

"Was his cousin a boy or girl?"

"A boy about my age, eleven or twelve."

"What was his cousin's name?"

"His name is Tommy Jones [not his real name]; he was on the news if you've been watching, in defense of Michael."

"Tommy Jones. He's thirteen now?"

"I think—no, I think he's twelve."

"And he went on the concerts?"

"On the tours."

"On the tours. And he was on the news saying what?"

"He said, 'I will admit that Michael and I are friends and we do sleep in the same bed, but Michael has never touched me,' and 'it's a really big bed.'"

"So he spoke about his cousin. And what did he say about Tommy Jones?"

"He said that, um, like, if he wanted me to do something with him, he would say that Tommy did that with him so that I would do it. And, like, if I didn't do it, then I didn't love him as much as Tommy did." [Jordie sighs heavily.]

"Are you okay?"

"Yeah."

"Okay, fine, you're doing very nicely. You know, we're going to take a break, but let's try to finish this and then we'll take a break."

"Do you think that Tommy Jones was lying when he went on television?"

"Yes."

"Why do you think he's lying?"

"Because Michael told me they did."

"Okay, but Michael said he did these things—"

"I mean it could be that Michael could be lying to me."

"Somebody is lying. Right? Because Michael was lying to Tommy by saying the opposite things, right?"

"Yeah, well, one of them is lying."

"Who do you think is lying?"

"Tommy."

"Why do you say that?"

"Because in public, when he's with Tommy, they're very close together physically and verbally and relationship-wise. And if one were to observe things in public, how they acted to each other, one would come to that conclusion, that it was more than just a friendly relationship."

"Now, let's go on. So that was the lip kissing. Then he cried—"

"He tries to make me feel guilty for—"

"And then what happened?"

"And then one time, when he was hugging me and kissing me, and he rubbed up against me. I don't know if he had an erection or not. I can't remember."

"Now was this in bed or what?"

"Bed."

"Was this all before the summer?"

"I don't remember. It may have gone into the summer."

"So you took what as the next step? You're talking about the gradual development; the next step was his rubbing against you?"

"Yes."

"With an erection."

"I think he had an erection. As it graduated he did."

"And then?"

"Then it graduated to where he had an erection and he would kiss me."

"Kiss you where?"

"On my mouth. By the way, he never put his tongue in my mouth again once I told him not to."

"What's the next step?"

"Let's see, I think the next step was, I had an erection and he rubbed up against me and that was it."

"You had an erection and he rubbed himself against—?"

"And he did, he did as well."

"Okay, and where was his erection and where was your erection? You both have an erection."

"We were on top of each other."

"Anything else?"

"That was it, and then it graduated to other stuff. Somewhere during that time we went to Florida."

"When did you go to Florida?"

"I don't know. My mom would know. [April 1993] And there we stayed in the same room."

"Where was your mother?"

"Same suite, different room, with Kelly."

"What happened in Florida?"

"Several things happened. One, he grabbed my butt, put his tongue in my ear—"

"He grabbed your butt; was he forcing you?"

"No. Well, he was kissing me and he grabbed my butt."

"It wasn't forced?"

"But, um, and then the third thing was that he was walking to the bathroom to take a shower, and he looked at me before he closed the door and he said, 'I wish I didn't have to do this,' and he shut the door, implying that he wished he could be so free as to be able to change in front of me."

"Changing from what to what? I'm a little confused. You said he grabbed your butt—"

"There are three different things."

"He grabbed your butt, put his tongue in your ear and walked into the bathroom and said, 'I wish I didn't have to do this.'"

"Then he shut the door."

"How long was he in the bathroom?"

"He took a shower, I don't know."

"Now, when he said 'I wish I didn't have to do this,' what was he referring to?"

"To shut the door behind him when he had to change."

"The implication being that he would like to be naked in front of you, is that what you're saying?"

"Right. But somewhere on the trip I said, 'I didn't like when you put your tongue in my ear and grabbed my butt.' Once again he started crying and making me feel guilty, and saying there's nothing wrong with it, and referring to the levitators and Tommy. I think he referred to Tommy and said Tommy wouldn't care if I did that to him."

"Then what's the next step?"

"By the way, he never did those either. The next step, we went back home to L.A. and he continued doing the things I hadn't stopped him from doing."

"Is this before the summer or during the summer?"

"I'm sure it was during the summer."

"The next step?"

"In L.A., he continued those things."

"Which things?"

"Rubbing up against me, having an erection and kissing for long periods of time."

"And having an erection?"

"Yes."

"Then what was the next step?"

"Then we went to Monaco."

"When did you go to Monaco?"

"During the summer, I think. My mom—" [Early May 1993]

"And in Monaco?"

"In Monaco, he and I both had colds, so we couldn't go out on the town or whatever and see the sights. We had to stay in and that's pretty much when the bad stuff happened."

"What happened?"

"I don't know. I think when he convinced me to take a bath with him or something. See, my mom and Kelly were gone, they were having fun and we were stuck in with colds.

And my mom, I remember, she offered to stay in and help us and take care of us, and Michael insisted that our colds shouldn't detract from them having fun. So we were alone and we took a bath together. That was the first time we ever saw each other naked. And during that time when we were alone in the room and they were gone, he talked about how all of his children friends masturbate in front of him."

"Did he say which children friends did it?"

"Yeah."

"Which children friends did he say masturbated him?"

"Masturbated in front of him."

"Oh, masturbated in front of him. Okay, who did he say masturbated in front of him?"

"He said [names omitted]—he was also on TV."

"He was also on TV and he said what?"

"'Michael and I do sleep in the same bed, but Michael has never touched me.'"

"He's lying or Michael's lying?"

"Well, I don't—as far as I know he's not lying. Michael never did touch him, as far as I know. But Michael said that [name omitted] masturbated in front of him."

"So Billy didn't say on TV anything about masturbation?"

"No. No. And so, other kids—Wait, I got to think of this kid's name, [name omitted]."

"Who's he?"

"A boy who went on the Bad Tour with him. That's the name of the tour before this one."

"You say, Bad Tour, is that the name of the tour?"

"Bad, yes."

"They called it the Bad Tour."

"Named after his album."

"So what else happened, if anything?"

"So he was talking about how all these kids masturbated in front of him, and he said that—Oh, by the way, I met Tommy and [name omitted] during that time period, and [name omitted] as well. So he was saying that all these kids masturbate and it feels really good, and so one time he masturbated in front of me. That was the first time."

"He masturbated in front of you?"

"Um, like, he didn't make me watch and like he was on the bed masturbating, and, I don't know, I was changing."

"This is when you had colds in Monaco?"

"Yeah. I don't know if I was standing in the same room or not, but it wasn't like he shut the door and closed everything."

"Where was he and where were you?"

"He was on the bed, in the room. I was, I may have been getting ready in the bathroom, or in the—We had a large closet and so I maybe was getting dressed in there."

"But you saw him?"

"Yeah."

"Go ahead, next thing."

"And so he continued that for, like, a lot of the trip. And he kept on saying, 'Tell me when you're ready and I'll do it for you.' Because up till then I had never masturbated or anything. And I had never, ever, indicated to him that I was ready, like, to be masturbated. And I guess that wasn't according to his plans, and so, one time he just reached over and said, "Okay, just tell me how this feels.' And he put his hand on my—"

"And this was in Monaco?"

"Right. And he put his hand on my shorts and he said, 'Now doesn't that feel good.' And he rubbed up and down. And I said, 'Yeah.'"

"Did he masturbate you to orgasm, to climax?"

"Well, then he said, 'Well, wait, it gets even better,' and he put his hand under my shorts and masturbated me to the end."

"Is that the very first climax you had in your life?"

"Yeah. Well, wait, during that summer I had a, what's it called, a wet something?"

"You mean at night, while you're asleep?"

"Yeah."

"You mean a wet dream."

"Yeah."

"Okay, these were spontaneous. Did you have orgasms in your wet dreams?"

"I had one and that was it."

"But it was the same feeling?"

"Yeah."

"So that was your first, was in the wet dream?"

"Right."

"And then so your first orgasm outside of a wet dream was when he masturbated you?"

"Right."

"Okay."

"What was the next step?"

"And he, like, continued that. He stopped everything else that we were originally doing together; we just took baths. And we went to Euro-Disney after we went to Monaco."

"Anything else at Monaco other than what you told me?"

"Uh-uh."

"About how many times would you say he masturbated you at Monaco?"

"I don't know."

"What were your feelings about it then?"

"Well, um, I said, this is really weird, like I never said I was ready then. But I said to myself, it feels good so, just, whatever, and he's my friend, so I can't be—"

"And while he was masturbating you, what was he doing?"

"Just that, nothing."

"Okay. Is there anything more about Monaco?"

"No."

"Okay, what's the next thing?"

"The next thing, we went to Euro-Disney."

"When was that?"

"After Monaco, because Monaco's in France as well as Euro-Disney, so we went from Monaco to Euro-Disney."

"And how long were you at Euro-Disney?"

"I don't know, a week or two at most."

"Was this during the summer?"

"I don't know. No, wait, no actually now that I remember, up 'til now, nothing was past the summer now that I remember, because—"

"So, Monaco was before the summer?"

"Everything."

"Euro-Disney was before the summer?"

"Yes, everything. Now I remember because I had a book to read for finals. It was called To Kill a Mockingbird. Supposedly that was one of his [favorite] books. And so he helped me study and he read the book to me and then he continued to masturbate me."

"By the way, if this was before the summer, this is the school time. When you're in all these other places, what's going on with school?"

"Well, I managed to still get all As; I brought my book with me."

"Did the school permit this?"

"Yeah."

"What happened at Euro-Disney?"

"He continued to masturbate me."

"About how many times do you think?"

"About once a day. And that was it for Euro-Disney—and France, in general."

"Okay, that was it with Euro-Disney. Anything else?"

"You mean Euro-Disney?"

"Yeah."

"I think we might have taken a bath together."

"On one occasion?"

"I don't know. It may have been one, it may have been not at all."

"Okay, next phase, next step."

"Next step, okay. We went home, back to L.A. again. Let's see, I remember, my dad, just as before, last year, was to help me study for finals, and so I was going to go to his house. And my dad and Michael, they had never met before, I don't think. And so, I was going to go to my dad's house and stay over there for, like, the weekend. And he was going to help me study. And that really saddened Michael that we would have to separate. So he stayed over there during that weekend."

"At your father's house?"

"That's right. That's the only time." [Actually, there were two weekends.]

"Okay, we're talking about June now? June of '93?"

"Late May."

"And then?"

"And then he masturbated me there, and one time when he was masturbating me, um, instead, he masturbated me with his mouth."

"So he put his mouth on your penis?"

"Yes. Then, um, from that point, till the end of our relationship, he masturbated me with his mouth. And that was as far as it went."

"About how many occasions did he do that?"

"I don't know but I can tell you where."

"Where did it take place?"

"In my father's house, his Hideout, my mother's house, and Neverland."

"Okay, so these are four different places, so obviously it had to happen at least four times. Right?"

"Oh yeah, of course."

"But I want you to give me a guess—"

"Okay. More than fifteen, that's safe. But he had me masturbate him."

"On how many occasions?"

"About ten. And he said that—he had me—he got me to twist one of his nipples while I sucked on the other and he masturbated himself."

"Was there ever any anal contact at any time?"

"No."

"Most men, when they masturbate—whether they be masturbated by someone else or doing it alone—most men have some thoughts in their mind. Sometimes they don't but most often they do. When he was masturbating you, what thoughts were in your mind?"

"Um, I thought, it's weird. It's like it didn't feel right but yet it felt good, and he was a friend so I didn't stop him."

"Most kids your age start, around your age, start to masturbate by themselves usually without any kind of experience with another person and kids who (inaudible). Have you continued to masturbate since those experiences?"

"I did, I believe, six times right after the end of our relationship."

"And not since?"

"And not since."

"I'm not saying you should, but I'm asking you why you did. I'm asking you what were your reasons?"

"Because, I remember that it felt good when he did it and—"

"Okay, why did you stop? I'm not saying you should or you shouldn't. I'm just saying why did you decide to stop?"

"I didn't (inaudible)."

"That's it. Let's separate the feeling from him."

"Let's do this. Let's take a break for about ten or fifteen minutes and then we'll continue. So you stretch your legs. Now I want to put it on the record that I'm not going to be talking to you between our meetings. All contact with you, all the things I'm going to say to you will be in this room on this tape. Do we agree that I haven't spoken to you prior to this day, right?"

"Right."

"So that's very important. Okay, so let's interrupt."

(Break)

"Do you miss him?"

"No."

"I'd like to talk to you about how this all came out. By the way, did he say to you that you should never talk to anybody?"

"Yes he did."

"What specific statements did he make to you in that regard?"

"He said that this—that we had a little box, and this was a secret, and it's a box that only him and I could share."

"He was not speaking literally?"

"It was a secret box, like, yeah, pretend we had a box and secrets go in there."

"A secret, like in a little box?"

"Yeah, you put the secret in the box and nobody can know about what's in the box but him and me. And he said, once again, he referred to, like, the unconditioned levitators. He said that we weren't conditioned, but if this box were revealed to other people, like regular people of today's society, they're conditioned and so they would believe it was wrong. And so that's why I shouldn't reveal what's in the box."

"Do you believe it's wrong?"

"Yeah."

"How did your parents learn about this?"

"I guess, after we had—Michael and I had stayed that night—"

"Where?"

"At my father's, during the finals. He saw that, like, it wasn't a healthy relationship for me."

"What did he observe directly in terms of the sexual activities?"

"No sexual activities."

"He didn't observe sexual activities? But there were sexual activities?"

"There was, but he didn't observe them."

"What did he observe?"

"He observed Michael and I having almost the same personality, the same interests, the same way of speech."

"When you say similar personality—"

"Like, I would act like him."

"Did you find yourself consciously doing that?"

"No."

"Did you make a decision or it just happened?"

"It just sort of happened. Like, the more we hung out together, his personality and his way of speech and everything else would rub off on me. And so he—Dad saw me alone one time at Cody's, his preschool graduation, and he told me 'You and Michael have lied to me,' and it seemed like he knew what was going on, without actually saying what was going on."

"So your father suspected. Is that what you're saying?"

"Yeah. And he said it in a stern, serious voice, not yelling."

"Was he speaking to you alone, or—"

"Alone."

"When did this happen?"

"I, like, right before my school graduation."

"That's May or June?"

"June." [June 9th, 1993]

"So what did you say then?"

"I didn't— He didn't ask me what did you and Michael do together."

"By the way, going back, did he say, 'It's a secret'?"

"Michael?"

"Yeah. In terms of . . . did he make any threats?"

"I think he may have said, like, if you tell—if people say 'Don't worry, just tell us, Michael will go to jail and nothing will happen to me you.' He said that wasn't true, and I could, like, go to juvenile hall or something."

"That he could go to jail but you'd go to juvenile hall?"

"Something like that."

"That he himself could go to jail?"

"I don't specifically remember. I'm almost positive, though, that he said about juvenile hall. I'm almost positive he said that, but I do indeed remember that he said that he would go to jail, and that, like, I wouldn't get off scot-free."

"Did you believe that?"

"Well, I didn't really believe it at the time, and I definitely don't now. But at the time I didn't really believe it but I said, okay, whatever, and just went along with it."

"Now let's see. When your father confronted you at first, what did you say?"

"Well, um, it was an intimidating circumstance, where he was talking to me, and he said, 'You've lied to me, as well as Michael.' And I said—I was like, fairly nervous. And he said 'What would you do if I said that I don't want you to go on the tour.' Because I was supposed to be on tour with him now. He's on the tour."

"Mmm-hmm."

"We were planning on going on the tour. And I said, like, 'I probably would go anyway because I don't know of any valid reason you have,' I said to my dad."

"You still wanted to go on the tour?"

"Yes, at the time."

"Why is that?"

"Because I was having fun. At the time, the things Michael was doing to me, they didn't affect me. Like, I didn't think anything was totally wrong with what he was doing since he was my friend, and he kept on telling me that he would never hurt me. But presently I see that he was obviously lying."

"You're saying you didn't realize it could hurt you? Is that what you're—"

"I didn't see anything wrong with it."

"Do you see the wrong in it now?"

"Of course."

"What is wrong as you see it?"

"Because he's a grown-up and he's using his experience, of his age in manipulating and coercing younger people who don't have as much experience as him, and don't have the ability to say no to someone powerful like that. He's using his power, his experience, his age—his overwhelmingness—to get what he wants."

"All right, so, you finally did tell your father. Who was the first adult you told?"

"My father."

"How many times did he have to ask you before you told him?"

"Once."

"The first time he asked, you told him?"

"Well see, at the graduation he said, 'You guys are lying to me,' and that was it, he didn't ask me any questions."

"And what did you say?"

"I just said, 'Huh?' like, 'I didn't know.'"

"You made believe you didn't know what he was talking about?"

"Right. And then he demanded me over to his house, because he knew that the circumstances were wrong. And he, like, I was with my mom and Michael, and he demanded me over to his house. So I went to his house, and he said just for a week and then you can go back. And I really started liking it there. And he had to pull my tooth out one time, like, while I was there. And I don't like pain, so I said could you put me to sleep? And he said sure. So his friend put me to sleep; he's an [anesthesiologist]. And um, when I woke up my tooth was out, and I was all right—a little out of it but conscious. And my dad said—and his friend was gone, it was just him and me—and my dad said, 'I just want you to let me know, did anything happen between you and Michael?' And I said, 'Yes,' and he gave me a big hug and that was it."

"And you never gave him the details?"

"No."

"Now you divulged this when? When did you tell him? In what month?"

"July. I believe July. I remember that because it was very close to my sister's birthday, which is July."

"Are you interested in girls?"

"Yes."

"Do you find yourself attracted to any boys?"

"No."

"Have you ever been attracted to boys?"

"No."

"You see, there are some kids who have an experience such as you describe, who shift from the heterosexual to the homosexual track. Do you know what I mean by that? If you ask them at five, six, seven, eight, they say, 'I'm going to be a fireman when I grow up and I'm going to get married and have children'—something like that—and then they stay on that track. But there are some kids, as a result of an experience like you're describing, that may shift and start moving down the homosexual track. Do you think that's going to affect you?"

"Well, it may, and I guess that's why I'm probably in therapy."

"Okay, but the question is, have you the feeling now that this may happen to you?"

"No."

"Why do you say that?"

"'Cause—I like girls!"

"Do you feel that you could have, somehow, prevented all this stuff with Michael?"

"Yeah."

"How?"

"Because originally— Remember I said there were a couple things he did and I said, 'Don't do that'?"

"Yeah."

"It worked those times, maybe I could have done it—"

"You could have been more forceful. Is that what you're saying?"

"Yeah."

"Why weren't you?"

"It was hard to do."

"Because?"

"Because he's an adult, he's overwhelming, he's famous, he's powerful."

"Were you in awe of him? Do you know what I mean by awe?"

"No."

"In awe of somebody means that you look up to them like they're almost a god, or something like that."

"No. Actually when our relationship got closer and closer I thought less of that. Like most people think that, wow, he's great, because he can dance and sing. But you know, he's just like, a regular person."

"Do you feel guilty about having participated in those acts?"

"Yeah. I regret doing it."

"What about fears? Any fears of any kind?"

"No."

"Sometimes people, after experiences of this kind, develop different kinds of fears. You have no fears?"

"Maybe of cross-examination, but that's all. I mean I have nothing to hide, it's just the thought of it."

[Jordie describes some of the nonsexual activities he and Michael did together.]

"It sounds to me, from what you're describing, he was functioning very much as a child."

"That's what he believed he was."

"You say, psychologically, he believed he was a child? When you were with him—you described the video games—he would play with you child games. Did he ever give any explanation as to why he did that?"

"Because he's, like, when he was young, like my age, his father would continuously make him work, and like, his father would like beat him and stuff, and he's trying to relive what he didn't have as a young boy. Peter Pan is his idol."

"Why is that?"

"Because Peter Pan is forever young, and he goes on adventures and stuff."

"He could relive all the experiences he didn't have, but what about the sexual part. How does that fit into reliving? Did he say he had sexual experiences of any kind as a child with some older person?"

"No, not that I know of."

"Did he say he loved you?"

"Mmm-hmm."

"You know how you look at a romantic movie sometimes and you see the man and the woman, and the man says how much he loves the woman, how much he adores her and praises her. You know about that?"

"Yeah."

"Would you say that was the way Michael was with you?"

"Like, it was sort of like a weird kind of love. Like, it was like that but he, he loved me selfishly. Like, regardless of the fact that what he was doing might hurt me, he continued."

"When you say it could have hurt you, how could it have hurt you?"

"Everybody thinks what he was doing could hurt, otherwise it wouldn't be a crime."

"Okay, how could it hurt? As you see it, how could it hurt you?"

"Because—that's a touchy subject, I guess. It separates you from any other people."

"How?"

"I don't know."

"Just your own guess."

"It could make me depressed or something, I don't know."

"Well, this is important. You say it's a crime. Why is it a crime?"

"Because, like I said before, he's using his experience, power, age—"

"How could this have left you? If this had gone on and not been interrupted, how could you have ended up?"

"According to his pattern, I believe he would have left me and, sort of dumped me, I guess you could call it. And I would be, sort of, a vegetable."

"Why a vegetable?"

"Because he would continue to do those things and I would have no knowing of what else is out there."

"Say that again. You wouldn't know what else is out there?"

"Right. Like, he didn't like it if I would want to call a girl or something. You know, I wouldn't know, like, there were other options."

"Are you saying that he would pull you off the track of going out with girls."

"Right."

"What would you say is the best thing that ever happened to you in your whole life?"

"When I told my dad what Michael was doing to me."

"Why do you say that?"

"Because once I told him, I knew that Michael would never be able to do that to me again. And when something horrible ends, it's most likely the best thing in your life."

"You say—"

"Like a prisoner being released from prison."

"But are you saying through all of this, although you enjoyed it, you felt a sense of pressure?"

"Yeah."

"Was it a big heavy on you? Do you know what—"

"Yeah."

"Could you describe—"

"Like, I couldn't be open with how I felt. Like if I didn't want to do something I couldn't just say 'I don't want to do that' because he would start crying or whatever. He wouldn't just say, 'Okay, whatever, we'll just be friends and play video games.' He'd start crying and do everything in his power to convince me that—"

"But you voluntarily went back there. You could have said, I don't want to go up to Neverland again, right?"

"Yeah."

"So why did you go back?"

"Because regardless of the fact that I went to Neverland, he would be with me. No matter what, he was always with me. It was like, I couldn't just say I don't want to hang out with you today."

"Why not?"

"It's not that easy. He would cry. He would say, 'You don't love me anymore.' It would be, like a whole deal, you know, it was hard."

"It's my understanding that your mother kind of facilitated things here."

"What's that mean?"

"Facilitate means, she made it easy for him. Another mother might not have believed him with this stuff about 'It's okay.' You know, some mothers would say, 'You're not sleeping in bed with my kid, I don't care what you say.' She got herself talked into it."

"Right."

"Is it correct she understands now what was going on?"

"Yes."

"It seems to me that your mother went along with him. She equally got fooled. Is that correct?"

"Yes."

"What are your feelings about your mother at this point?"

"She was fooled, just like you said."

"Any feelings about that?"

"That I'm sure if she knew what was going on, that she would say there's no way."

"Have you discussed this with her?"

"No."

"No!"

"Wait, discussed?"

"This whole thing. About her being fooled."

"No, 'cause, I mean, I personally don't like talking about it more than I have to."

"Do you have any other feelings besides she was fooled?"

"No."

"I understand from your parents that you're not spending that much time at your mother's house. Is that correct?"

"That's right."

"And at your age and at your intelligence they are basically letting you make that decision yourself. But there are reasons for everything, and what I want to know from you is, what are your reasons why you want to spend so little time at your mother's house?"

"It's not really that I don't want to spend time at my mother's house. It's, there's, I don't know."

"There's always a reason for everything. Guess."

"I would say it's because there's not so many rules at my father's house."

"And what is the reason for that?"

"I don't know. I guess their values, maybe."

"What about their values?"

"My father doesn't believe, for example, in eating the right food every night. You can have candy."

"Your mother is kind of a stickler?"

"What does that mean?"

"Stickler? Your mother's fussy and your father's less fussy about the food. Is that what you're going to say?"

"Yeah."

"Any other reasons?"

"It's not the food specifically, it's her rules in general."

"What about her rules?"

"My mom's rules are more strict. Like, go to bed this time, do homework right when you come home from school."

"Any other reasons why?"

"Well, also, at my mom's house—the house specifically, or her?"

"Both."

"Well, I don't want to spend time at that house because Michael's presence is still there."

"It's like his ghost is still in the house, his aura?"

"Yeah."

"Any other reasons with your mother?"

"Why?"

"You see, because I'm trying to find out what psychological problems or reactions, if any, you had to this experience—which was a mind-blowing experience. I'm sure you agree on that. When you think of all the kids in the world, to have had this experience with that guy, you know, it's reasonable to say that if you lived to be a thousand you wouldn't forget it. Am I correct?"

"Right."

"Okay. And it's got to have some effects on people: you're not immune to it. It's probably the case that it's not going to affect your sex life. You know it could, but it can have more subtle effects. They're not as obvious but they are nevertheless effects. I'm trying to find out—like one of them is, now you have a—you can't walk into your mother's house feeling relaxation and comfort because the aura of Michael is there. It's not a sexual effect, but it's an effect. And it compromises your relationship with your mother. And I'm just wondering about other things, of those effects. That's why I'm asking you these questions. Do you think it has anything to do with your mother having facilitated. Do you know what I mean by facilitated?"

"No."

"Your father thinks, and I'm in agreement with him, that she didn't show enough—although he was such a convincing and seductive guy—that she should have earlier seen that there was some hokey-pokey stuff going on here and pulled you out of there quicker. Do you agree with that?"

"Well, he had me under his spell. So, you know—"

"His spell? Do you think she was under his spell?"

"Well, he got me under it, so I imagine he could get other people under it."

"I'm wondering whether you do feel some resentment toward her, and that may be a factor why you're not seeing her."

"No. I don't think so."

"Okay. You know, as I understand it from your parents, and as I can see from what you say, when you're under his spell he became like, the—you were being pulled away from your father, from your mother. You know, you were almost like a, you know, drawn in under his web and taken away from your family, and you viewed him as the most important person in your life. Right?"

"Yes."

"And under those circumstances you often take on the traits and the qualities of that person. Did you take on any of his qualities?"

"I did when I was with him, but I thankfully got rid of them."

"What were the qualities?"

"His way of speech."

"Can you imitate it?"

"He would use words like 'hook me up.' That means get me something. An erection was 'lights.'"

"Lights was an erection. Go ahead."

"Cum was 'duck butter.'"

"Duck butter? That was semen, ejaculate?"

"Yeah."

"So those were his words and you were using those words?"

"Yeah."

"Anything else that became part of you?"

"No."

"I want to get clarification with girls. What's your situation with girls at this point? Your father says that you're on the phone a lot."

"Mmm-hmm."

"Do you talk a lot with girls primarily? Do you spend a lot of time with girls?"

"Mmm-hmm."

"I see you smiling. Do you have a [girlfriend] at this point?"

"I'm sort of in the process of chasing after one."

"So you got your eye on her?"

"Yeah, I guess you could call it that."

"Have you kissed anybody yet?"

"I kissed this one girl."

"Okay. So, your father seems to think in your relationship with the girls you ask a lot of questions; you're very controlling. Do you think that has anything to do with Michael?"

"No—Well, yeah."

"How does it relate to Michael?"

"Because, I hadn't thought of it this way previously, but now that I think of it, since I put too much trust and gave control to Michael in our relationship, now I watch out for myself."

"What about trust of your mother? Do you think any trust of your mother has been affected?"

"Well, not because she, as people would say, she wanted to pimp me out. More because of maybe, I tried to tell her one time and she didn't believe me."

"When was that? Do you remember?"

"No."

"How do you feel about that?"

"I feel that if there's any remote, itty-bitty thing in your mind that your kid may be getting hurt, you should put an army together, you know, if there's a suspicion as strong as that, that my dad had carried out this far. She should have at least listened to what I had to say."